MOTHER EARTH, MOTHER AFRICA
and
MISSION

EDITORS
Seblewengel Daniel
Mmapula Diana Kebaneilwe
Angeline Savala

SUN PRESS

Mother Earth, Mother Africa and Mission

Published by African Sun Media under the SUN PReSS imprint

This publication was subjected to an independent double-blind peer evaluation by the publisher.

The editors and the publisher have made every effort to obtain permission for and acknowledge the use of copyrighted material. Refer all enquiries to the publisher.

Views reflected in this publication are not necessarily those of the publisher.

First edition 2021

ISBN 978-1-991201-30-0
ISBN 978-1-991201-31-7 (e-book)
https://doi.org/10.52779/ 9781991201317

Set in Adobe Garamond Pro 11/14

Cover design, typesetting and production by African Sun Media

SUN PReSS is an imprint of African Sun Media. Scholarly, professional and reference works are published under this imprint in print and electronic formats.

This publication can be ordered from:
orders@africansunmedia.co.za
Takealot: bit.ly/2monsfl
Google Books: bit.ly/2k1Uilm
africansunmedia.store.it.si *(e-books)*
Amazon Kindle: amzn.to/2ktL.pkL

Visit africansunmedia.co.za for more information.

This book is dedicated to Christina Landman,

a founding member of the Circle of Concerned African
Women Theologians

CONTENTS

ACKNOWLEDGEMENTS

The Circle of Concerned African Women Theologians (henceforth Circle) has benefited from various contributions from its members over the years, both in kind and in cash. For this, we are truly grateful to our Circle members. In particular, Dr. Musimbi Kanyoro has supported various fund-raising opportunities, including substantial contributions of her money and time. At the time of the All Africa Circle celebration in Botswana (July 2019), Musimbi was wrapping up her responsibility as the President and CEO of the Global Fund for Women, and therefore was unable to attend the conference in person. Keeping her commitment as one of the founders of the Circle, she decided to take a step of faith and contributed to the Circle's 30th anniversary celebration through a considerable amount of money which included her end-of-service bonus and some funds raised through Global Fund for Women. For this, we are truly grateful to her and to the Global Fund for Women. We are also grateful to the University of Botswana, Global Challenges Research Fund, World Council of Churches, The Church of Holland and the Ecumenical HIV and AIDs Alliance for their contributions towards the conference. Our gratitude also goes to the Botswana Circle Chapter for successfully organising and hosting a splendid conference. Special thanks to Professor Musa W. Dube for her sterling leadership in the overall organising of the conference. The friendships and contributions of Prof. Johanna Stiebert and Dr. Katie Edwards were truly divine. We heartily thank them. We extend our gratitude to all the book contributors and peer reviewers who made this project a success by devoting their time and expertise. Last, but not least, we would like to thank African Sun Media for enabling this project to be calcified in a publication.

PREFACE

By Beverley Haddad[1]

The Circle of Concerned African Women Theologians was launched in 1989 in Accra, Ghana and celebrated its 30th anniversary in 2019 in Gaborone, Botswana. These anniversary celebrations brought together women (and some men) from across the world to the University of Botswana under the theme, 'Mother Earth and Mother Africa in Theological, Religious, Cultural, and Philosophical Imagination.' The imperative behind the theme of this celebratory conference was twofold. First was the recognition that the land, the Earth, is a gendered space. For centuries, women across the African continent have been dispossessed of their right to own land despite the fact that they have often been, and still are, significant carers of the Earth and need the Earth to survive. Second, the mounting global ecological crisis is driven by anthropocentric religious, cultural and theological perspectives. The essays in this volume respond to these two imperatives, drawing on indigenous, cultural and theological resources to re-imagine a different world in which the Earth and women are honoured and respected by the whole of humanity – honoured by both women and men and the children of generations to come.

The Circle has always tried to respond theologically in a proactive manner to current issues confronting the continent. To date, it can be argued, the body of work by African women theologians on HIV is some of the most significant theological reflection on the crisis faced by people, and particularly women throughout the African continent. The volumes that were first published in the early 2000s were amongst the first attempts to respond theologically to the emerging HIV crisis. As the epidemic developed and changed, bringing new challenges, the Circle theologians have responded and offered some of the most astute critique of patriarchal culture and its implications for women, who were increasingly infected and affected by HIV.

So it is not surprising that the Circle has once again been proactive and has engaged with the issue of the ecological destruction of the Earth. This volume is but one of a series of volumes through which the Circle seeks to engage the topic in a sustained way. These volumes take up the trajectory of earlier work that intersects gender and ecology. As early as 1996, a pivotal volume edited by Rosemary Radford Ruether,

---

1   Professor Beverley Haddad is based at the University of Kwazulu-Natal, South Africa.

Women Healing Earth: Third World Women on Ecology, Feminism and Religion,[2] addressed the issue and placed the voices of women from the South on the theological agenda. In this volume, voices of global women, including African women, argued that ecological destruction was a matter of life and death. Impoverishment of the environment meant real poverty for women, resulting in longer hours doing back-breaking work as they sought to find wood, water, and food to feed their families amidst issues of drought and deforestation. This spelt the destruction of rural livelihoods for women that led to the worse alternative of urban migration and rising unemployment. Nonetheless, these voices went largely unheeded. The need to conserve the environment and halt climate change only began to take central stage on the global agenda when a young adolescent woman from Sweden, Greta Thurnberg, addressed the 'United Nations Climate Change' conference in 2018. African women had been making the same argument twenty years earlier!

African women theologians have also argued that women play a key role in addressing ecological destruction. They have pointed to expressions of religious practices where women have been central in nurturing and caring for the Earth, such as the Mwari people[3] and the Karanga people of Zimbabwe.[4] Others have been inspired by the environmental activist work of Wangari Maathai, who started the Green Belt Movement in Kenya in 1977 and was the first African woman to be awarded the Nobel Peace Prize for this lifelong work.[5] As far as a theological and cultural focus was concerned, the 30th anniversary celebration of the Circle, with its attendants from almost every continent, as well as subsequent publications considerably advanced the discussion on ecological degradation far and wide. The conference brought the importance of this theological reflection into sharp focus.

This volume is part of the re-positioning of Mother Earth on the global theological agenda. The chapters in the volume cover a wide range of topics which address central theological themes that need to be re-imagined, key ways in which the issue of land rights is central to the care of Mother Earth, and case studies of indigenous and Christian forms of environmental activism. Our world needs to be re-imagined into a place where the forces of life reign over the forces of death. Our world needs to be re-imagined into a place where the whole of creation is protected and nurtured through the dismantling of unjust structures of gender, race, and class that impoverish communities, particularly women and children. Our world needs to be re-imagined into a place where women and men stand together in solidarity as agents of change. May this volume be a contribution to this quest for an eco-gendered just world.

2   Ruether, R.R. 1996. Women Healing Earth: Third World Women on Ecology, Feminism and Religion. Maryknoll, NY: Orbis Books.

3   Mukonyora, I. 1999. Women and Ecology in Shona Religion. *Word & World*, XIX(3):276-284.

4   Chirongoma, S. 2012. Karanga-Shona Women's Agency in Dressing Mother Earth: A Contribution towards an Indigenous Eco-Feminist Theology. *Journal of Theology for Southern Africa*, 142:120-144.

5   Rakoczy, S. 2013. Wangari Maathai: Discerning a Call to Environmental Justice. *Journal of Theology for Southern Africa*, 145:75-91.

INTRODUCTION

Mmapula Diana Kebaneilwe[1]

Background

This publication is one of a number of publications that were born out of the 5th Pan African Circle of Concerned African Women Theologians conference, which was held in Gaborone, Botswana in July 2019. The theme of the conference was 'Mother Earth and Mother Africa in Theological, Religious, Cultural, and Philosophical Imagination.' The publication of this volume comes at a difficult time for the inhabitants of Mother Earth who have been apprehended by the devastating effects of the novel Coronavirus pandemic, also known as COVID-19. The virus, which attacks the human respiratory system, was first reported in Wuhan, China, in late 2019 and has now spread across the globe, causing the deaths of millions of people.[2]

Papers that were presented at the said conference, including the chapters in this edited book, did not say anything about COVID-19 because it was non-existent at the time. They do, however, explore the interconnectedness of life on Mother Earth, and the vulnerability of human life to natural disasters and pandemics. In this way, COVID-19 has proven to be a natural disaster that knows no boundaries of colour, race, gender, social standing or any of the labels that serve to differentiate between people on Mother Earth. As a result, all of life has been affected. Human life has particularly been disrupted with an impending global economic recession as countries continue to undergo movement restrictions or lockdowns, halting economic activities across the globe. According to one recent publication, Pope Francis recently gave an email interview in which he makes a connection between climate change and COVID-19.[3] In the interview, the Pope conceives the pandemic as "nature's response" to climate change.[4] He quotes a Spanish expression translated as

---

1   Mmapula D. Kebaneilwe specialises in Hebrew Bible studies at the University of Botswana.

2   https://who.int/emergencies/diseases/novel-coronavirus-2019/question-and-answers-hub/q-a-detail/q-a-coronaviruses

3   Green, M.C. 2020. Introduction. In M.C. Green and M. Haron (eds). *Law, Religion and the Environment in Africa*. Stellenbosch: African Sun Media. ix-xv. Citing Ivereigh, A. 2020. 'A Time of Great Uncertainty': An Interview with Pope Francis, *Commonwealth Magazine*, 8 April.

4   Green, Introduction, ix.

"God always forgives, we sometimes forgive, but nature never forgives."[5] Therefore, it is possible that due to human beings' ravaging activities on Mother Earth, nature could be responding with COVID-19.

The importance of the subject of this book cannot be overemphasised. Studies preceding it have shown that Mother Earth has suffered devastating effects due to climate change and the subsequent global warming in the last few decades, and that there has been an impending ecological crisis threatening the twenty-first century inhabitants of planet Earth.[6] As a member of the global Earth community, Africa has not been spared from the ravages of the ecological crisis of the present era. As we shall see below, everyone and everything that shares life on Earth, both fauna and flora, have to this day been adversely affected by the ecological decline of planet Earth.

Mother Earth, Mother Africa and Mission: A Three-Way Intersection

According to the Merriam-Webster dictionary, Mother Earth refers to the planet Earth as a woman or a goddess.[7] As a goddess, the concept comes from a "Greco-Roman personification of nature that focuses on the life-giving and nurturing aspects of nature."[8] 'Mother Africa' draws from the same understanding that planet Earth and its continents are mothers to their inhabitants. In the words of Joseph Patmury:

> The Earth nourishes us while we live and reclaims us when we die. It is from the dust of the Earth that God formed us and from the same dust he fashioned all the beasts of the field and birds of the air (Gen 2:17). Humans are not beings fallen from heaven, but taken from the ground. Hence we have a very profound relationship with the Earth as well as with other earthly creatures.[9]

We may then ask, what is mission? The term mission has been broadly defined as "what the Christian community is sent to do."[10] According Andrew Kirk, however, mission can be defined in five specific ways, namely: 1) announcing the good news in a culturally authentic way, 2) struggling to right the wrongs caused by economic malfunction, environmental degradation and conflict, 3) engaging with people of different beliefs, 4) establishing new communities of disciples, and 5) seeking the

---

5   Green, Introduction, ix.

6   Kebaneilwe, M.D. 2016. Law, Religion and Ecological Issues: A Theological Approach. In P. Coertzen, M.C. Green and L. Hansen (eds). *Religious Freedom and Religious Pluralism in Africa: Prospects and Limitations*. Stellenbosch: African Sun Media, 257-268.

7   Merriam-Webster, https://www.merriam-webster.com/dictionary/Mother%20Earth. Accessed 24 Aug. 2020.

8   https://en.wikipedia.org/wiki/Mother_Nature

9   Patmury, J. 2008. Mission in Relation to Mother Earth In: J. Mattam and J. Valiamangalam (eds). *Building Solidarity-Challenge to Christian Mission*. Delhi: FOIM/ISPCK. 83-98.

10   Kirk, J.A. 2000. *What is Mission? Theological Explorations*. Minneapolis: Fortress Press, 233-234.

unity of Christians and human communities.[11] What concerns us here is mission as humanity's duty towards planet Earth (and in our case, towards Africa). Chapters in this book explore at different levels and from different angles some, or all, of the aspects entailed in the title of this book.

The book calls for re-imagined perspectives targeted at achieving a different and more balanced world than is currently the case. Towards that end, it constructs a three-way intersection between ecology, gender, and mission. The questions that one may ask then is, what is the ecological status of the Earth? How is the ecological landscape of our planet related to issues of gender? And what should we do to rectify the situation? This book places special focus on the African continent, with scholars from different parts of Africa and the African diaspora each addressing the subject in relation to their specific contexts.

As observed by Angeline Lotsuro, the entire universe is built on relationships and its well-being is dependent on keeping these relationships in balance.[12] The well-being of our planet Earth and all her inhabitants is also dependent on orderly and balanced relationships.[13] Furthermore, an imbalance in these relationships results in disasters.[14] Sadly, human beings are invariably culprits in destroying their relationship with the Earth.[15] Thus, as observed by Lucjan Pawlowski, the current ecological crisis is a result of reckless technical and technological exploitations in which human beings have given themselves power to transform the Earth to an almost unlimited degree.[16] The trend is said to have begun at the time of the industrial revolution, which was founded on the principle of dominance over and objectification of nature, subjugating it to the human will and mind.[17] Human beings have degraded the Earth by treating it as an insensitive object worth only what it could benefit us. Now it is dying under our watch.[18] Leornardo Boff shares similar sentiments when he asserts that the ethic of the dominant society of today is utilitarian and anthropocentric.[19] Human beings believe that they are lords over nature, and deny

---

11   Kirk, What is Mission? 234.

12   Lotsuro, A. 2008. Gender Relation. In J. Mattam and J. Valiamangalam (eds). *Building Solidarity-Challenge to Christian Mission*. Delhi: FOIM/ISPCK, 63-82.

13   Lotsuro, Gender Relation, 63.

14   Lotsuro, Gender Relation, 63.

15   Lotsuro, Gender Relation, 63.

16   Pawlowski, L. 2015. Where Is the World Heading? Social Crisis Created by Promotion of Biofuels and Nowadays Liberal Capitalism. *Rocznik Ochrona Środowiska* [Yearbook of Environmental Protection], 17(1):26-39. Cited by Kebaneilwe, M.D. 2020. Do Not Pollute the Land Where You Are: Hebrew Bible Teaching on Environmental Conservation. In: M.C. Green and M. Haron (eds). *Law, Religion and the Environment in Afric*a. Stellenbosch: African Sun Media, 17-29.

17   Patmury, Mission in Relation to Mother Earth, 87.

18   Patmury, Mission in Relation to Mother Earth, 87.

19   Boff, L. 1997. *Cry of the Poor, Cry of the Earth*. Maryknoll: Orbis Books, 7.

nature's intrinsic value over the false conviction that the rest of nature is at their service and created for their pleasure.[20]

Today we talk of global warming, which is a result of complex activities and events that all point to the pressures that humanity exert on Mother Earth and her resources. In a nutshell, climate change is a result of pollution, industrialization, population growth, deforestation, land degradation, and the depletion of the ozone layer.[21] Pollution is caused by the emission of greenhouse gases, which result from energy use such as carbon dioxide produced by the burning of fossil fuels, methane and nitrous oxide in the course of industrial activities.[22] All of the above and more result in climate change with its subsequent global warming, which is felt across the globe in tangible ways, such as extremes in temperature and precipitation, diminished water supply, and polluted water.[23] It also changes the amount of seasonal rainfall and perennial snow, ice cover, and sea level.[24] Another study indicates rapid temperature rise and particular habitat destruction, which have the potential to disrupt the interconnectedness among creation and lead to possible extinctions of some species.[25] Expressing similar sentiments, Jingcheng Xu and his colleague assert that "Mother Nature has seen devastating changes and the ecosystem in a vicious circle has been suffering myriads of ecological disasters."[26] All of these are attributed to atmospheric concentrations of carbon dioxide and have adverse implications for human and other species' survival.[27] Therefore, as asserted earlier, these human-induced atmospheric changes are causing ecological disasters, which in turn have adverse implications for all Earthly life. Because humanity has failed to act in just ways in relation to non-human communities of Mother Earth, there is environmental degradation. In summary, the ecological crisis suffered by Mother Earth is due to the imbalance in the relationship between humanity and the environment.

The above leads us to the next important question that this book seeks to explore, namely, the issue of gender. It is now compelling to explore to what extent humans

---

20   Boff, Cry of the Poor, 7.

21   Karl, T.R. and Trenberth, K.E. 2003. Modern Global Climate Change. *Science*, 302(5651):1719-1723 [https://doi.org/10.1126/science.1090228], cited by Kebaneilwe, M.D., Do Not Pollute the Land, 18.

22   Karl and Trenberth, Modern Global Climate Change, 1721.

23   Karl and Trenberth, Modern Global Climate Change, 1721.

24   Karl and Trenberth, Modern Global Climate Change, 1719.

25   Root, T.L., Price, J.T., Hall, K.R. et al. 2003. Fingerprints of Global Warming on Wild Animals and Plants. *Nature*, 421(6918):57-60. Citing: Baldo, M. O'Brien, D.F., You, Y., Shoustikov, A., Sibley, S., Thompson, M.E. and Forrest, S.R. 1998. Highly Efficient Phosphorescent Emission from Organic Electroluminescent Devices. *Nature*, 395:151-154.

26   Xu, J. and Gong, M.N. 2012. A Study of the Social Ecological Wisdom in H.W. Longfellow's Poetry. *TPLS*, 2(1):24-30.

27   Kebaneilwe, M.D. 2020. Do Not Pollute the Land Where You Are: Hebrew Bible Teaching on Environmental Conservation. In: M.C. Green and M. Haron (eds). *Law, Religion and the Environment in Africa*. Stellenbosch: African Sun Media. 17-29.

have been able/unable to deal fairly amongst themselves as men and women. Many studies indicate that gender-justice has an important bearing on the ecological crisis. For instance, ecofeminists have observed a link between the exploitation and degradation of the natural world and the subordination and oppression of women.[28] According to Radford Ruether, women's denigration in contrast to men's is modelled after the denigration of non-human nature by 'man.'[29] Ruether further argues that the term 'man' itself is to be understood as an androcentric false generic which actually elevates the elite male as the normative human being.[30] Woman is a derivative auxiliary to be dominated and ruled by the latter.[31] In such a scenario, women are seen and treated as less human and likened to 'body' in the dichotomy of mind and body, and 'animal' in the dichotomy of human and animal.[32] Thus, the oppression of people (especially women) is often, if not always, linked to the oppression of the Earth and her less powerful inhabitants.[33] Therefore, justice, mission, salvation, gender relations and ecclesiology must be re-imagined in the context of the current global environmental crisis.[34] This is what this book aims to do. In particular, the volume foregrounds African women's voices on the interface between religion and the environment but does not exclude male voices.

The interface between the fields of religion and the environment has received considerable scholarly attention in the last few decades,[35] and yet African women's voices are not as widely represented as those of male African scholars from the continent. Chitando, in mapping out eco-theology in Africa, describes the current situation expressly as follows:

> Although African Theologians from diverse contexts have drawn some attention to the need to address the environmental crisis, it is not yet possible to refer to a well-defined body of writing that could be labelled African ecotheology."[36]

The above statement, in a way justifies continuing efforts as the ones made by this particular edited volume, by African scholars and faith practitioners to further explore the field of ecotheology.

---

28 Mellor, M. 2007. Ecofeminism: Linking Gender and Ecology. In: J. Pretty, A. Ball, T. Benton, J. Guivant, D.R. Lee, D. Orr, M. Pfeffer, H. Ward (eds). *The Sage Handbook of Environment and Society*, Los Angeles: SAGE. 66-77.
29 Ruether, R.R. 2012. Ecofeminism: The Challenge to Theology. *DEP*, 20:22-33.
30 Ruether, Ecofeminism, 25.
31 Ruether, Ecofeminism, 25.
32 Ruether, Ecofeminism, 28.
33 Boff, L. 2014. *Ecology and Liberation: A New Paradigm*. Maryknoll: Orbis Books, xi.
34 Boff, Ecology and Liberation, xi.
35 Chitando, E. 2020. Ecotheology in Africa: an Overview and Preliminary Assessment. In Green M. C. and M Haron, eds. *Law, Religion and the Environment in Africa*. Vol. 7. Stellenbosch: African Sun Media, 2020, 3-16.
36 Chtando, Ecotheology in Africa, 4-5.

Mission re-imagined calls for a reassessment of especially communities of faith (and everyone else), to ask themselves what it really means to be a people of faith in this age of globalization and climate change. How should scriptures be re-read in the light of the global environmental crisis? What does it mean to do mission? What is salvation? How is the Divine/God imagined in the Creation community? How should gender relations be imagined so as to harmonise and heal all relationships? The above are some of the pivotal questions that the chapters in the proposed edited volume seek to address.

In the first section of this book, 'Re-imagining Theological Perspectives on Women and the Earth,' the authors explore theological aspects of re-thinking and re-reading biblical texts in the light of environmental oppression and gender injustice. The overarching theme in this section is the interrogation of what salvation means and what it might mean in a world so characterised by environmental degradation and marginalization of women. In the first chapter, Mmapula Diana Kebaneilwe and Kgomotso Scotch make a call to contemporary or neo-Pentecostal mission, which they argue is the hallmark of Christianity in modern-day southern Africa, to join hands with other stakeholders in an effort to save Mother Earth. They maintain that current or neo-Pentecostal movements, especially in southern Africa, are engaged in inculturation hermeneutics which gives pre-eminence to the believers' situational context. Scripture is read to address the physical needs of believers, including but not limited to poverty, sickness, marital issues and other ills that plague people in the African and southern African context. The authors acknowledge that such a stance is commendable but that there is need to include environmental conservation in the agenda. They maintain that an inculturated reading of Jesus' mission or ministry reveals his love for an intimate connection with the natural world. Hence, the mission of the church should be re-imagined as inclusive of all of creation and not just focused on the well-being of humans at the expense of the natural world.

Peggy Mulambya-Kabonde takes up the theme of calling for a re-thinking of salvation as not just the saving of souls, but one that specifically takes cognisance of gender justice and ecological justice. Mulambya-Kabonde maintains that a holistic view of salvation is one that underscores the interconnectedness of all of creation, both human and non-human. She calls for a re-construction of such a theological understanding of salvation where everyone and everything ever created is appreciated as an important part of God's creation beyond the divides of gender and the dichotomy of human vs non-human. Houssou Gandonou argues that protection of Mother Earth is more than an imperative given to human beings at creation, but is a theological mission that must be carried out by all human beings. According to her, human beings must start by appreciating the interconnectedness of life on Earth and by understanding that as the Earth nourishes us, we too must nurture and protect her. Thus, if humans selfishly exploit the Earth and her creatures, eventually she will fail to sustain human life and all of life on Earth will become impossible.

In the second section of this book, 'Re-imagining Women's Oppression and the Earth,' authors pick up the theme of Mother Earth and Mother Africa. By further illustrating the interconnection between the oppression of Mother Earth and Mother Africa, where the latter is represented in the oppression of African women, the authors provide examples from their different contexts. Esther Mombo underscores the role of Kenyan women as food producers for their families and demonstrates how the women are marginalised and exploited. Mombo claims that with the advent of missionary work in Kenya, women were further pushed to a marginal existence through mandatory vegetable gardening that served to isolate them from one another and from the rest of society. She maintains that the women had to do this work along with other domestic chores of fetching wood, carrying water, weeding and harvesting, grinding, cooking and caring for the children. She further objects to the situation where the women were denied any land ownership rights and makes a connection between their oppression and that of the land. Mombo makes some critical recommendations to avert the ecological crisis in contemporary Africa.

Master Matlhaope asserts that the dualistic approach to spirituality and materiality has exacerbated women's marginalization in land ownership rights. He argues that God the Creator never envisioned a disparity between spirituality and materiality and that the disconnection of the two has led to imbalances, including gender inequality, subjugation of the physical world by humans, the wide gap between rich and poor, and all kinds of unjust dealings amongst God's creatures. He calls on the Christian faith to act to redress especially women's marginalization with regards to land ownership. Matlhaope further maintains that Christ, in a distinctly patriarchal context, upheld women's dignity and hence a Christocentric faith should endeavor to bring about gender equality that would afford women the right to land ownership. Also taking up the theme, Angeline Savala suggests that there is need to theorise on female headship as a possible paradigm shift aimed at attaining a harmonious and sustainable ecosystem. Savala interrogates headship as a concept that is generally associated with masculine power. She argues that such a stance has led to male domination over women and over the natural world. Her conviction is that stripping headship or leadership off masculinity would enable women to participate in decision making. Savala proposes that since women are nurturers and care givers, allowing them positions of leadership and decision making will go a long way in addressing the ecological crisis. She maintains that after all, women are proactive in environmental activities but operating as backbenchers disadvantages them from full participation to achieve a harmonious and sustainable ecosystem.

The final section of this book, 'Re-imagining Women as Change Agents Who Care for the Earth,' pays special attention to women as capable agents of change in the environmental crisis. Jennet Tabe sets the stage by re-telling the story of the Ngbokondems who were the female ancestors of the Ejagham of Cameroon. Tabe is adamant that the female ancestors were conservationists whose careful usage of nature – trees, water, animals and birds – helped in environmental preservation. She laments that the early missionaries who came to the place condemned the Ngbokondems' tradition as demonic and that even some contemporary Christian communities still uphold the view. Tabe claims that Ngbokondems were sacred spaces for communing with Ndem for the well-being of the land. She argues that colonial missionaries and later patriarchal infringements in the Ngbokondems and its traditions ruined everything, and the destruction has left little to be desired as Mother Earth is still weeping in environmental waste.

Nelly Mwale decries the muted voices of women in her Zambian Kasisi Agricultural Training Centre. Following two women's trajectories, Mwale not only interrogates the silencing of the women in the Kasisi's Agricultural project, but also explores the mission of the church to Mother Earth and women's participation in the mission. According to Mwale, the Kasisi project is part of the Jesuit initiative in Zambia which began in the 1970s. The aim of the project is to empower women in rural areas in sustainable agriculture for the sake of their livelihood and for the conservation of Mother Earth. Following the trailed trajectories of two women who benefited from the project revealed a significant improvement in their livelihoods and those of their families. Mwale discovered that the women formed support groups among their rural communities, training others in the trade whose lives also improved. According to Mwale, when given opportunities, women can transcend heights to change their communities for the better and, as in the case of the two women, their efforts will go a long way in environmental conservation. She advocates for the celebration of heroines whose stories, if buried, may not have an impact on others. In the final chapter, Maitseo Bolaane and Gwen Lesetedi explore the roles of women in some contemporary neo-Pentecostal churches, also known as 'Fire Churches,' in Botswana. They argue that in some of the said churches women are re-positioning themselves as leaders and thereby bringing changes to the religious landscape, which until now has been dominated by male headship. Consequently, they assert that the women are acting as agents of change.

References

Boff, L. 2014. *Ecology & Liberation: A New Paradigm*. Maryknoll: Orbis Books.

Boff, L. 1997. *Cry of the Poor, Cry of the Earth*. Maryknoll: Orbis Books. 7.

Chitando, E. Ecotheology in Africa: an Overview and Preliminary Assessment in Green M.C. and Haron M. (eds). *Law, Religion and the Environment in Africa*. Stellenbosch: African Sun Media, 3-16. https://doi.org/10.18820/9781928480570/01

Green, M.C. 2020. Introduction. In: M.C. Green and M. Haron (eds). *Law, Religion and the Environment in Africa*. Stellenbosch: African Sun Media. ix-xv. https://doi.org/10.18820/9781928480570/00

Ivereigh, A. 2020. 'A Time of Great Uncertainty': An Interview with Pope Francis. *Commonwealth Magazine*, 8 April.

Karl, T.R. and Trenberth, K.E. 2003. Modern Global Climate Change. *Science*, 302(5651): 1719-1723. https://doi.org/10.1126/science.1090228

Kebaneilwe, M.D. 2020. Do Not Pollute the Land Where You Are: Hebrew Bible Teaching on Environmental Conservation. In: M.C. Green and M. Haron (eds). *Law, Religion and Environment in Africa*. Stellenbosch: African Sun Media. 17-29. https://doi.org/10.18820/9781928480570/02

Kebaneilwe, M.D. 2016. Law, Religion and Ecological Issues: A Theological Approach. In: P. Coertzen , M.C. Green and L. Hansen (eds). *Religious Freedom and Religious Pluralism in Africa: Prospects and Limitations*. Stellenbosch: African Sun Media.

Kirk J.A. 2000. *What is Mission? Theological Explorations*. Minneapolis: Fortress Press.

Lotsuro, A. 2008. Gender Relation. In: J. Mattam and J. Valiamangalam (eds). *Building Solidarity-Challenge to Christian Mission*. Dehli: FOIM/ISPCK, 63-82.

Mellor, M. 2007. Ecofeminism: Linking Gender and Ecology. *The Sage Handbook of Environment and Society*, 66-77. https://doi.org/10.4135/9781848607873.n4

Merriam-Webster, https://www.merriam-webster.com/dictionary/Mother%20Earth. Accessed 24 Aug. 2020.

Mother Nature. 2021. *Wikipedia*. Available at: https://en.wikipedia.org/wiki/Mother_Nature. Accessed: 25 August 2020.

Patmury, J. 2008. Mission in Relation to Mother Earth. In: J. Mattam and J. Valiamangalam (eds). *Building Solidarity-Challenge to Christian Mission*. Delhi: FOIM/ISPCK. 83-98.

Pawlowski, L. 2015. Where Is the World Heading? Social Crisis Created by Promotion of Biofuels and Nowadays Liberal Capitalism. *Rocznik Ochrona Środowiska* [Yearbook of Environmental Protection], 17(1):26-39.

Root, T.L., Price, J.T., Hall, K.R., Schneider, S.H., Rosenzweig, C. and Pounds, J.A. 2003. Fingerprints of Global Warming on Wild Animals and Plants. *Nature*, 421(6918):57-60. Citing: Baldo, M. et al. Highly Efficient Phosphorescent Emission from Organic Electroluminescent Devices. *Nature*, 395(1998):151-154. https://doi.org/10.1038/nature01333

Ruether, R.R. 2012. Ecofeminism: The Challenge to Theology. *DEP*, 20:22-33. https://doi.org/10.1177/0966735012436915

WHO. 2020. *Coronavirus disease (COVID-19)*. Available at https://www.who.int/emergencies/diseases/novel-coronavirus-2019/question

-and-answers-hub/q-a-detail/q-a-
coronaviruses (Accessed: 20 Dec 2020).

Xu, J. and Gong, M.N. 2012. A Study of
the Social Ecological Wisdom in H.W.
Longfellow's Poetry. *TPLS*, 2 (1):24-30.
https://doi.org/10.4304/tpls.2.1.24-30

PART ONE

Re-imagining Theological Perspectives on
Women and the Earth

RE-IMAGINING MISSION THROUGH INCULTURATION

Pentecostalism and Sustainable Environment

Mmapula Diana Kebaneilwe[1]
Kgomotso Scotch[2]

Abstract

African Pentecostalism of the twenty-first century is characterised by prophecy, exorcism, miracles, focus on prosperity, deliverance from malevolent spirits, demons, and so on. Sexual scandals, money laundering, fake resurrections and other ills have also been reported in some circles. Many of the adherents to Pentecostal mission engage in cross-border pilgrimages in search of certain 'men of God or prophets' believed to be uniquely endowed with the power of God to set people free from the multifaceted challenges of contemporary life. Without necessarily condemning the said activities, we endeavour to call Pentecostals' attention to yet another topical issue that seems to be side-lined, namely, ecological crisis. The Earth is currently in a state of emergency, needing urgent rescue from possible collapse. We will argue that there is need for a shift from anthropocentric practices evident in Pentecostal missions to joining hands with other stakeholders in efforts to save our environment. The chapter advocates for a close examination of Jesus' mission and ministry with special emphasis on his affinity with nature/environment. We propose an inculturation perspective.

Introduction

One scholar describes African, in particular Southern African, Pentecostalism of the present century as follows:

---

1   Mmapula Diana Kebaneilwe (PhD). She obtained her PhD in Old Testament Studies from the University of Murdoch in Perth, Australia in 2012. The title of her PhD thesis was *This Courageous Woman: A socio-rhetorical Womanist Reading of Proverbs 31:10-31.* She is a Senior Lecturer of Hebrew and Old Testament Studies in the Department of Theology and Religious Studies at the University of Botswana. Her research interests include the following: Women and the Hebrew Bible, HIV and AIDS and the Hebrew Bible, The Bible and the Environment.

2   MA Student of Theology, University of Botswana.

A spirit is haunting Southern Africa – the spirit of Neo-Pentecostalism. For some time now Pentecostal ministries have been changing, other churches are changing as well, and even outside Christianity we see a similar spirit moving, a spirit which I call here the spirit of neo-Pentecostalism.[3]

Gregory Deacon and Gabrielle Lynch define neo-Pentecostalism as a strand of Christianity that believes in, affirms and promotes the experiential presence of the Holy Spirit as part of a normal Christian life and worship.[4] It is a stream of charismatic churches that emerged in sub-Saharan Africa during the neo-liberal era from the 1980s-1990s.[5] They are closely associated with prosperity gospel which holds that prosperity of all kinds is the right of every Christian[6] and hence wealth and health are central to their preaching and belief. Thus neo-Pentecostals preach a gospel of prosperity promising instant wealth and health.[7] They emphasise healing, deliverance, prosperity and the anointing power of church leaders.[8]

In the past, the church was focused on the saving of souls from personal sins.[9] They practised resignation from the present world and its material concerns in order to keep themselves holy for the invisible spiritual world of God.[10] Thus, historically, Christianity advocated for what Norman Habel calls "heavenism" which is literally alienation from the Earth.[11] Habel further maintains that what was passed down to believers was that:

> The world of heaven was a world apart, where God dwelt in splendour and majesty. That world was not only more glorious than Earth; it was also more valued and pure. This valuing of heaven as God's abode above meant a consequent devaluing of Earth as a mere foot stool.[12]

Contrary to the above, current Pentecostal churches, especially in southern Africa, if not in all of Africa, have shifted their message from obsession with the heavenly world and its demands to a more worldly involvement. In his analysis of neo-Pentecostal movements in southern Africa, Kroesbergen asserts that in the said churches,

---

3   Kroesbergen, Neo-Pentecostalism in Southern Africa, 1.

4   Deacon, G and Lynsh. G. 2013. Allowing Satan in? Moving toward a Political Economy of Neo-Pentecostalism in Kenya. *Journal of Religion in Africa*, 43(2):108-130.

5   Deacon, and Lynch, Allowing Satan in? 109.

6   Deacon, and Lynch, Allowing Satan in? 109.

7   Kramer, E. 2005. Spectacle and the Staging of Power in Brazilian neo-Pentecostalism. *Latin American Perspectives*, 32(1); 15-120.

8   Deacon, and Lynch, Allowing Satan in? 109.

9   Habel, N. 2010. Earth-Mission: The Third Mission of the Church. *Currents in Theology and Mission*, 37(2): 114-125.

10   Kroesbergen, Neo-Pentecostalism in Southern Africa, 7.

11   Habel, Earth-Mission, 116.

12   Habel, Earth Mission, 116.

the context of the reader is given pre-eminence.[13] A two-storied world picture is presented: a visible material world and an invisible spiritual world.[14] Emphasis now is on the former (the visible/material world) and the latter (invisible/spiritual world) is used for achieving worldly material goals.[15] Sharing similar sentiments, Eric Gbote and Selaolo Kgatla insist that the prosperity gospel, which is characteristic of current Pentecostals, teaches that God wants his people to be healthy and wealthy.[16] This is what Habel argues is the second mission of the church, which emphasises the power of Christ in saving people from whatever forces oppress them.[17]

The focus on the heavenly world to the present state of the believer is a landmark of current Pentecostalism. Such is a welcome development. We cannot, as members of the Earth community, pretend that Earthly endeavours do not matter to us, for they do. However, the chapter decries that there is a missing and yet critical and timeless link between the current state of affairs in Pentecostalism and ecological activism. As asserted by Augustinus Dermawan, there is a lack of concern and an attitude of avoidance toward environmental issues by many Christians.[18] Consequently, there is need to re-examine and re-imagine the Pentecostal mission (and indeed the church mission) and to determine how to develop responses to environmental stewardship.[19] For instance, natural disasters that have become commonplace in the present century affect us all. It is undeniable that such are a result of the declining status of the environment, and that the situation demands urgency. According to Habel, the church is called to a third mission, which he calls the Earth Mission.[20] It is a call for commitment to be custodians and advocates of the deteriorating Mother Earth.[21]

On the contrary, contemporary Pentecostal movements, while emphasizing the welfare of people on Earth, tend to pay little or no attention to the welfare of the very Earth that sustains life. The question is, can people really find peace and justice when their very dwelling is deficient of the same? If our home is polluted, ravaged in

---

13   Kroesbergen, Neo-Pentecostalism in Southern Africa, 18.

14   Kroesbergen, Neo-Pentecostalism in Southern Africa, 18.

15   Kroesbergen, Neo-Pentecostalism in Southern Africa, 23.

16   Gbote, E.Z.M. and Kgatla, S.T. 2014. Prosperity Gospel: A Missiological Assessment. *HTS Theological Studies,* 70(1):1-10.

17   Habel, Earth Mission.114.

18   Dermawan, A. 2003. The Spirit in Creation and Environmental Stewardship: A Preliminary Pentecostal Response toward Ecological Theology. *Asian Journal of Pentecostal Studies (AJPS),* 6(2):199-217.

19   Dermawan, The Spirit in Creation, 201.

20   Habel, Earth Mission, 114.

21   Habel, Earth Mission, 114.

some ways or other, will we not suffer along with it?[22] The ecological predicament is thus not only about flora and fauna but a people issue and a justice issue as well, for as the Earth community, we share a finite home.[23]

A Call to Re-imagine Pentecostal Mission

Twenty-first century Pentecostalism need to re-imagine their mission with the aim of reconciling all parties involved, taking into cognisance that healing and justice for the people cannot be achieved without healing and justice for Mother Earth, who is the host. The chapter advocates for a critical reflection by contemporary Pentecostal movements to break away from anthropocentric views of the world in which creation is valued only for what it can offer humanity. The consequent human superiority has resulted in environmental destruction. Dermawan sums up the concern expressly in the following statement:

> For the past three years I have had the opportunity to attend various Pentecostal services in Baguio, Philippines, including services at the seminary chapel, but I have not heard a single sermon which communicates any concern regarding environmental issues.[24]

Expressing similar concerns, Aaron Swoboda asserts that little or no attention has been given to the intersection between prosperity theology and ecological issues, such as global warming and its associated ills.[25] He further argues that the uncritical reception of the theology has the potential to create ecologically destructive, if not anti-ecological, modes of thought and action within its adherents.[26] This is not to deny the positive impact of the prosperity gospel and theology as one that speaks to real life needs and experiences of people.[27] However, there seems to exist a vacuum and a missing link between people's physical needs for survival and the environmental crisis. There is need to establish and harmonise such an intersection in order to create the balance needed for the good of all Earth inhabitants – flora and fauna alike. To that end, Habel challenges the church as a whole to develop worship patterns that reflect on the status of Mother Earth, which he calls "the very sanctuary in which we live and move and have our being."[28] Continuing the same

---

22   Edwards, D. 2005. *Jesus the Wisdom of God: An Ecological Theology*. Oregon: Wipf and Stock Publishers, 4.

23   Edwards, Jesus the Wisdom of God, 4.

24   Dermawan, The Spirit in Creation, 202.

25   Swoboda, A.J. 2015. Posterity or Prosperity? Critiquing and Refiguring Prosperity in an Ecological Age. *Pneuma*, 37(3):394-411.

26   Swoboda, Posterity or Prosperity? 394.

27   Swoboda, Posterity or Prosperity? 394.

28   Habel, Earth-Mission, 117.

slant, the chapter challenges Pentecostals of twenty-first century southern Africa to re-imagine their mission based on observation and 'inculturated' understanding of Jesus's mission and ministry, especially with regards to nature as a whole.

We shall, in what follows, provide a brief overview of the theoretical framework for our chapter, which is inculturation hermeneutics. Our conviction is that the hermeneutic here proposed will enable us to see Jesus's ministry in a different light. We hope to be able to establish his ecological activism and advocacy by viewing his ministry from an eco-just perspective. We shall then explore Pentecostalism's involvement in ecological issues or the lack thereof, before positing that an inculturated perspective on Jesus' association with the environment could be resourceful in dealing with the current environmental predicament.

Inculturation Hermeneutics as a Theoretical Framework

Inculturation has been defined variously by its many proponents. As explained by Jean-Claude Loba-Mkole, inculturation hermeneutics acknowledges the sacred status of the biblical text and its normative value for believers.[29] It seeks to dynamically re-read the text against the cultural context of the present readers.[30] Paulinus Odozor maintains that the encounter allows the Bible or biblical text(s) to inform, transform and even alternate the culture of the current reader.[31] It is the process whereby the faith in one culture encounters another culture and infuses with it.[32] Notably, the process involves interaction of mutual critique and affirmation-acceptance or rejection of certain modes of thoughts, practices and attitudes by and between the cultures involved.[33] In inculturation hermeneutics, Christianity dialogues with the cultures and/or contexts it encounters and results in a novel religious-cultural reality.[34] Consequently, through inculturation, the biblical faith responds to the aspirations and anxieties of the people it is propagated in and seeks to make them recover their identity as well as their dignity.[35]

---

29   Loba-Mkole, J.C. 2008. Rise of Intercultural Biblical Hermeneutics in Africa. *HTS Teologiese Studies/ Theological Studies*, 64(3):1347-1364.

30   Loba-Mkole, Rise of Intercultural Biblical Hermeneutics, 1347.

31   Odozor, P.I. 2008. An African Moral Theology of Inculturation: Methodological Considerations. *Theological Studies*, 69(3):583-609.

32   Magesa, L. 2014. Anatomy of Inculturation: Transforming the Church in Africa. Maryknoll: Orbis Books, 7.

33   Magesa, Anatomy of Inculturation, 7.

34   Magesa, Anatomy of Inculturation, 7-8.

35   Kiariem, G. and Mouki, J.S. 2016. The Changing Understanding of the Eucharist among the Kikuyu Communicants of the Thika Diocese in the Anglican Church of Kenya. *Stellenbosch Theological Journal*, 2(2):295-320.

Worth noting is that inculturation is an African biblical hermeneutic that is informed and shaped by elements in the African context.[36] We note that, although Africa is a vast continent with diverse peoples and cultures, there are several factors that give the continent a distinguishable flavour when it comes to the interpretation of the Bible.[37] Andrew Mbuvi argues that despite the diversified contexts of Africa, cultural trends reflect enough overlaps that we can cautiously retain the branding of African biblical studies (ABS).[38] Ultimately, ABS translates into inculturation hermeneutics as it entails the encounter between the Bible and the African context(s).

Thus, at the heart of inculturation hermeneutics is the concern to make the Bible relevant to the context in which it is read. Such a stance allows for a conversation between the Bible and the situational context of the reader/interpreter. We have already indicated that in the current Pentecostal missions in our part of the world, the situational context of the followers/believers is taken seriously. One scholar, in describing current Pentecostals, asserts that "neo-Pentecostal churches represent prosperity as a God-given blessing and resent the mainline churches for legitimizing poverty by referring to Jesus as a poor man."[39] Our point of departure, therefore, is that contemporary Pentecostal missions, particularly in Africa, is unapologetically engaged in inculturation hermeneutics in their evangelism. We add that the inculturation should include ecological evangelism and advocacy.

Inculturation and Pentecostal Mission in Africa: An Evaluation

African Pentecostal movements have taken it upon themselves to directly address tangible and intimate issues faced by Africans. They undertake the task by preaching a gospel of deliverance, prosperity, healing and hope to their adherents. Thus, as expressed by one scholar, "African Pentecostalism has benefitted from processes of vernacularization and inculturation."[40] It has re-examined and redefined theological concepts of salvation, health and healing, poverty and wealth, deliverance, generational curses, sorcery, etc.[41] Accordingly, the aforementioned constitute inflictions to God's people which can be overcome by deliverance and exorcism through faith. The central theology in the gospel of prosperity is that God does not want to see his children afflicted. Consequently, Pentecostalism in Africa

---

36   Omenyo, C.N. and Arthur, W.A. 2013. The Bible Says! Neo-Prophetic Hermeneutics in Africa. *Studies in World Christianity*, 19(1):50-70.

37   Mbuvi, A. 2017. African Biblical Studies: An Introduction to an Emerging Discipline. *Currents in Biblical Research*, 15(2):149-178.

38   Mbuvi, African Biblical Studies, 152.

39   Kroesbergen, Neo-Pentecostalism in Southern Africa, 20.

40   Kalu, O.U. 2009. A Discursive Interpretation of African Pentecostalism. *Fides es Historia*, 4(1):71-90.

41   Kalu, A. Discursive Interpretation, 71.

is rooted in the varied contexts and experiences of the people. It seeks to address existential challenges holistically for the benefit of believers and their communities. It is a religion for the total person. It has a three-dimensional conception of the human person being soma, psyche and pneuma.[42] It is notable that the majority of those who participate in services rendered by contemporary Pentecostal churches are those who are troubled, desperate and in need of urgent solutions to their present ordeals.[43] As such, Pentecostalism in African contexts enables believers to make the best of rapid social change and to come to terms with and maximise their benefit from modernity's dominant values and institutions.[44] That is, given that in the current century everything has been reduced to monetary value, Pentecostals have not been left behind by the bandwagon of such change. We conclude that by providing services aimed at resolving visible, tangible and hence worldly needs for their adherents, the said missions are involved in inculturation hermeneutics in their reading, interpretation and appropriation of the Bible, making it relevant here and now.

We, however, want to highlight that in addition to the challenges mentioned above, there is the reality of an impending ecological crisis and possible collapse of Mother Earth. Mwiturubani and van Wyk caution that the climate change phenomenon is a global concern which threatens the sustainability of livelihoods of the majority of the population, especially in developing countries.[45] Still another scholar points out that Mother Nature has seen devastating changes and the ecosystem has been suffering numerous ecological disasters.[46] The growing global environmental crisis has profound implications for the long-term viability and welfare of natural environments and human social and economic systems.[47] Sadly, African Christianity, if not Christianity in general, displays some troubling tendencies, especially the separation of salvation from creation and the consequent lack of participation

42 Kalu, A. Discursive Interpretation, 71-72.

43 Kebaneilwe, M.D. 2018. Neo-Pentecostalism in Southern Africa: Some Critical Reflections. In: H. Kroesbergen (ed). *Neo-Pentecostalism in Southern Africa: Some Critical Reflections*. Lusaka: Word and Context. 44-58.

44 Maxwell, D. 1998. Delivered from the Spirit of Poverty: Pentecostalism, Prosperity and Modernity in Zimbabwe. *Journal of Religion in Africa*, 28(3):350-373.

45 Mwiturubani, D.A. and Van Wyk, J.A. 2010. Climate Change and Natural Resources Conflicts in Africa. *Institute for Security Studies Monograph*, 170:1-3. The authors here have further noted that members of the African Union have acknowledged Africa's vulnerability to climate change and the possible dangers posed by the changes on the continent's population, ecosystems and socio-economic progress.

46 Xu, J. and Gong, M.N. 2012. A Study of the Social Ecological Wisdom in H.W. Longfellow's Poetry. *Theory & Practice in Language Studies*, 2(1):24-30.

47 Edwards, M., Biloslavo, R. and Kwaymullina, A. 2013. Big Picture Wisdom: Metatheorising Ancient, Scientific and Indigenous Wisdom Perspectives for Global Environmental Leadership. *Journal of Spirituality, Leadership and Management*, 7(1):13-32.

in environmental issues.[48] Conspicuously, the material space within which the redeemed person lives, moves and has his/her being has been taken for granted.[49] Therefore, there is urgent need to mobilise all stakeholders, including churches, to awaken to the needed efforts to address the ecological challenge before us. In the words of Habel, we must figure out "how we can be contemporary prophets who give voice to the sufferings of Earth in a meaningful way."[50] For this reason, we call for an awakening of Pentecostal churches to incorporate ecological advocacy in their agenda as they seek to liberate their adherents from oppressive challenges of poverty, sickness and other injustices. We contend that dealing with the said issues without attending to the eminent issue of ecological decline renders all efforts meaningless in the long run. Simply put, social justice and ecological justice are interconnected.[51] For life to thrive holistically, Mother Earth must be alive and healthy, but currently:

> The forests, rivers, arable lands, atmosphere, and the oceans are all suffering degradation at the hands of humans. They are calling for someone to hear their cries and articulate their plight. The Earth, in turn, summons us to hear the cries for justice rising from the poor, weak and vulnerable.[52]

An Ecological Advocacy Rooted in Inculturated Reading of Jesus's Ministry

This section gives an overview of some random biblical texts which give initial reference to the mission and ministry of Jesus in the world. Attention is called to all references to nature or its members in our texts as well as Jesus's involvement with such, both in word and action. We shall begin with the very idea of Jesus coming into the world as the incarnate God. Our argument being that, that move on its own renders Earth sacred, valuable and worthy of love and care as the very dwelling of the son of God and hence God himself.

The Incarnation as God on Earth: A Call for Environmental Conservation

John 1:1-3 and 9-10

> In the beginning was the Word, and the Word was with God, and the Word was God. He was with God in the beginning. Through him all things were made; without him nothing was made that has been made. The true light that gives

48   Golo, B.W.K. 2014. The Groaning Earth and the Greening of Neo-Pentecostalism in the 21st century Ghana. *PentecoStudies: An Interdisciplinary Journal of Research on Pentecostal and Charismatic Movements*, 13(2):197-216.

49   Golo, B.W.K. 2012. Creation and Salvation in African neo-Pentecostalist Theology. In: E.M. Conradie (ed). *Creation and Salvation: A Companion on Recent Theological Movements*. Munster: LIT Verlag. 334-339.

50   Habel, Earth Mission. 119.

51   Habel, Earth Mission. 119.

52   Habel, Earth Mission. 119.

light to everyone was coming into the world. He was in the world, and though the world was made through him, the world did not recognise him... (NIV).

Scholars agree that the above verses, which form part of the prologue to John's gospel, are indicative of the presence of God in the world. For instance, Elaine Pagels asserts that in the text, John envisions a successful revelation of the Divine which appears in the world in human form.[53] Likewise, John Pryor maintains that the pronunciations of John 1:9 support a time in the incarnate history.[54] Thus, the enfleshment of the *Logos*/Word is God's way of dwelling in the world so as to make visible the invisible Creator of the world.[55] Noteworthy is that the very essence of Christianity is rooted in the concept of the incarnate God, which is the idea expressed by this prologue of the gospel of John. The argument raised here is that if Pentecostals today still uphold the idea that God became flesh (which they undoubtedly do) in the person of Jesus as John here claims, then it is even more compelling for them to recognise the importance of environmental advocacy and activism in their mission. Thus, not only creating the universe and all in it, with love and adoration as indicated in the creation account of Genesis 1, God also descended to become part and parcel of the created world/nature and to dwell with the Earth community. By choosing to be in the form of humanity, in and through Jesus, God can be said to show humanity that the Divine is inseparable from the worldly realm. It follows that, if that be the case, humanity is obligated to act towards nature/creation/environment/Earth with the same fellowship, love, respect and care as shown by the Creator God from its inception to the point of choosing to make it the abode of Divine presence.

Expressing similar sentiments, Musa Dube asserts that in Genesis 1, the human being is mandated to keep the Earth community in the same good state as God created it.[56] The point is, who are we as humanity to despise, disrespect, abuse and exploit that which the Creator loves, cherishes and deems as very good? Consequently, there is a justifiable demand to see commitment to environmental activism and advocacy from custodians of biblical faith, like Pentecostals. After all, everyone alive today is a culprit in environmental degradation, for research shows that human action has contributed to the undesirable changes in the atmosphere, summed up in the global warming phenomenon.[57]

53   Pagels, E. 1999. Exegesis of Genesis 1 in the Gospel of Thomas and John. *Journal of Biblical Literature*, 118(3):477-496.

54   Pryor, J.W. 1990. Jesus and Israel in the Fourth Gospel: John 1: 1-11. *Novum Testamentum*, 32(3):201-218.

55   Keinzer, M. 1998. Temple Christology in the Gospel of John. *Society of Biblical Literature Seminar Paper*, 37:1-2.

56   Dube, M.W. 2015. And God Saw that It Was Very Good: An Earth-friendly Reading of Genesis 1. *Black Theology*, 13(3):230-246.

57   Ring, M.J., Lindner, D., Cross, E.F. and Schlesinger, M.E. 2012. Causes of the Global Warming Observed since the 19th Century. *Atmospheric and Climate Sciences*, 2(4):401-415.

We have reiterated that the current state of our environment requires concerted efforts as it is in a crisis that not only threatens the non-human Earth community but humanity as well. Habel, in reference to Isaiah 6:3, emphasises that Earth is a sanctuary filled with God's presence, which compels all of humanity to develop strategies for protecting it.[58] Continuing the same slant, it may be argued that in ancient Israelite thinking, God has always dwelt on Earth as much as he dwells in heaven. There are numerous scriptures throughout the Bible which either directly or indirectly suggest the same idea. For instance, in Gen. 3:8,

> Then the man and his wife heard the sound of the LORD God as he was walking in the garden in the cool of the day, and they hid from the LORD God among the trees of the garden.

The above text illustrates that according to Israelite primeval history, the Creator God belonged in the land and the land belonged to him. By implication, God loves nature. He placed the first human couple in his garden and charged them with accountability for all his creation (Gen. 1-3), to be custodians thereof. It follows that he desired and still desires that humanity as descendants of Adam and Eve should be nurturers and guardians of nature and the natural world for him. The text presupposes that God is ever-present on Earth. Such an understanding is contrary to anthropocentric readings of Gen. 1:28 which emphasise humanity's 'dominion' over all other creation. Accordingly, the hush language which implies humanity's domineering status over all of God's creation, which in the Hebrew is denoted by the term *kabash* "dominion" and *radah* to "subdue," is rather problematic when considered within the entire scheme of events at creation in Gen. 1 and 2.[59] This is no less important today as the global Earth community struggles with environmental crises of high magnitude, making the liveability of Mother Earth questionable with every passing moment. We who are alive in the twenty-first century need to be proactive in finding and enacting readings of Gen. 1:28 (and the entire Bible) that are Earth friendly and leave no room for anthropocentricism. Current Pentecostal mission is therefore urged to become the mouthpiece of God's creation, which includes not just humanity but plants, animals and the soil. It suffices to indicate that in Africa, generally, the church commands large followings and contemporary Pentecostals are leading in that regard.[60] As observed by J. Kwabena Asamoah-Gyadu, the growth of Pentecostalism in Africa is a result of its ability to adapt to different African cultures and societies and its focus on contextualised expressions of the

---

58   Habel, Earth Mission, 115.

59   Kebaneilwe, M.D. 2015. The Good Creation: an eco-Womanist Reading of Genesis 1-2. *Old Testament Essays (OTE)*, 28(3):694-704.

60   Golo, B.W.K. 2012. Redeemed from the Earth? Environmental Change and Salvation Theology and African Christianity. *Scriptura: Journal for Contextual Hermeneutics in Southern Africa*, 111:348-361.

Christian faith.[61] That places Pentecostals in a good place to be the leading prophetic voice for inclusive justice that is not human-centred but Earth-centred. In fact, the involvement of the entire church and all Christian communities in environmental conservation through preaching will address the need for mass communication that aims to improve public understanding of environmental issues.[62]

Through an inculturated reading of the Bible, that aims to appropriate and contextualise all of Scripture in order to address current concerns, Pentecostal missions today cannot afford to ignore the cries of Mother Earth due to abuse and domination by humanity. The cries are presented in what we call global warming and the effects thereof, a phenomenon that simply may not be ignored. Adverse effects of ecological degradation are continually being felt throughout the world. That is, contemporary citizens of Mother Earth have and will at one point or another experience droughts, earthquakes, tornadoes, water shortages and other uncountable extreme weather conditions that have not only claimed human life but animals and vegetation as well.[63] The point is that inculturation requires us to pause and consider the believer as well as the non-believer's immediate context, which as indicated here includes environmental crisis and presents it as a topical reality that commands immediate attention. Finally, there are numerous texts expressing the idea that God has his dwelling on Earth, including Gen. 3:8; 28:15, 2 Chron. 16:9; Deut. 4:39; Num. 35:33-34 etc. All that is needed is for custodians of faith and all other interested parties or stakeholders of life on planet Earth to see to it that God's dwelling place – Mother Earth – is treated justly not just for God's sake but for sustenance of all Earthly life. Importantly, we need to remember, as Harry Hahne explains, that it is humanity's sin (Gen 3) that defiled the Earth and caused some aspects of nature not to operate as God originally intended.[64] God holds humans accountable for their sins against the Earth and animals. Nature is a victim of human sin and cries out in suffering and pain.[65] It follows necessarily that as humans we are obliged to fix our own chaos by devising strategies for environmental sustainability if Mother Nature is to continue to carry us all.

61   Asamoah-Gyadu, J.K. 2013. Contemporary African Pentecostal Christianity: Interpretations from an African Context. Oregon: WIPF & Stock Publishers. xiii.

62   Keith, R., Stamm, K.R., Clark, F. and Eblacas, P.R. 2000. Mass Communication and Public Understanding of Environmental Problems: The Case of Global Warming. *Public Understanding of Science,* 9(3):219-238.

63   Karl, T.R. and Trenberth, K.E. 2003. Modern Global Climate Change. *Science,* 302(5651):1719-1723.

64   Hahne, H.A. The Whole Creation Has Been Groaning. https://www.baylor.edu/content/services /document.php/106707.pdf

65   Hahne, The Whole Creation Has Been Groaning, 1-2.

Nature Ushers Jesus into Ministry: The Interconnectedness of Heaven and Earth

We must hasten to show that at the start of his ministry, Jesus demonstrated close affinity and intimacy with nature. We read in Matthew 3:16-17 that:

> As soon as Jesus was baptised, he went up out of the water. At that moment heaven was opened, and he saw the Spirit of God descending like a dove and alighting on him. And a voice from heaven said, "This is my Son, whom I love; with him I am well pleased." (NIV)

Considering that the events stated in the above text are an allusion to what happened right at the beginning of Jesus's ministry to the world, we can see that there is close association between him and nature. First, he gets baptised in water, which is a natural phenomenon. The baptism marks a pivotal point in Jesus's life and ministry. Water baptism in this case introduces Jesus to his life's sole mission as one sent to reconcile and restore all of creation back to the Creator God, as indicated in Romans 5:17 thus:

> For if, by the trespass of the one man, death reigned through that one man (Adam), how much more will those who receive an abundance of grace and of the gift of righteousness reign in life through the one man, Jesus Christ!... (Study Bible)

Water serves as a vehicle through which the son, Jesus is connected to the father-God, to humanity and to nature. We are told that the spirit of God descended on Jesus in the form of a dove (Matt. 3:17) and that, at that juncture, God spoke words of affirmation, out of the heavens, declaring that he is well pleased in and with his son. We may conclude that by so doing God the Creator confirms, albeit indirectly, that all things, i.e. humankind and God now both embodied in the person of Jesus, are connected to both the heavens and the Earth through the spirit that descended on Jesus at baptism. The same spirit is promised by Jesus to his disciples at the end of his Earth mission, "I will ask my father to give you another helper, to be with you forever ..." (John 14:16). Consequently, the circle of interconnection between the divine and natural will not be broken by Jesus's death and ascension back to the father.

Animals are also part of this connection as represented in the form of the dove that carried or symbolised the spirit of God. Consequently, Jesus's baptism was a phenomenal event that sealed the connection of all created beings with their creator so that we can no longer see heaven as separate from Earth. While God has always been part of both heaven and Earth (as discussed earlier), it is through Jesus as revealed at his baptism that the imagined barrier between heaven above and Earth below was ultimately demolished.

Furthermore, it is the same natural phenomenon, namely, water, through which humankind and by extension all of creation will continue to be reconciled with the Creator. This is not a far-fetched idea, given that in Matt. 28:19 we read, "Therefore go and make disciples of all nations, baptizing them in the name of the Father and of the Son and of the Holy Spirit." Thus, water stands as a connecting thread between Christ, God, humanity and nature. Through water baptism, the opportunity for all of creation to be restored back to the harmonious unity with the Creator expressed at creation and lost at the fall is made available to all nations (Matt. 28:19). The scenario here should become a guiding stick directing humanity toward Earth justice that seeks to preserve water and by implication all natural resources. Today, water baptism is still a widespread ritual throughout Christendom. Nonetheless, due to the effects of global warming, there is water shortage, water pollution and other human-induced ills that are threatening this vital natural resource without which there cannot be any life on Mother Earth.

Still in Matt. 3:16-17 above, we should underline the connection between heaven and Earth which exists through the act of baptism, for at that moment "heaven was opened, and he saw the Spirit of God descending like a dove ..." One can argue that reference to the opening of heaven at that juncture points to a link between God and Mother Earth through his spirit as it descended on Jesus, who at this stage was part of the Earth community. Not only that, but cognisance must also be taken that the events referred to here involved the appearance of a dove. Could this mean that all of creation was being reconciled through this connection between heaven and Earth? We assume it is a possibility and that read this way, we cannot help but feel obliged as humanity to see and treat all of creation with awe, adoration and respect. This emphasises the interconnectedness of all living species, including the Divine which through Jesus takes human form in order to demystify God's dwelling as not just in heaven but also on Earth. In the given scenario, animal kingdom and plant kingdom can no longer be seen as only valuable in so far as they benefit the human kingdom and will instead be seen as having intrinsic value in their own right. The Creator God, God's Son and God's Spirit are all partakers of the earthly dwelling. Therefore, humanity has to be cautious of this presence and avoid defiling the abode of God. Indeed, in Numbers 35:34, God makes it an imperative to "not defile the land where you live and where I dwell, for I, the LORD, dwell among the Israelites."

Do Not Turn All Stones into Bread: Environmental Sustainability

Still as an indication of Jesus's close association with nature in his earthly mission, we read in Matt 4:3-4 that:

> Jesus was led by the Spirit into the wilderness to be tempted by the devil. After fasting forty days and forty nights, he was hungry. The tempter came to him and said, "If you are the Son of God, tell these stones to become bread." Jesus answered, "It is written: 'Man shall not live on bread alone, but on every word that comes from the mouth of God." (NIV)

The term "wilderness" has been defined by the Longman dictionary as "a large area of land that has not been developed or farmed."[66] By implication, this is land that does not belong to a particular individual and therefore is natural and undisturbed. We learn that after baptism Jesus retreated to such a land and during the forty days and nights out there, he was tempted by the devil. Of interest to us is that when he was asked to turn a stone into bread, he reasoned that he would not do such a thing because "humans shall not live on bread alone..." (v. 4).

To Jesus, it is more valuable to be in communion with the creator, by communicating with and hearing from God, than to indulge in food all the time. Bread in this case may be understood as much more than food but perhaps materialism in general. By analogy, therefore, it may be argued that Jesus is here advocating for a sustainable use of environmental resources so that 'not all stones may be turned into bread.' Sustainability of natural environments and all of nature is a feasible project only if humanity stops turning every stone into their bread. As explained by John Morelli, we need to use the environment and natural resources in ways that will achieve a balance that allows ecosystems to sustain humanity while they continue to regenerate themselves rather than getting depleted.[67]

This is contrary to what is happening in our world today, where people selfishly want to own land so badly that eventually there will be hardly any land left unused. It constitutes greed and will eventually lead to unsustainable use of land, once all land has been developed for personal use and consumption. This is not to say that people may not own land, but that developments take place at the expense of natural resources, including land itself, water, plants and animals. The situation can be explained as follows:

> An individual's or community's consumption behaviour translates into an environmental footprint. Given the huge variation in consumption patterns and related environmental burdens and the world's limited natural resources and assimilation capacity, an increasingly pressing question is, who takes the biggest part of the pie and what actually is a "fair share"?[68]

66 https://www.ldoceonline.com/dictionary/wilderness

67 Morelli, J. 2011. Environmental Sustainability: A Definition for Environmental Professionals. *Journal of Environmental Sustainability,* 1(1):1-9.

68 Hoekstra, A.Y. and Wiedmann, T.O. 2014. Humanity's Unsustainable Environmental Footprint. *Science,* 344(6188):1114-1117.

As developments take place around the world, in every human community, they are done at the expense of the environment and its natural resources. No wonder studies show that pollution, which is one of the leading causes of global warming, is a result of economic growth.[69] In the said scenario, big cities are major contributors to regional and global pollution due to the extent of their industrialization and human population.[70] Simply put, when industries grow, more land is developed into buildings and roads, leaving no 'wilderness' and no 'stone.' A lot of natural resources such as wood and water, for example, also go into building. This happens simultaneously with the production of more greenhouse emissions as machinery used for construction become heavily involved, leading to more damage to the atmosphere as well as to the land. Non-human life gets destroyed in the process of digging, cutting down of trees and the use of chemicals that usually accompany the construction of buildings and roads.

It is high time that human beings reconsidered their use of natural resources and exploitation of Mother Nature in general. An inculturated reading of Jesus's response in Matthew 4:3-4 indicates that there is need for the wilderness to continue to exist. Such is a call for sustainable environment. As suggested by Arjen Hoekstra and Thomas Wiedmann, a sustainable use of natural resources means using them in a way that allows them to regenerate or to be able to sustain pressure from such use.[71] For instance,

> The ecological footprint (EF) measures both the appropriation of land use and the land needed for waste uptake (CO_2 sequestration)...The water footprint (WF) measures both the consumption of fresh water and the use of fresh water to assimilate waste.[72]

Sustainable use of environmental resources, therefore, calls for accountability. Not only is it for humans to be able to retreat to untouched lands, for instance, to connect with the divine, but also, as science has proven, for nature to regenerate. The spirit which descended on Jesus at his water baptism (Matthew 3:16-17) led him to the most natural, undisturbed place where he showed such utter dependence on God that he refused to turn a stone into bread. He was in intimate communion with God. The moral of the story is that some natural resources must be protected so that they remain natural and are not turned into commodities for human consumption. This is a call for humanity to limit their footprints on the environment, namely, the pressure humans exert on the environment resulting in ecological degradation.[73]

---

69   Karl and Trenberth, Modern Global Climate Change, 1719.

70   Karl and Trenberth, Modern Global Climate. 1719.

71   Karl and Trenberth, Modern Global Climate. 1719.

72   Hoekstra and Wiedmann, Humanity's Unsustainable Environmental Footprint, 1114.

73   Hoekstra and Wiedmann, Humanity's Unsustainable Environmental Footprint, 1114.

Genesis 1 speaks of the mandate of multiplication as given to the entire created world, so that humanity should allow other creatures to multiply as well. By limiting human action that otherwise prevents the rest of creation from thriving, there will be room for plants to flourish more, leading to healthy forests, animals and the rest of the natural world.

It goes without saying that Pentecostal churches and especially contemporary Pentecostals have become the face of Christianity in Africa in the current century. As noted by Asamoah-Gyadu, it has become the most exciting and dominant stream of Christianity, especially in Africa and other non-Western third world countries.[74] The situation has contributed to further damage of natural environments because, as indicated earlier, construction of buildings and roads affect our environments negatively, as it involves de-bushing areas, using heavy plant machineries and using chemicals for soil treatment prior to putting up buildings. We are convinced that Jesus would have been adamant that some of our lands should be left undisturbed and undeveloped, rather than all of them being turned into buildings etc. We want to encourage Pentecostal missions and humanity as a whole to start emphasizing the planting of forests, the protection of all animals and sacred sites, and the preservation of rivers and other water sources from pollution or extinction. There is need for more forests and wildernesses than buildings. As such we should hear and put into practice what Jesus meant when he said "not all stones should be turned into bread," in which 'stones' represent all of God's non-human creation.

Conclusion

In this chapter, we have attempted to show that the environmental crisis forms part of the situational context of the global community of the twenty-first century. This includes faith communities such as contemporary Pentecostal missions. However, we have noted that the church generally has not paid due attention to environmental issues. We have particularly focused on contemporary Pentecostalism in Africa and southern Africa, which is our context. Pentecostal missions in our part of the world engages in what is described as inculturation hermeneutics, which expresses the contextual nature of their endeavour. As a result, it has been observed that their efforts in appropriating the Bible and its faith to address tangible issues and challenges of the African people, which include persistent poverty, disease and other injustices, are commendable. Nonetheless, we have raised the concern that the same missions have neglected yet another pressing issue which forms part of the context of the people of Africa (as well as people elsewhere in the world), namely, the environmental crisis.

74 Asamoah-Gyadu, Contemporary Pentecostal Christianity: 1.

In their inculturation, Pentecostal churches and movements, especially in southern Africa, have focused more on what is popularly known as prosperity gospel. The theology of this type of gospel aims at addressing pertinent and intimate concerns of their adherents in order to come up with solutions of deliverance from poverty, lack and disease. Our argument throughout the chapter is that there is need to incorporate environmental issues in their work. Our suggestion and conviction is that if Pentecostals (and the church at large) could contextualise or inculturate Jesus's affinity, love and appreciation of nature in his ministry, they would gain a different perspective with regards to Mother Earth. We have shown that throughout his ministry Jesus revealed his connectedness with the natural world and the interconnectedness of all reality. When he came into the world in human form, while still a part of the divine, Jesus showed that the heavenly and the Earthly realms are infinitely interconnected. The revelation was further shown through his baptism and temptation. Therefore, Pentecostal evangelism would do well to become custodians of Mother Earth and all her inhabitants, fauna and flora alike. A commitment to environmental justice and advocacy is a demonstration of love for the God who loves his creation and wants to dwell within it eternally.

References

Asamoah-Gyadu, J.K. 2013. *Contemporary African Pentecostal Christianity: Interpretations from an African Context*. Oregon: WIPF& Stock Publishers. https://doi.org/10.2307/j.ctv1ddcp37

Deacon, G., & Lynch, G. 2013. Allowing Satan in? Moving toward a political economy of neo- Pentecostalism in Kenya. *Journal of Religion in Africa*, 43(2), 108-130. https://doi.org/10.1163/15700666-12341247

Dermawan, A. 2003. The Spirit in Creation and Environmental Stewardship: A Preliminary Pentecostal Response toward Ecological Theology. *Asian Journal of Pentecostal Studies (AJPS)*, 6(2):199-217.

Dube, M.W. 2015. And God saw that It was Very Good: An Earth-friendly Reading of Genesis 1. *Black Theology*, 13(3):230-246. https://doi.org/10.1179/1476994815Z.00000000060

Edwards, D. 2005. *Jesus the Wisdom of God: An Ecological Theology*. Oregon: Wipf and Stock Publishers.

Edwards, M., Biloslavo, R. and Kwaymullina, A. 2013. Big Picture Wisdom: Metatheorising Ancient, Scientific and Indigenous Wisdom Perspectives for Global Environmental Leadership. *Journal of Spirituality, Leadership and Management*, 7(1):13-32. https://doi.org/10.15183/slm2013.07.1113

Freston, P. 1999. Neo-Pentecostalism in Brazil: Problems of Definition and the Struggle for Hegemony. *Archives de sciences sociales des religions*, 145-162. https://doi.org/10.3406/assr.1999.1082

Gbote, E.Z.M. and Kgatla, S.T. 2014. Prosperity Gospel: A Missiological Assessment. *HTS Theological Studies*, 70(1):1-10. https://doi.org/10.4102/hts.v70i1.2105

Golo, B.W.K. 2014. The Groaning Earth and the Greening of

Neo-Pentecostalism in the 21st century Ghana. *PentecoStudies: An Interdisciplinary Journal of Research on Pentecostal and Charismatic Movements*, 13(2):197-216. https://doi.org/10.1558/ptcs.v13i2.197

Golo, B.W.K. 2012. Redeemed from the Earth? Environmental Change and Salvation Theology and African Christianity. *Scriptura: Journal for Contextual Hermeneutics in Southern Africa*, 111:348-361. https://doi.org/10.7833/111-0-17

Golo, B.W.K. 2012. Creation and Salvation in African neo-Pentacostalist Theology. In: E.M. Conradie (ed). *Creation and Salvation: A Companion on Recent Theological Movements*. Munster: LIT Verlag. 334-339.

Habel, N. 2010. Earth-Mission: The Third Mission of the Church. *Currents in Theology and Mission*, 37(2):114-125.

Hahne, H.A. The Whole of Creation Has Been Groaning. https://www.baylor.edu/content/services/document.php/106707.pdf

Hoekstra, A.Y. and Wiedmann, T.O. 2014. Humanity's Unsustainable Environmental Footprint. *Science*, 344(6188):1114-1117. https://doi.org/10.1126/science.1248365

Kalu, O.U. 2009. A Discursive Interpretation of African Pentecostalism. *Fides es Historia*, 4(1):71-90.

Karl, T.R. and Trenberth, K.E. 2003. Modern Global Climate Change. *Science*, 302(5651):1719-1723. https://doi.org/10.1126/science.1090228

Kebaneilwe, M.D. 2018. Neo-Pentecostalism in Southern Africa: Some Critical Reflections. In: H. Kroesbergen (ed). *Neo-Pentecostalism in Southern Africa: Some Critical Reflections*. Lusaka: Word and Context.

Kebaneilwe, M.D. 2015. The Good Creation: an eco-Womanist Reading of Genesis 1-2. *Old Testament Essays(OTE)*, 28(3):694-704. https://doi.org/10.17159/2312-3621/2015/v28n3a8

Keinzer. M. 1998. Temple Christology in the Gospel of John. *Society of Biblical Literature Seminar Paper*, 37:1-2.

Kiariem, G. and Mouki, J.S. 2016. The Changing Understanding of the Eucharist among the Kikuyu Communicants of the Thika Diocese in the Anglican Church of Kenya. *Stellenbosch Theological Journal*, 2(2):295-320. https://doi.org/10.17570/stj.2016.v2n2.a14

Keith, R. Stamm, K.R., Clark, F., and Eblacas, P.R. 2000. Mass Communication and Public Understanding of Environmental Problems: The Case of Global Warming. *Public Understanding of Science*, 9(3):219-238. https://doi.org/10.1088/0963-6625/9/3/302

Kramer, E.W. 2005. Spectacle and the Staging of Power in Brazilian neo-Pentecostalism. *Latin American Perspectives*, 32(1), 95-120. https://doi.org/10.1177/0094582X04271875

Kroesbergen, H. (ed). 2018. *Neo-Pentecostalism in Southern Africa: Some Critical Reflections*. Lusaka: Word and Context.

Loba-Mkole, J.C. 2008. Rise of Intercultural Biblical Hermeneutics in Africa. *HTS Teologiese Studies/Theological Studies*, 64(3):1347-1364. https://doi.org/10.4102/hts.v64i3.77

Longman Dictionary of Contemporary English. https://www.Idoceonline.com/dictionary/wilderness

Magesa, L. 2014. *Anatomy of Inculturation: Transforming the Church in Africa*. Maryknoll: Orbis Books.

Maxwell, D. 1998. Delivered from the Spirit of Poverty: Pentecostalism, Prosperity and Modernity in Zimbabwe. *Journal of Religion in Africa*, 28(3):350-373. https://doi.org/10.2307/1581574

Mbuvi, A. 2017. African Biblical Studies: An Introduction to an Emerging Discipline. *Currents in Biblical Research*, 15(2):149-178. https://doi.org/10.1177/1476993X16648813

Morelli, J. 2011. Environmental Sustainability: A Definition for Environmental Professionals. *Journal of Environmental Sustainability*, 1(1):1-9. https://doi.org/10.14448/jes.01.0002

Mwiturubani, D.A. and Van Wyk, J.A. 2010. Climate Change and Natural Resources Conflicts in Africa. *Institute for Security Studies Monograph*, 170:1-3.

Odozor, P.I. 2008. An African Moral Theology of Inculturation: Methodological Considerations. *Theological Studies*, 69(3):583-609. https://doi.org/10.1177/004056390806900305

Omenyo, C.N. and Arthur, W.A. 2013. The Bible Says! Neo-Prophetic Hermeneutics in Africa. *Studies in World Christianity*, 19(1):50-70. https://doi.org/10.3366/swc.2013.0038

Pagels, E. 1999. Exegesis of Genesis 1 in the Gospel of Thomas and John. *Journal of Biblical Literature*, 118(3):477-496. https://doi.org/10.2307/3268185

Pryor, J.W. 1990. Jesus and Israel in the Fourth Gospel: John 1:1-11. *Novum Testamentum*, 32(3):201-218. https://doi.org/10.1163/156853690X00070

Ring, M.J., Lindner, D., Cross, E.F. and Schlesinger, M.E. 2012. Causes of the Global Warming Observed since the 19th Century. *Atmospheric and Climate Sciences*, 2(4):401-415. https://doi.org/10.4236/acs.2012.24035

Swoboda, A.J. 2015. Posterity or Prosperity? Critiquing and Refiguring Prosperity in an Ecological Age.

Pneuma, 37(3):394-411. https://doi.org/10.1163/15700747-03703002

Xu, J. and Gong, M.N. 2012. A Study of the Social Ecological Wisdom in H.W. Longfellow's Poetry. *Theory & Practice in Language Studies,* 2(1):24-30. https://doi.org/10.4304/tpls.2.1.24-30

SALVATION RE-IMAGINED

Theological Perspectives on Gender and Ecology

Peggy Mulambya-Kabonde[1]

Abstract

This chapter presents a gendered analytical and contextualised study on salvation that is re-imagined for both human beings and the rest of God's creation.[2] It provides Ernst Conradie's (2011) theoretical framework. In his theory, Conradie concedes that "the earth is a sacred gift to us from God."[3] This framework is employed because there is some unequal partnership between humankind and the rest of God's creation. Conradie's lens will assist in examining how societies have contributed to destroy God's creation. Most of all, Conradie's framework is of great importance to this chapter because it provides a platform for a theology of Salvation re-imagined, with particular reference to gender and theological understanding of salvation. For example, Conradie emphasises that with regard to the way human beings destroy the earth, "we have to confess our sins in this regard and alter our ways."[4] Firstly, while the chapter argues against this view, it tries to answer the following question: *What is the holistic understanding of the word "Salvation" from a Theological and gender perspective?* Secondly, the chapter utilises other sources to probe the degradation of Mother Earth by exploring the unequal relationship between human beings and the rest of God's creation.

---

1   Peggy Mulambya-Kabonde obtained her PhD in Gender and Theology from the University of KwaZulu-Natal in South Africa in 2014. The title of her thesis was Ordination of Women: Partnership, Praxis and Experience of the United Church of Zambia. Her research interests include issues of gender justice and inclusivity of all God's creation. She served as first female General Secretary of the United Church of Zambia and is currently serving as minister of the word and sacraments in the United Kingdom. She is also the Southern African Circle coordinator.

2   Please note, the words "creation", "ecology", "earth" and "Mother Earth" will be used interchangeably in this chapter.

3   Conradie, E.M. 2011. Christianity and Earthkeeping: In Search of an Inspiring Vision. Stellenbosch: African SUN MeDIA. 95.

4   Conradie, Christianity and Earthkeeping, 5.

Introduction

Conradie proposes that "the reason why Christians should engage in earthkeeping should be based on faith in the Creator God."[5] For Conradie, all human beings are confronted with issues such as acid rain, ozone depletion, floods, deforestation, climate change, pollution, population growth and insurmountable waste dumps.[6] It is for these reasons that he calls all Christians to engage in earthkeeping to exercise their faith in God. He observes that "… the earth is seen here as a sacred gift from God – which has to be treasured and preserved because God's own presence may be detected in nature."[7] The chapter focuses on the notion that assurance of salvation to human beings does not rest in our hands, but in God's own hands. It reminds humanity to re-imagine their salvation with the potential of utilizing Christian ethics for social change, particularly, in relation to ecology.

The word *salvation* is defined as preservation or deliverance from harm, ruin or loss.[8] In Christian circles, salvation is deliverance from sin and its consequences. It is achieved by faith in Christ. The Christian gospel of salvation as I understand it, is for all humankind and the rest of God's creation. It provides personal dignity that is closely related to independence, interdependence and dependence. Human beings are naturally subject to moments of interdependency, for one cannot work in isolation. Christians, for example, are dependent on God through faith. Therefore, since Christians follow in the footsteps of the Lord Jesus as their model, they cannot work effectively without the assurance of salvation in Christian Discipleship. Thus, this chapter will look at two dimensions, namely, salvation as re-imagined in the life of an individual and as re-imagined in the rest of creation as recorded in Romans 8:19-25:

> **19** For the creation waits in eager expectation for the children of God to be revealed.
>
> **20** For the creation was subjected to frustration, not by its own choice, but by the will of the one who subjected it, in hope.
>
> **21** that the creation itself will be liberated from its bondage to decay and brought into the freedom and glory of the children of God.
>
> **22** We know that the whole creation has been groaning as in the pains of childbirth right up to the present time.

---

5   Conradie, Christianity and Earthkeeping, 17.

6   Conradie, Christianity and Earthkeeping, 11.

7   Conradie, Christianity and Earthkeeping, 95.

8   This definition is according to Clarkson S & Russell LM (eds). 1996. *Dictionary of Feminist Theologies*. Louisville: Westminster John Knox Press, 194. They also explain that the word salvation means the act of saving or the state of being saved.

23 Not only so, but we ourselves, who have the first fruits of the Spirit, groan inwardly as we wait eagerly for our adoption to childship, the redemption of our bodies.

24 For in this hope we were saved. But hope that is seen is no hope at all. Who hopes for what they already have?

25 But if we hope for what we do not yet have, we wait for it patiently.[9]

Of particular concern in the above Pauline passage is the use of the word "creation" and the phrase "… in this hope we were saved." In my view, the above Bible quotation suggests that salvation does not only apply to human beings but also to the rest of God's creation. In other words, God's creation, apart from human beings, awaits liberation from its bondage to decay. This is my objective statement for re-imagining salvation that is inclusive of all God's creation instead of the anthropocentric salvation of human beings alone. Additionally, this chapter will give an exegetical aspect towards some selected biblical texts namely, Psalm 24:1-2; Genesis 1:26-27; Mark 4:34-38 and Philippians 1:6. These biblical texts illustrate salvation being re-imagined, God's creation and God's love for humanity.

Over the years, the Circle of Concerned African Women Theologians, hereafter 'the Circle,' has convened in creative ways as part of the driving energy behind African women's scholarly contributions on theological, social, ecumenical and gender issues in Africa and globally. The Circle has enriched the witness and leadership of women in church and society. As a result, African contextual feminist theologies have emerged in many social locations, critically analyzing and identifying the root causes of women's oppression, unmasking and deconstructing patriarchal ideologies, and working to change the social systems which contribute to the unequal partnership of men and women in church, society and the rest of God's creation.

To provide an overview, this section is followed by a discussion on the earth as a sacred gift to us from God. It includes the church's promotion of holistic salvation, that is, on caring of human souls and the rest of God's creation. Since this chapter includes some gender-related issues, the section on the church's promotion of holistic salvation deals with patriarchal issues. Furthermore, it highlights issues on salvation re-imagined, since this is the core of the chapter. Salvation and the Earth are sacred gifts that are gendered or shared. They are discussed in the section before the conclusion. I will conclude this chapter by highlighting an alternative model for the church to work beyond her tradition of human relationships alone. This is a model of ecumenism, viz., of being all-inclusive that also retains an understanding of God's creation. The church must work towards an inclusive community, which

---

9   Holy Bible. 2012. *New Revised Standard Version.* The United Kingdom: The British and Foreign Bible Society Press. Romans 8:19-25.

holds all the members of the body of Christ together as well as the rest of God's creation, thereby bringing them together to the whole household of God.[10] The following section outlines Ernst Conradie's theoretical framework on the earth as a sacred gift that undergirds this chapter.

Theoretical Framework

Theologians such as Conradie acknowledge that "one reason why Christians should engage in earth-keeping is from a sense of guilt for the ecological damage that we as humans have collectively caused. We have to care for the environment because we have failed to do so in the past."[11] Conradie is of the view that human beings need to understand that one of the aims of Christ's death is to counter the environmental injustice. For Conradie, human beings contribute to God's creation which is the earth and everything that is in it. He invites all theologians to continue affirming that there is a clear need to transform the Christian faith into a more ecological faith and Christian theology into an ecological theology.[12] Conradie warns us that "the integrity of creation is regarded as sacred and it must therefore be protected through an ecological vision and ethos."[13] Conradie encourages humanity to observe the divine nature of the earth and protect the earth by coming up with godly rules and principles. He thus calls both women and men to work together in caring and treating the earth as a sacred place where justice should prevail and right relationships are formed because it is from the earth that human beings receive their blessings from God.

For Conradie, this is what it means when he states that the earth is a sacred gift to us from God. He concedes that,

> [t]he world exists as an intricate balance of parts. Human beings must recognise this balance and strive to maintain and stay within this cosmic balance. The earth is regarded as a living being which must be treated with respect and loving care. Everything, from hunting to healing, is a recognition and affirmation of the sacredness of life.[14]

---

10 Conradie maintains that the whole household of God has been employed for an ecological doctrine of creation based on the indwelling of God's Spirit in creation and in the ecclesial community, an anthropology of stewardship (the *oikonomos*), or one of being at-home-on earth, a soteriology and an ecclesiology focusing on the way of becoming members of the household of God (Eph 2:19-22), an eschatology expressing the hope that the house which we as humans inhabit (the earth) will indeed become God's home, (See Conradie E.M. *The Whole Household of God (OIKOS): Some Ecclesiological Perspectives. Scriptura*, 2007:2).

11 Conradie, Christianity and Earthkeeping, 5.

12 Conradie, Christianity and Earthkeeping, 8.

13 Conradie, Christianity and Earthkeeping, 95.

14 Conradie, Christianity and Earthkeeping, 96.

Conradie advocates for churches, communities and the entire world to become places where even the marginalised are embraced, where even the environment becomes a safe space for human beings to live in.[15] In one hand, Russell concurs with Conradie as she states that hospitality is part and parcel of the gospel message of caring and welcoming all human beings, including those that are in the margins and are discriminated against, to invite them to the sacramental round table.[16] This is in accordance with the parable of the Good Samaritan in the Gospel of Luke 10:30-37. Additionally, Conradie's work provides a space for human beings to live and appreciate the sacred gift of nature and the environment that they live in. He asserts that "if life becomes a struggle for basic survival, as is often the case in Africa, it will be increasingly difficult to resist environmental destruction. Only where there is hope, life can become meaningful."[17] In order for churches and communities to become safe spaces, human beings need to be hopeful, and faithful, so as to share in justice, equality, and a safe environment within their communities and churches.[18]

To this end, the chapter proposes the above theoretical framework located within power, culture, creation, Christian and gender studies. Since this chapter is located within African culture, an analysis of the salvation re-imagined concept from the African theological perspective on gender and ecology will be explored. Conradie's theory of the earth, being a sacred gift to us from God will be used as a framework. As Olssen, Codd and Neill have noted, central to such a framework is "a conception of policy as a politically, socially and historically contextualised practice."[19] Hence, this chapter will analyze and contextualise the problem of salvation that is experienced in the church and society so as to create room for churches to formulate policies and principles that will safeguard equal and just societies in caring for the environment. The following section outlines how the church has promoted the holistic salvation of human souls and the rest of God's creation.

How the Church in General Has Promoted Holistic Salvation: Caring of Human Souls and the Rest of God's Creation

The key question in this chapter is: *what is a holistic understanding of the word Salvation from a Theological and gender perspective?* This question is guided by the

---

15 Russell L.M. 1993. Church in the Round: Feminist Interpretation of the Church. Louisville: John Knox Press. 25.

16 Russell L.M. 2001. Hot-house Ecclesiology: A Feminist Interpretation of the Church. *The Ecumenical Review*, 53.

17 Conradie, Christianity and Earthkeeping, 100.

18 See Russell, Hot-house Ecclesiology, 52-54

19 Olssen, M. Codd J. and O'Neill A. 2004. *Education Policy: Globalisation, Citizenship and Democracy.* London: Sage Publications. 3.

hypothesis that the church has encouraged preaching on the saving of human souls alone. There are no clear policies and practices that support the liberation of both human beings and the rest of God's creation in sermons and in the mission of the church. To some extent these forms of dichotomizing can be termed as "patriarchy," which is also described as a violent system of domination in which women, children and creation are subordinate.[20] Patriarchy has been perpetuated throughout human history through the institutionalization of domination in the social, cultural and religious practices of societies. Prachar Hutanuwar, who writes about domination of one group over another, states that:

> When we look at this world view in the context of Globalization, we can see that it has created a kind of civilization that victimises its own people; people of other worldviews and other sentient beings. Over the last few hundred years this has been happening in the name of Industrialization, colonization and development in both capitalist and communist frameworks.[21]

Hutanuwar's view is that our worldviews have been submerged within the context of globalization to an extent that whatever we do as human beings, we view reality in the form of unequal power relations, class and gender.[22] Whatever human beings do is about competition and marginalization. For Hutanuwar, patriarchy is still at work in this context of globalization because issues of sex, class, gender and power are experienced in our everyday lives.[23] Patriarchy is legitimised through nature, the media, politics and legal, economic and education systems. It is so complex, with its interplaying factors of sex, gender, class, age, ability, ethnicity, and religion, that it encircles women and men in its exploitative, discriminatory and oppressive control.[24] Patriarchy prevents both men and women from being fully human.

Our different experiences and traditions can become the starting point in the search for the full humanity of women and men and renewal of creation. The church also needs to be involved as a healing community to both human beings and the rest of God's creation. In this context the participation of women in different ministries of the church empowers them rather than subordinates them, when women are empowered, so is the whole community – equality as well as inclusivity are reinforced. But as the present partnership stands, with stories coming from above of neglecting the rest of God's creation, Duchrow and Gerhard observe that:

20 Ruether, R.R. 1983. *Sexism and God-talk: Toward a Feminist Theology*. Boston: Beacon Press, 73.
21 Hutanuwar, P. 2000. Globalisation from Buddhist perspective. In *Globalisation and its consequences*. 50. June. Geneva: Warc, 4.
22 Hutanuwar, Globalisation from Buddhist perspective, 5.
23 Hutanuwar, Globalisation from Buddhist perspective, 6.
24 Hutanuwar, Globalisation from Buddhist perspective, 6.

> The situation of the majority of peoples in the present economic, political, and military systems clearly indicates that the point of departure for theological penetration cannot be 'the good creation' but the suffering and oppression of humanity and other sentient beings. Here we see even more easily than in the case of creation that in our present situation the weaker 'partner' must endure the ruthless violence of the wealthy, 'the haves.'[25]

Duchrow and Gerhard's concern stems from the societal norms that entail that the poor should always submit to the rich. Thus, they observe that power is always in the hands of those that are stronger, and the weaker parties should be submissive.[26] Duchrow and Gerhard insist that when doing theology in a community, one has to remember that the suffering and oppression of humanity and other sentient beings must be taken into consideration.[27] Where the voices of the 'suffering and oppression of humanity' are not heard, it is important to ask them questions so that they share what they know, especially anything to do with God's creation for the earth is part of god's creation, which is a sacred gift to us from God. The usual demonstration of power over the weaker partner in religious circles help to perpetuate the inferiority in the minds of growing boys and girls. This is in agreement with Comaroff and Comaroff's argument on issues of power.[28] They argue that power comes across to humanity basically as a collection of ideas that reflect the interests of those who are ruling. They are similar to the most violent coercion that has to do with shaping, directing and dominating social thoughts and actions.[29]

An interpretation of Mark 4:34-38, shows that for the house of Christ to be completely built, it has to be erected by unity in diversity. Diversity means that the church of God is supposed to value different gifts in whatever form. Unequal power dynamics should be avoided. In Mark 4:34-38, we observe that the teaching of the Lord Jesus Christ attracted a lot of people in Palestine. The high class, middle, and the marginalised had a place in his teaching. As a result, crowds of people were following Jesus Christ.[30] The large following of people characterised Jesus Christ's ministry. This shows that the ministry of Jesus Christ flourished on the aspect of assurance of salvation. The salvation that the church must preach is a salvation that encompasses the rich and the poor, the strong and the weak, female and male, embraces humanity and teaches humanity to embrace God's creation. Therefore, the

25 Duchrow, U. and Gerhard, L. 1987. *Shalom: Biblical Perspectives on Creation, Justice & Peace.* Geneva: WCC Publication. 55.

26 Duchrow and Gerhard, Shalom: Biblical Perspectives on Creation, 56.

27 Duchrow and Gerhard. Shalom: Biblical Perspectives on Creation, 58.

28 See Comaroff, J. and Comaroff, J. 1991. *Of Revelation and Revolution: Christianity, Colonialism, and Consciousness in South Africa.* Vol. 1. London: The University of Chicago Press. 22.

29 Comaroff and Comaroff, Of Revelation and Revolution: Christianity, Colonialism, and Consciousness in South Africa. 22.

30 Holy Bible. 2012. *New Revised Standard Version.* Mark 4:34-38.

ministry of Jesus did not discriminate but forgave sins and assured people that they were free indeed.

Similarly, the word of God assures our salvation as recorded in Philippians 1:6, "He who began a good work in you will carry it on to completion until the day of Christ Jesus."[31] This is one of the roles of assurance of salvation that the church ought to be preaching to humanity. Suffice it to say, this is vital in that regardless of challenges a person goes through in life, he or she must find comfort in the Lord who began the good work in him or her and extend it to the rest of God's creation. For the church to be the way it was meant to be, all humanity, regardless of their talents, need to be seen as sacred assets that should be given room to nourish God's creation. In light of the above, it is the duty of the church to preach salvation to her members so that humanity can take control of re-imagining it.

Salvation Re-imagined

It is very important to study and understand the strategy of winning more souls to Christ through the nice enticements towards Christ's salvific agenda. Most human beings in this world have different understandings and perception of the whole economy of being saved and why they should be saved. There is an urgent call and prompting of the church to be a hub for clear and convincing plans for salvation. This call articulates why human beings should let go of their different beliefs, faiths, or religions and be the disciples of Christ in taking a "sacramental approach to Christian earthkeeping."[32] This is the reason this chapter uses the model of the earth as a sacred gift to us from God. This includes all human beings who are faced with issues of unjust communities. Many human beings would ask, why join Christianity? Why not continue with my beliefs that my forefathers or mothers left me with? What are the advantages or the benefits of abandoning my beliefs? Surely, there must be an assurance of Salvation for one to be fully convinced to forsake or abandon one's faith and follow the Christian way. Hence, the criticality of this chapter in discussing the subject matter of the assurance of salvation re-imagined from the gender and theological perspectives. The following verses from Psalm 24:1-2 show us that both human beings and the rest of God's creation belong to God and are important.

> **1** *The Earth is the LORD's and everything in it, the world, and all who live in it;*
>
> **2** *for he founded it on the seas and established it on the waters.*[33]

---

31 Holy Bible. 2012. *New Revised Standard Version*. Philippians 1:6.

32 Conradie, Christianity and Earthkeeping, 96.

33 Holy Bible. 2012. *New Revised Standard Version*. Psalm 24:1-2.

An exegesis of the above text is self-explanatory, although the psalmist in this regard reminds us that generally, God is the ultimate ruler and Creator over this world. God is the Creator and is present in every part of the world. The psalmist further declares that God's special presence in God's tabernacle is an indication that the fullness of life is provided by God, "and the fullness thereof" means that all the creatures belong to God and are thus, sacred. We ourselves are not our own; our bodies, our souls, are not ours. Even the children we have are God's.[34] We are souls that know and consider their own nature, and for this we must live to cherish the environment that has been provided to us by God. To this end, the statement, "human life is inseparably bound to nature,"[35] means that there is a divine connection between humanity and nature. All Creation is interconnected and as such, human beings cannot survive without nature. That is the reason human beings are being cautioned to preserve nature. Conradie is of the view that, "there is an almost overwhelming emphasis on interrelatedness, mutual dependence, reciprocity, ecological balance, wholeness, the integrated web of life and, especially, community."[36]

Therefore, "the Earth is the Lord's, and the fullness thereof ...,"[37] viz., the whole universe; both land and water, and the skies, the wind or air, and all that is therein; the fishes of the sea, the fowls of the air, the beasts of the field, all plants and vegetables that spring out of the Earth, and metals and minerals in the bowels of it; all these are the riches of God. Human beings live, plough and make use of the Earth, yet it belongs to God, not to humanity. Human beings are tenants of the Earth because the sole proprietor is God. This means "we have to be concerned not only with the question as to how Christianity can respond to environmental concerns,"[38] but we have to be sure of how we can preach the assurance of salvation to our communities in relation to God's Creation.

The Longman Dictionary of the English Language defines assurance as, "The quality or state of being sure or certain; freedom from doubt. It is the confidence of mind or manner. Assurance is to be secured in the face of risk; to inform positively, it is characterised by certainty or security; satisfied as to the certainty or truth of the matter."[39] From the above definition, we are able to ascertain how we are to disciple human beings into Christianity. It is very important to assure them of finding salvation for their souls and their entire lives in God. The critical part is to define salvation. What then is Salvation? What benefit does it have in the lives of

---

34   Matthew, H. https://biblehub.com/commentaries/psalms/24-1.htm accessed on 19 April 2020.
35   Conradie, Christianity and Earthkeeping, 97.
36   Conradie, Christianity and Earthkeeping, 96.
37   See Psalm 24 above.
38   Conradie, Christianity and Earthkeeping, 8.
39   The Longman Dictionary of the English Language. 1992. Amazon: Addison-Wesley Longman Ltd. 87.

human beings? Whatever the definition of salvation, it is very critical to make sure that human beings are assured of being saved. Salvation must also be contextual and dependent upon different individuals, their beliefs, way of life, environment, culture, and generally their entire life. The key word before anyone can fully commit themself is to get this assurance of being saved, but being saved from what?

Let us broadly find out what the word 'salvation' means. Ronald Nicolson states that "… the Hebrew word usually translated as Salvation, 'yasha' has its root in the idea of broadness and liberation from that which constrains and imprisons."[40] This is an eye opener because it means that anything that inhibits someone from attaining the true worthiness of being human, any depravity of humankind in anyway, should be broken by the word of God that saves and changes lives. Human beings should find healing, hope, and deliverance from social, political, ecological and economic woes that put them into bondage. Human beings should see light in the word of God for them to have that desire of joining it. Otherwise, it will be like any other religion which is just systematically placed to record its existence without making tangible positive impact on the lives of the masses.

The further probing questions could be; does Christianity offer itself as a solution to the many challenges that society today is facing? Can Christianity offer hope of being saved from the many dangers which society is grappling with today like disease, poverty, unemployment, nepotism, death, climate change and economic challenges? Indeed, Christianity should show some positive signs of this assurance, meaning that salvation is being freed from that which limits someone from attaining freedom and development. Freedman affirms that salvation "involves being delivered from slavery, separation from one's family, and the threat of death."[41] The Israelites were at one time in bondage in Egypt, and God through Moses had to liberate them from the Egyptians. In this sense, it can be seen that the Israelites attained salvation through being redeemed from slavery in Egypt so that they could go to the Promised Land. Another example can be taken from marriage where the wife lives in bondage if she is regularly beaten by her husband, and when she is divorced, this is seen as attaining salvation from being beaten.

Conradie notes that "we are confronted with statistics about deforestation, the extinction of species, climate change, population growth"[42] and other natural disasters. Equally, when people in my context learn not to cut trees or fish indiscriminately,

---

40   Nicolson, R. 1990. *A Black Future? Jesus and Salvation in South Africa*. London: SCM and Philadelphia: Trinity Press International. 91.

41   Freedman, H. 1992. *The Phenomenology of Information on Salvation*. Ramat Gan Israel: Bar Ilan University. 124.

42   Conradie, Christianity and Earthkeeping, 11.

that will be salvation brought to nature. The changes in rainfall patterns and other forms of precipitation could be some of the most critical factors determining the overall impact of climate change. The cutting down of trees for charcoal has heavily affected weather patterns. As these changes occur, one will see that rainfall is much more difficult to predict than expected. However, there are some statements about the future that scientists can make with confidence, especially with the cutting of trees for charcoal. There is evidence to show that regions that are already wet are likely to get wetter, but details on how much wetter and what the impact will be on a local scale are more difficult to ascertain. Conradie terms the preservation of Creation by human beings as a sacramental approach to Christian earthkeeping. He reiterates that, "in such a sacramental approach to Christian earthkeeping the focus is less on normative religious texts and more on the sacred and even revelatory character of nature itself."[43]

God has greatly blessed us with various natural resources, such as land, trees, rivers and lakes. These are the revelatory character of nature. When these are depleted, there will be changes in weather patterns that make predicting rainfall particularly difficult. Different climate models are in broad agreement about future warming on a global scale, when it comes to predicting how these changes will impact on the weather, rainfall and the environment. In this case, one wonders about human beings' behaviour when they are the ones who are supposed to care for and be prudent with all the natural resources that God has entrusted to them. As the rest of creation groans, human beings are supposed to listen and deliver it from all manner of oppression. The Israelites complained and cried out to God to rescue them when the Egyptians were pursuing them as they headed towards the Red sea. God heard and delivered them from the hand of their enemies. Similarly, human beings should hear and become prudent stewards of the rest of God's creation.

If a human being in life has attained all the required freedom, then he or she has salvation. Teresa Hinga argues that in order to gain salvation, many Africans gained access to the various images of Christ enshrined in the New Testament.[44] Africans appropriated one or several of these images of Christ and made them their own, despite the distortions apparent in missionary praxis. She further suggests that:

> While not ruling out the possibility of some Pharisaism, the image of Jesus as a personal friend has been one of the most popular among women, precisely because they need such a personal friend most. (Thus, the image of Christ

43   Conradie, Christianity and Earthkeeping, 95.

44   Hinga, M.T. 2001. Jesus Christ and the Liberation of Women in Africa. In: M.A. Oduyoye and M.R.A. Kanyoro (eds). *The Will to Arise: Women, Tradition and the Church in Africa*. Maryknoll: Orbis Books. 190.

who helps them to bear their griefs, loneliness and suffering is a welcome one indeed).[45]

For Hinga, many African women have adopted the image of Jesus as a personal friend and a personal saviour simply because they have come to accept Jesus as a saviour to the needy, the poor, the sick and the marginalised. They need a friend in whom they can find comfort. Hinga sees that the image of Christ that many African women [and men] believe in as the one that "… is actively concerned with a lot of victims of social injustice and the dismantling of unjust social structures."[46] However, she cautions many African women [and men] to formulate a relevant Christology and to be critical and on the alert; to be suspicious "…of any versions of Christology that would be inimical to their cause."[47] It is only by doing this that many African women and [men] will be confident enough to confess Christ as their liberator and one who would grant them salvation.

Salvation in this case meets both the physical and spiritual realms of African women. For the children of Israel, whenever they won a battle against their enemy, it was believed to be salvation and God was their Saviour. The redemption and restoration of Israel after the Babylonian captivity illustrated strikingly the spiritual aspects of salvation.[48] They held out that hope of enjoying the Lord's intimate presence in the temple and as renewed people were free again with God amidst them. This is in line with the time when the Israelites had no freedom of worship during their captivity in Babylon. After their liberation, they were in their own land, and, could worship Yahweh freely. That was their salvation on Earth.

Salvation, Gender and the Earth – Matthew 15:19-20

> For out of the heart come evil thoughts – murder, adultery, sexual immorality, theft, false testimony, slander. These are what defile a person; but eating with unwashed hands does not defile them.[49]

Matthew 15:19-20 informs us that sin keeps separating humanity from God. For us human beings, salvation is necessary because we are created in the flesh that causes us to sin. Therefore, salvation is necessary because of sin. With reference to the text, Psalm 24:1-2 above, it simply means 'everything in the world' belongs to God; whereas in the second verse, its inhabitants refer specifically to land, creatures and to humans.

---

45   Hinga, *Jesus Christ and the Liberation of Women in Africa*. 191.
46   Hinga, *Jesus Christ and the Liberation of Women in Africa*. 192.
47   Hinga, *Jesus Christ and the Liberation of Women in Africa*. 192.
48   Holy Bible. 2012. *New Revised Standard Version*. Jeremiah chapter 30.
49   Holy Bible. 2012. *New Revised Standard Version*. Matthew 15:19-20.

Today, there are so many disasters faced by humanity. Some are natural while others are caused by human beings. These disasters are social, political, economic, spiritual and ecological. One of the recent natural disasters was cyclone Idai that left Mozambique, Zimbabwe and Malawi devastated.[50] Idai claimed many lives. As believers, we must always approach the throne of God with a conviction that God cherishes a repentant heart and an attitude that is ready to be seen as a humble person ready for good use. We can be cleansed from our sins and renewed into God's holiness. In this case, therefore, we become the people of God. Those who seek the divine purpose in their hearts will ultimately be seen as children of God and receive salvation. The church should attract the masses and be a voice for the voiceless, including all of God's creation, in order to be relevant and attractive to many. Only then will it attract many people. Salvation from all human oppression must be key to winning many souls to Christ. Different initiatives and tactics must be used in order for the church to look attractive and useful in the economy of winning souls in this present generation.

Women were made to share with men in the service of God and in the custodial caring of the Earth. The woman was indeed made to live side by side with her counterpart. It was for this reason that God had to find a companion and fellow worker rather than to meet the man's need to use a woman as an object. But Mananzan[51] observes that humans have distorted the original plan of God in as far as God's creation is concerned. She states:

> The morality that has evolved in patriarchal society has crippled women's minds and produced guilt complexes that have infringed on their freedom. So pervasive has this been in the home, in education and indeed in all areas of life – that it has become a structural sin. There is a need to develop a cosmic spirituality by returning to our life-giving roots and actively participating in creating a society based on just, right and harmonious relationships.[52]

With regards to Mananzan's point above, human beings have caused sin to become hierarchical. Women have accepted the human-made norm that men are superior to them. This has resulted in men being in control or becoming rulers of everything, namely the home, the church, community, the environment and all areas of life. For Mananzan, the control of men over women has led them to commit sinful acts, forcing women to learn to be silent even in the midst of abusive relationships. In the nature of things, the creation of a woman by God meant that both men and women should live together in harmony. It meant that God created both men and women

50 Otto-Mentz V. 2019. Cyclone Idai and the importance of resilience. *Money Marketing*, 5. May, 16. Online: https://hdl.handle.net/10520/EJC-15bb39c220 accessed 24 March 2020.

51 Mananzan M.J. 1995. Feminist Theology in Asia: An overview in Ortega O. (ed). *Women's Visions, Theological Reflection, Celebration,* Action. Geneva: WCC Publications. 35.

52 Mananzan, Feminist Theology in Asia: An overview, 35.

to partner together and serve their societies in a just manner. That is the reason Watson[53] urges women to see and eradicate unjust social, political, religious and other structures which are indeed sinful and dehumanise them. Additionally, during her interview, Oduyoye asserts that "… men are what they are because women don't give them enough work to do. They make them feel like they are 'the all'." [54] Oduyoye invites all women to unlearn the socialization of being second-class human beings to men because this is not God's intention.[55]

God's intention was to see man and woman enjoy companionship with the rest of God's Creation. He commanded man and woman to take care of the rest of creation and not to dominate one another. God neither instructed Adam to be above Eve, nor Eve to be above Adam. Both were created equal to love and to help each other. Any relationship that dominates one another or God's creation is not a true relationship. It is like slave and master. The exegesis of biblical scriptures from the feminist view could be the point of departure to guide Christians to interpret the word of God that has been distorted, such as on the domination of the rest of creation as recorded in Genesis 1:26-27:

> Then God said, let us make man in our own image, after our likeness; and let them have dominion over the fish, the seas, and over the birds of the air, and over the cattle and over the Earth and over every creeping thing that creeps upon the Earth. So, God created man [sic] in [God's] own image, in the image of God, [God] created them, male and female, [God] created them.[56]

Humanity's likeness to God is part of the creation process. Human beings have the privilege of being like God. This is the privilege of enjoying everything that God has made possible for us to receive from the ground, as in Genesis 3:22-23. In both creation stories, the image of God is located on the ground. Therefore, the ground, or rather, land, is important because it can be understood to mean that human beings are meant to take care of it just as they take care of themselves. The relationship between woman and man is one of equality and mutuality. This is the reason Conradie's model of the earth as a sacred gift is useful because it includes everything in the world as being created by God. The model of the earth being a sacred gift is also a symbol of hospitality that humanity should embrace, and a metaphor for gathering, sharing and dialoguing with one another without excluding or denying anyone a share of resources and privileges to make decisions. This is a model of ecumenism that the church and community need to adopt. The model

---

53   Watson, N.K. 2002. Introductions in Feminist Theology: Introducing Feminist Ecclesiology. New York: Sheffield Academic Press. 109.

54   Oredein O. 2016. Interview with Mercy Amba Oduyoye: Mercy Amba Oduyoye in Her Own Words. *Journal of Feminist Studies in Religion*, 32(2):153-164.

55   Oredein, Interview with Mercy Amba Oduyoye, 162.

56   Holy Bible. 2012. *New Revised Standard Version*. Genesis 1:26-27.

returns the understanding of *oikoumene* (the household of God to that of the whole inhabited Earth). Conradie declares that:

> Such ecumenical discourse on the whole household of God is best understood within the context of the whole work of God (creation, providence, redemption, completion) which has traditionally been described as the "economy of the triune God" (*oikonomia tou theou*), from which the term "economic trinity" has also been derived.[57]

In a world at ecological risk, the church should deepen its existing partnerships for the sake of healing of God's Creation. For Conradie, the earth is the whole household of God. For this reason, human beings are at liberty to utilise the earth's resources in a mutual way. My understanding is that when the members of the church get together as one body of Christ, it signifies a decisive turning away or *metanoia* (changing of one's mind) from the powers and principalities of person and systemic oppression. "The environmental crisis has therefore not only led to the claim that Christianity could and should make an important contribution to a more adequate understanding of the role of humanity in nature."[58] It will mean that we abandon the destructive powers of those who are ruling, and reject their hold over our lives and over other sentient beings. We have to recognise that the principalities of evil go beyond our conscious control. They have been ingrained into the thick layers of our conscious minds. So, we continue to obey them without realizing it. As such, they manifest in political, economic, religious, social and ecological systems that we do not control or entirely escape, and they continue to exist.

Conclusion

This chapter focused on the notion that the salvation of human beings is not for us to decide but comes from God. The chapter has reminded us that human beings should re-imagine their salvation by utilizing the Christian ethics for social and ecological change. Salvation has been defined as preservation or deliverance from harm, ruin or loss, which is really deliverance from sin and its consequences through faith in Christ. The chapter employed Ernst Conradie's (2011) theoretical framework. Conradie's theory states that the earth is a sacred gift to us from God. In this framework, Christians are called to maintain, care for, celebrate and respect God's creation in harmony. Since Conradie maintains that there is divine connection and a cycle of interrelations between living things and nature, the framework also calls human beings to a critical reassessment of the Christian faith with regard to God's creation. The chapter included some exegesis on some biblical texts such as

---

57   Conradie, The Whole Household of God (OIKOS), 2.
58   Conradie, Christianity and Earthkeeping, 8.

Romans 8:19-25; Psalm 24:1-2; Genesis 1:26-27; Matthew 15:19-20; Mark 4:34-38 and Philippians 1:6. By trying to interpret these texts, the chapter tried to answer the following question: what is the holistic understanding of the word 'salvation' from a theological and gender perspective? The approach to this question was that the church has encouraged preaching on the saving of human souls without necessarily tackling issues of policy formulation in order for humanity to work on equality and equity. For this reason, a model of ecumenism of inclusivity that also returns the understanding of God's entire creation has been proposed. This means that the church must work towards an inclusive community, which holds all the members of the body of Christ together as well as the rest of God's creation, thereby bringing them together to engage in earthkeeping. It is my understanding that people concerned with justice yearn for healing of all God's creation, including the environment. This calls for the church to go beyond its traditional relationships to make common cause with people of good-will throughout the world who are committed to compassion, peace and justice for all and the rest of creation.

The church of Jesus Christ should be understood in the light of a theology, which has recognised both an objective and a subjective side of the saving power of Christ. In other words, this means that all people who have passed through the saving power of Christ, regardless of their gender, are children of God. The objective side is God's liberating love, which is given to both men, women and the rest of God's creation as an unmerited gift from beyond our historical nature, and which transforms the self into a new being in communion with God. The subjective side is the process of personally examining the saving power of Christ by making this journey of *metanoia* and transformation meaningful in one's own life. The church must work towards creating an inclusive community, which holds all the members of the body of Christ together as well as the rest of God's creation. Conradie's framework will assist in bringing the community of Jesus Christ together to create one united body which have many gifts, including the rest of creation.

Nonetheless, the church continues to fail in its efforts to embrace the many gifts and theological contributions of women. Through the institutionalization of domination based on gender injustice, power is used as a tool to control and reinforce the oppression of women in the social, cultural, political, economic, ecological and religious systems of our time. This injustice persists at all levels of our lives because patriarchy survives in contexts where it is not questioned but is legitimised through the many institutions in church and society. Women's theologies that address these gender and ecological injustices are therefore needed to critically question and analyze such human-made structures that dehumanise other people and the rest of creation. It is when we confront and deconstruct these human-made structures that human beings may enjoy living in just, peaceful and healthy communities where men who are in partnership with women and where the rest of God's creation may become a safe place to live in.

To this end, I have attempted to show the role of salvation in a human being but also how it extends to the rest of God's creation if we are to live in harmony. I have also briefly discussed the prophetic role of the church in ensuring that all God's creation is liberated from all manner of destruction and oppression. As St Paul puts it in Romans 8:19-25, the whole creation groans, yearning to be liberated from bondage. God's creation needs to be saved from all manner of plundering. The whole Earth and all that is in it needs to be delivered. This is because the earth is a sacred gift to us from God.

References

Clarkson, S. and Russell, L.M. (eds). 1996. *Dictionary of Feminist Theologies.* Louisville: Westminster John Knox Press.

Comaroff, J. and Comaroff, J. 1991. *Of Revelation and Revolution: Christianity, Colonialism, and Consciousness in South Africa.* Vol. 1. London: The University of Chicago Press. https://doi.org/10.7208/chicago/9780226114477.001.0001

Duchrow, U. and Gerhard, L. 1987. *Shalom: Biblical Perspectives on Creation, Justice & Peace.* Geneva: WCC Publication.

Freedman, H. 1992. *The Phenomenology of Information on Salvation.* Ramat Gan Israel: Bar Ilan University Press. 908-909.

Conradie, E.M. 2011. *Christianity and Earthkeeping: In Search of an Inspiring Vision.* Stellenbosch: African SUN MeDIA. https://doi.org/10.18820/9781920338589

Conradie E.M. 2007. The Whole Household of God (OIKOS): Some Ecclesiological Perspectives. *Scriptura.* 94:1-9. https://doi.org/10.7833/94-0-1431

Hinga, M.T. 2001. Jesus Christ and the Liberation of Women in Africa. In M. A. Oduyoye, and M. R. A. Kanyoro (eds), *The Will to Arise: Women, Tradition and the Church in Africa.* Maryknoll: Orbis Books. 183-194.

Holy Bible. 2012. *New Revised Standard Version.* The United Kingdom: The British and Foreign Bible Society Press.

Hutanuwar, P. 2000. Globalization from Buddhist perspective. *Globalization and its Consequences,* 50(2), June. Geneva: Warc.

Mananzan, M.J. 1995. Feminist Theology in Asia: An overview. In O. Ortega, (ed). *Women's Visions, Theological Reflection, Celebration, Action.* Geneva:

WCC Publications. https://doi.org/10.1177/096673509500001003

Matthew Henry Concise Commentary. https://biblehub.com/commentaries/psalms/24-1.htm

Nicolson, R. 1990. *A Black Future? Jesus and Salvation in South Africa.* London: Trinity Press International.

Olssen, M., Codd, J. and O'Neill, A. 2004. *Education Policy: Globalisation, Citizenship and Democracy.* London: Sage Publications.

Oredein, O. 2016. Interview with Mercy Amba Oduyoye: Mercy Amba Oduyoye in Her Own Words. *Journal of Feminist Studies in Religion,* 32(2):153-164. https://doi.org/10.2979/jfemistudreli.32.2.26

Otto-Mentz, V. 2019. Cyclone Idai and the importance of resilience. *Money Marketing,*

16. https://hdl.handle.net/10520/EJC-15bb39c220 [Accessed 24 March 2020].

Ruether, R.R. 1983. *Sexism and God-talk: Toward a Feminist Theology.* Boston: Beacon Press.

Russell, L.M. 2001. Hot-house Ecclesiology: A Feminist Interpretation of the Church. *The Ecumenical Review,* 53(1): January, 48-49. https://doi.org/10.1111/j.1758-6623.2001.tb00072.x

Russell, L.M. 1993. *Church in the Round: Feminist Interpretation of the Church.* Louisville: John Knox Press.

The Longman Dictionary of the English Language. 1992. Amazon: Addison-Wesley Longman Ltd.

Watson, N.K. 2002. *Introductions in Feminist Theology: Introducing Feminist Ecclesiology.* New York: Sheffield Academic Press.

LA PROTECTION DE LA TERRE UNE MISSION POUR L'ÉGLISE

Fifamè Fidèle Houssou Gandonou[1]

> Nous n'héritons pas de la Terre de nos parents, nous l'empruntons à nos enfants. Antoine de Saint-Exupéry

> La terre donnera ses fruits, vous mangerez à satiété et vous mènerez une existence paisible. Lévitique 25, 19[2]

Introduction

La terre est polluée principalement par les déchets ménagers et l'activité humaine surtout industrielle. Les produits chimiques toxiques produits tels que les cendres de charbon, les herbicides et les pesticides, les sachets plastiques sont des sources importantes de pollution de la terre et du sol. Or, la terre a une importance capitale pour la production agricole et la vie des humains. Ainsi, la terre contaminée est synonyme de cultures et de produits infectés ; ce qui a des répercussions directes ou indirectes sur la production agricole, l'alimentation et la santé humaine.[3] En outre, la terre est un don, une ressource naturelle à protéger. Souvent traitée comme une chose et parfois comme une marchandise, la terre n'est pas comme un tapis : on ne

---

[1] Elle est professeure associée à l'Université ¨Protestante d'Afrique de l'Ouest (UPAO/Porto-Novo), au département de la Faculté de théologie et des sciences religieuses. Elle est aussi est membre du cercle des théologiennes africaines engagées et du Réseau des théologiennes africaines et européennes, Tsena Malaka. Elle a obtenu son doctorat en éthique à l'Université Protestante de l'Afrique Centrale (UPAC/Yaoundé) en 2014 avec une recherche sur les fondements éthiques du féminisme dans le contexte africain. Depuis des années, elle est impliquée dans plusieurs initiatives au service des femmes et des enfants dans la société béninoise à travers l'ONG Déborah. Elle est auteure de plusieurs articles scientifiques et d'ouvrages, notamment : Les fondements éthiques du féminisme : une réflexion à partir du contexte africain, Globethics.net. 2016 ; La violence sexuelle parmi les adolescents : une réflexion théologique et éthique, PBA, 2018.

[2] Les références bibliques sont de la version « Bible d'étude », Version du Semeur 2000, Excelis, 2005.

[3] Http://web.unep.org/environmentassembly/fr/terres-et-sols.

peut pas la rouler et l'emporter avec soi où l'on veut. Il y a une interdépendance qui existe entre l'être humain, les autres espèces vivantes et la planète terre sur laquelle nous vivons tous et toutes. Pour créer des usages productifs de la terre, il est donc nécessaire d'en prendre soin. Car la terre et ses écosystèmes nous soutiennent et nous nourrissent durant toute notre vie.

- La Protection de la terre : une mission de l'Église ;
- Est-ce que l'Église accomplit cette mission (état des lieux) ?
- Que doit-elle faire de plus ?

La mission de l'Église dans la protection de la terre

Il y existe une interdépendance entre l'être humain, les autres espèces vivantes et la planète terre. Car la terre et ses écosystèmes les portent et les nourrissent durant toute la vie, c'est la terre nourricière. Elle est partout dans le monde le lieu propice à la culture et l'éclosion de toute production agricole comme le maïs, l'arachide, le manioc, le niébé, le piment, la tomate, le riz, la patate douce, le taro, etc. Sans la terre, la production agricole n'existerait pas et par conséquent la nourriture non plus. Ce qui implique un lien étroit entre la terre et la souveraineté alimentaire. Ce lien est très remarquable dans le livre de Lévitiques où il est fait un rappel sur quelques pratiques agricoles qui affectent positivement la terre afin d'obtenir une bonne production agricole. Par exemple, la pratique de la jachère qui consiste à faire reposer la terre pendant quelques années (Lévitiques 25, 2-7, 18-22). Ce lien entre la terre et la nourriture est symbolisé dans le récit de la chute au Jardin d'Eden, où Dieu notifie à la femme que sa nourriture proviendra de la terre (Genèse 3, 17b-18).

La protection de la terre est une garantie de la nourriture, elle est donc une action urgente interpellant les chrétiennes et les chrétiens. C'est pourquoi au cœur de la réflexion chrétienne et théologique, la protection de la terre trouve sa place. Plusieurs textes[4] font référence à la responsabilité et à l'engagement chrétien pour le souci et la bonne gestion de la terre. Ce souci est lié à la mission de l'Église incluant la dimension personnelle (l'appel évangélique à se repentir, à croire et à mener une vie de disciple), la dimension sociale (charité pour les nécessiteux et justice pour les opprimés, mais aussi pour la génération future) et la dimension écologique (souci de la protection de la création tout entière) liée à l'éthique environnementale.

---

4   On peut citer : Genèse 1, 1-26 ; 2, 4-17 ; 3, 17-19 ; Proverbes 8, 22-31 ; Psaumes 8 ; 19, 1-7 ; 104 ; Job 38 ; Lévitiques 25, 1-12 ; Ésaïe 19, 1-12 ; 24, 1-6 ; 58, 6-11 ; 65, 16-25 ; Ezéchiel 21, 1-6 ; Joël 1 ; Amos 8, 4-14 ; Marc 4, 30-32 ; Romains 1, 20-21 ; 8, 18-25.

La protection de la terre : une théologie d'un monde interconnecté

La protection de la terre pose le problème du rapport à la nature et de la responsabilité humaine. Les relations de l'être humain avec la terre et la chaîne de provenance de la nourriture constituent des préoccupations au cœur de la théologie de la création. L'approche théologique qui soutient la lutte pour la protection de la terre s'enracine dans la logique de Dieu qui crée l'être humain après avoir tout créé. Dieu y a mis une interconnexion de manière à ce que le soin que l'être humain ferait de cette création permette son épanouissement et la floraison de toute la création. Dès lors, une relation existe entre les humains et les autres créatures ; c'est sur la terre et avec la terre que l'être humain s'épanouit dans la nature. Et *Dieu dit : voici, je vous donne pour vous en nourrir, toute plante portant sa semence et qui partout sur la terre, et tous les arbres fruitiers pourtant leur semence. Je donne aussi à tout animal vivant sur la terre, aux oiseaux du ciel, et à tout ce qui se meut à ras de terre, et à tout être vivant, toute plante verte pour qu'ils s'en nourrissent.* (Genèse 1, 29-30) D'ailleurs, Genèse 8, 22 souligne la permanence des lois et des saisons régissant la création. « *Aussi longtemps que la terre subsistera, semailles et moisson, froid et chaleur, été, hiver, et jour et la nuit ne cesseront jamais* . »

Le monde créé et donné par Dieu est un monde interconnecté. Il est facile de se rendre compte que la nourriture vient de l'interconnexion entre la terre, le soleil, les pluies, l'environnement et toute une chaîne de personnes. Tous ces acteurs, naturels et humains, contribuent à la croissance et au développement holistique et clément. L'interdépendance entre les micro-organismes est une réalité indéniable. Que ce soient les êtres vivants du sol, ceux sous la terre, qui fertilisent les plantes ou ceux d'insectes comme les abeilles qui permettent la pollinisation des fleurs, fruits et graines pour créer la nouvelle plante ou encore ceux du courage, qui facilitent la digestion ; il y a une interconnexion. Il faut un orchestre de plusieurs musiciens, de la plus petite des créatures à une plus grande étoile appelée soleil, pour créer la symphonie de délicieux aliments, dans une belle, dynamique, diversifiée et fragile planète bleue appelée terre, mère nourricière. Chaque créature a son rôle à jouer dans la chaîne alimentaire, montant de la terre pour finalement retourner à la terre, après avoir terminé sa mission de vie. Voilà pourquoi, il faut une terre saine et propre pour une nourriture saine et une vie appropriée et équilibrée.

Dans son encyclique *Laudato Si*, le Pape François rappelle cette interconnexion en situant la problématique de la crise écologique dans l'urgence de la conservation, de la préservation et de la sauvegarde de la création.[5]

---

5   Pape François, Laudato Si », Lettre encyclique sur la sauvegarde de la maison commune, 2015.

La protection de la terre : un appel prophétique au développement

Le souci de la protection de la terre et de la justice est au cœur du développement. La Bible enseigne l'intégralité de la création et invite les êtres humains à prendre soin du jardin d'Eden (Genèse 2,15). Le Dieu de la Bible est un Dieu de justice, qui protège et aime ses créatures, les plus vulnérables et veille sur elles.

Les Prophètes Michée et Esaïe ont prédit que le jour où le règne de Dieu sera établi, où il y aura la paix et la justice, les nations renonceront aux guerres pour s'investir dans le développement et dans l'agriculture. *Chacun habitera en paix sous sa vigne et sous son figuier, il n'y aura personne qui puisse le troubler. C'est l'Eternel qui a parlé, le Seigneur des armées célestes.* (Michée 4,4)

Cette politique de consommation et de transformation locale que soulève ce verset est une grande économie pour l'être humain, sa santé et son environnement conduisant à la paix et à la sérénité. Ceci implique la protection de la terre pour une nourriture localement produite, plus fraîche et plus nutritive. Ce sont là déjà des signes de croissance, car la paix et le développement ne peuvent se réaliser que lorsque les communautés vivent avec leurs ressources propres et bénéficient des fruits de leur travail, dans leur propre environnement sans peur ni domination.

Au-delà du droit humain,[6] la protection de la terre pour un accès à la nourriture saine et nutritive est une grâce divine ; un moyen pour la consolidation de la paix ; alors tout ce qui peut l'empêcher doit être dévoilé et dénoncé publiquement. De ce fait, les institutions ecclésiales doivent être des espaces pour la promotion de la protection de la terre. Le prophète Esaïe apostrophant toute injustice exhorte à la bienveillance et l'équité : *le jeûne qui me plaît est celui qui consiste à détacher les liens de la méchanceté, à délier les courroies de toute servitude, à mettre en liberté tous ceux que l'on opprime, et à briser toute espèce de joug. C'est partager ton pain avec ceux qui ont a faim, et offrir l'hospitalité aux pauvres sans abri, c'est donner des habits à celui qu'on voit nu, ne pas se détourner de ton prochain.* (Esaïe 58, 6-7). Ce texte énonce très bien le rôle que peuvent jouer les communautés de foi dans l'atteinte des Objectifs du Développement Durable (ODD). La campagne pour la protection de la terre en vue de la souveraineté alimentaire est intrinsèquement liée à la perspective missionnaire de l'Église et constitue un appel à la paix.

---

6   Toute personne, en tout temps, devraient avoir l'accès physique et économique à une nourriture suffisante, saine et à des aliments nutritifs pour répondre à ses besoins alimentaires et ses préférences alimentaires pour mener une vie active et saine. Cf. . FAO, le Sommet mondial de l'alimentation, Plan d'action, 1996.

La protection de la terre : un cri pour la paix

Afin de rétablir la dignité humaine et environnementale, supprimer l'injustice, la pauvreté, la malnutrition, la faim et les migrations clandestines, il est nécessaire de comprendre que la protection de la terre est un des signes du royaume de Dieu au milieu de nous; et se situant dans le cadre du *Shalom* qui signifie la vie dans toute sa plénitude, une vie abondante (Jean 10,10). Le *Shalom* commence par la protection de la terre, notre mère nourricière qui met en valeur la dignité humaine dans toute sa dimension holistique.

Dans le monde actuel, l'Église a une mission globale basée sur le développement durable qui prend la forme d'un triangle : - *Dieu et l'être humain – l'être humain avec lui-même – l'être humain et la création (le prochain et tout son environnement).* Ces trois sommets du triangle sont nécessaires pour un développement durable et plénier. Pendant, longtemps, un pan des sommets du triangle, être humain et création, a été négligé. La théologie développée sur l'agroécologie dans le jardin d'Eden qui consiste à garder, cultiver la terre et la protéger doit être amplifiée et appliquée pour assurer la souveraineté alimentaire et le développement humain durable de manière holistique. Cette théologie commence par la lutte pour la protection de la terre à travers le juste accès aux domaines arables, le respect et l'équité dans le traitement et la gestion de la terre et ses composantes. Cependant, la connaissance et la formation sont importantes pour une transformation durable dans les habitudes vis-à-vis à la terre. Ce qui implique l'engagement de l'Église.

La protection de la terre : une action ecclésiale

La protection de la terre nécessite une action ecclésiale. Ceci implique un engagement efficace des membres et fidèles de l'Église mais aussi et surtout des actions de mobilisation, de formation, d'éducation et de plaidoyer. Pour la protection de la terre, l'Église est appelée à s'engager:

- dans l'utilisation raisonnable des ressources de la terre pour répondre aux besoins des hommes et des femmes, et assurer le bien-être pour tous et toutes ;

- dans la sauvegarde et la restauration des habitants et des espèces de la terre par des actions de mobilisation, de formation, d'éducation; et de plaidoyer en vue de la protection de la terre et de toutes ses composantes.

Ces deux types d'engagements visent en fait, le même but : le service du Dieu créateur même, mais aussi le bien-être de l'être humain et de la nature entière.

La bataille ecclésiale pour la protection de la terre et de toute la biodiversité constitue la louange à Dieu, lui-même, et à toute la création. Le théologien de la Société des Missions africaines, le Père Donald Zagore, exprime cet engagement en ces termes : *« Le principe de la mission en tant qu'engagement écologique consiste fondamentalement à transmettre à nos dynamiques politiques, économiques, culturelles, sociales, ecclésiales, le cri de la terre, notre maison commune, qui est un cri de souffrance et d'agonie.*[7] » La mission de l'Église consiste à éviter ce qui constitue la tentation de tous les temps, à savoir présenter exclusivement le salut de la terre comme prisme d'une authentique conversion écologique de l'être humain. Des actions de protection de la terre font partie intégrante de la mission de l'Église, celle qui prend en compte, les humains, la société et la création. Il s'agit d'une metanoia, comme on dit en grec, une transformation par rapport à la compréhension que nous avons de la conversion ; celle qui consiste à séparer la conversion personnelle de la conversion écologique. C'est à cette expérience de transformation que le Pape François nous invite son encyclique Laudato Si.

S'il est une réalité que ces trois cibles (Dieu, humains et création) sont brisées dans leur relation et souffrent à cause du péché, de la maltraitance de la terre et de l'environnement, alors protéger la terre signifie guérir les blessures qui lui sont infligées.

L'engagement à la protection de l'environnement n'est qu'une marche vers la réalisation du refrain de la louange dans la bouche de Dieu juste à la fin de la création dans le récit de Genèse 1, 31, « *et c'était très bon.* » En traitant bien la terre voire la création, le cœur de Dieu se réjouit et celui des humains aussi.

S'engager donc dans la lutte pour la protection de la terre, c'est honorer et rendre gloire à celui par qui et pour qui toutes choses sont créées. C'est l'adorer et agir en tant que disciple répondant à la vocation d'espérance.

L'apôtre Paul nous parle de cette espérance dans Romains 8, 22 en comparant la création à une femme enceinte qui souffre des douleurs de l'enfantement. Et c'est l'espérance en Christ (Colossiens 1, 15-20), puisqu'il est considéré comme l'*origine* de la création, comme le *soutien* de la création et comme le *sauveur* de tout l'ordre établi. Cette espérance nous conduit à faire de la terre un présent convenable et magnifique pour le Seigneur, une espérance qui doit nous mener non à un excès de confiance, mais à une action de sauvegarde de la terre accomplie dans la joie et l'humilité (Habacuc 2, 14 et Philippiens 2, 10-11.)

La protection de la terre est ainsi une obligation pour la foi chrétienne. Le Pape Jean Paul II l'avait rappelé en ces termes nous avons donc l'obligation en tant que chrétiens, de conserver la nature, nos forêts et nos animaux, de protéger « les créatures et les éléments de toute violation ». Et cela sera fait dans la mesure où on

---

7   Donald Zagore, Laudato Sì et la mission en tant qu'engagement en faveur de la Création dans www .fides.org/fr/news/67971, Agence Fides, 23/05/2020.

les considérait comme des êtres à l'égard desquels l'homme est lié par devoirs.[8] Mais bien souvent, cette mission n'est pas toujours une réalité vécue à voir tous les dégâts causés à la terre par les actions des humains, chrétiens ou non.

Quelques dégâts causés à la terre

La terre constitue cette entité composée d'êtres vivants et de matière inerte entourant l'être humain. Dans cette perspective, elle est un lieu qui met l'être humain en relation, en interdépendance avec les autres composantes. La dégradation de la terre est alarmante et observable partout. Cette dégradation s'exprime par l'action des femmes et des hommes sur la terre. Au lieu de prendre soin de la terre, les humains, en général, exploitent la terre et oublient de l'alimenter en retour. Dans ce sens, Ibrahim Seck du Sénégal observe que : *nos parents se nourrissaient de la terre et la nourrissaient. Nous avons maintenant détruit la terre.*[9] Ce faisant, la destruction de la terre n'est rien d'autre que le manque de soins à la terre. C'est-à-dire le refus de considérer la dimension réciproque du traitement dans la relation de l'Homme à la terre. Ainsi comprise, la destruction de la terre est un synonyme de l'écroulement de l'humain et de toute la création. Les humains en subissent non seulement les effets, mais aussi les récoltes et les bétails en sont des victimes et des témoins.

Les dégâts causés à la terre agissent sur les systèmes alimentaires, l'écosystème et la vie sociale, mais aussi sur la relation avec Dieu. Le Béninois, enseignant d'éthique, Daniel D. DOSSOU commente ces dommages que l'humain cause à la terre en ces termes : *Sur le plan purement climatique, par exemple, l'ampleur du dégât dépasse l'entendement. Car déjà, nous parlons d'exilés ou de « réfugiés » climatiques et les terres, de plus en plus arides, ne semblent pas pouvoir « accepter » davantage de « polluants chimiques » pour produire suffisamment « à manger » pour plus d'une dizaine de milliers de « bouches », d'ici à là. Le paradigme économique actuel n'augure nullement d'un lendemain meilleur ; ni pour la nature ni pour la race humaine.*[10] La terre est malade des activités humaines entraînant ainsi de graves répercussions sur la souveraineté alimentaire et la vie sociale. Les problèmes de la dégradation de la terre sont les effets de la production de l'économie capitaliste globalisée et globalisante. La perte de la pluriculture et de la biodiversité sont souvent le résultat d'une monoculture intensive traduite par une déforestation massive, et laissant place à des champs à perte de vue de caféiers, de cotonniers et d'acajou … Les sols, propriétés de grandes

---

8   Jean Paul II, « Lettres aux Ministres Généraux des Divers Ordres Franciscains », 15 août 1982, Théo, p. 721 dans Ka Mana et Jean Blaise Kenmogne, Éthique écologique et reconstruction de l'Afrique, Cipcre/Clé, Bafoussam/Yaoundé, 1997, p. 18.

9   Cité par Daniel Dotu Dossou, Pratique éthique et management socialement responsable, OBA, 2019, p. 94.

10   Ibid.

multinationales, se sont appauvris rapidement et c'est le cycle des insecticides-fertilisants et des pesticides. L'accaparement des terres, le refus d'accès des femmes à la terre, la mauvaise gestion des déchets sont des problèmes liés à la maltraitance de la terre.[11] Dans la représentation africaine, comme le précise Daniel Dotu DOSSOU, la terre, la forêt et l'eau sont des données sacrées pour certains peuples. Et dans certaines cultures, les hommes et les femmes vénèrent ou divinisent la terre. Tout ce que l'être humain fait à la terre, il le fait à lui-même, pensent certains peuples.

L'Afrique ferait certainement sienne cette déclaration! Mais le doigt accusateur est omniprésent et ne semble pas épargner l'Africain. Néanmoins, la sagesse populaire dit : la terre donne ce qu'on lui donne. Tout se fait comme si le sens du caractère sacré de la personne et de l'environnement n'est plus à l'ordre du jour. L'esprit de conservation et de protection ne se remarque plus au sein des ceux et celles qui sont sensés savoir que *« de même qu'il y a des choses qu'on ne fait pas, de même qu'il y a des espaces qu'on ne détruit pas, même si c'est pour avoir des profits.*[12] Ce faisant, nous avons coupé tous les arbres autour de nous pour fabriquer nos maisons et aussi pour le bois de feu. Nous savions qu'il y aurait une fin, néanmoins nous n'avions pas d'alternative. Maintenant, tout est nu. D'ailleurs, les récits bibliques en donnent le témoignage et expliquent clairement que la terre forme un système entier avec les autres créatures et le créateur.

Ce faisant, le mauvais traitement infligé à la terre et le péché des humains affectent non seulement la relation avec Dieu, mais aussi, avec les autres créatures, endommageant ainsi le bon fonctionnement de la terre elle-même ainsi que celui du climat, etc. Le récit de Genèse 3, 17-19 relève que le péché d'Adam et d'Ève a eu comme conséquence la séparation d'avec Dieu, mais aussi la dégradation de la terre qui se met à produire des épines, et rendant l'agriculture difficile. Dans Jérémie 12, 14, il est dit que la terre *souffre,* et Osée 4, 1-3 précise que la terre *pleure* à cause du péché du peuple de Dieu.[13] Ces récits exposent avec évidence que la maltraitance infligée à la terre est une véritable cause de désorganisation de l'écosystème et du monde ainsi que de la relation avec Dieu. Puisque les hommes et les femmes maltraitent la terre qui les porte, il importe de rappeler la relation des humains à la terre. Car la terre nous porte, nous supporte et nous nourrit tout au long de notre existence.[14]

---

11 Comme maltraitance à la terre, on peut citer : la coupure désordonnée des arbres, les feux de brousse tout azimut, la culture avec les engrais chimiques, l'utilisation des sachets plastiques, la destruction des forets, les constructions anarchiques, etc.

12 Ka Mana et Jean Blaise Kenmogne, Éthique écologique et reconstruction de l'Afrique, p. 23.

13 Dave Bookless, « Vers une théologie du changement climatique », dans Émile HOBBS, Jean-François Mouhot et Chris Walley, Évangile et Changement climatique, Vivre n° 40, Je Sème 2017, p. 17.

14 Daniel Dotu Dossou, op.cit. p. 95.

Enjeux anthropologiques liés à la protection de la terre

La protection de la terre est une question sociale et ses enjeux sont importants. La véritable sécurité sociale se comprend comme la paix intérieure, l'absence de crainte, le manque de toute inquiétude, d'un danger ou d'un mal à venir. Elle demeure une exigence humaine qui doit être satisfaite sur tous les plans.[15] Cette sécurité est effective lorsqu'il y a une harmonie entre les êtres humains et les autres créatures de la nature en particulier la terre. Selon l'ontologie africaine, l'être humain est au centre de son bien-être et pourtant en relation avec les autres éléments de la créature. Joe M. Kapolyo le signale si fortement en ces termes, *dans presque tous les mythes africains de la création, le lien qui existe entre les hommes et Dieu apparaît clairement : Dieu est le créateur des hommes et celui qui pourvoit à leurs besoins afin de les maintenir en vie. Pourtant, l'univers — Dieu y compris — n'est là que pour expliquer la place de Umuntu (l'homme) au centre de la création.*[16] La création n'est là, pour ainsi dire, que pour la jouissance et le bien-être de l'être humain. Toutefois, cette création, exclusivement la terre, développe avec l'être humain plusieurs types de relations.

La terre n'appartient pas aux humains

Selon l'ordre de la création décrit dans le récit de Genèse 1, il est dit qu'au 3e jour, Dieu créa la terre et les mers, ensuite la végétation fut créée (Genèse 1, 9-13). Elle est une création de Dieu tout comme les humains. La terre appartient à Dieu. Elle n'est donc pas une propriété des humains pour qu'ils en abusent sans restriction. Le Psaume 24, 1 le proclame assez bien : la terre et ses richesses appartiennent à l'Éternel. Ce faisant, la terre est une formidable ressource naturelle à protéger, à laquelle le respect et le bon traitement sont dus. Dans Lévitique 25, il est stipulé fortement que la terre appartient à Dieu ; on ne peut la posséder. L'être humain n'est pas propriétaire de la terre, elle lui a été confiée, comme à un hôte de passage. Le texte de Lévitique 25 le stipule si bien ; chaque Israélite aura droit à sa parcelle et pour empêcher l'endettement et la perte de son usage, Moïse avait prescrit que tous les sept ans, toutes les dettes soient remises et aux sept fois sept ans, à la cinquantième année, une réforme agraire redistribuerait les terres aux paysans dépossédés, c'est l'année jubilaire. Si la terre appartient à Dieu (Lévitiques 25, 23), les humains ont tout de même un lien étroit avec la terre.

Lien entre l'être humain et la terre

Il y a trois formes de relation qui lient l'être humain à la terre :

---

15   G. Durozoi et A. Roussel, Dictionnaire de philosophie, Paris, Nathan, 1987, P. 352.

16   Joe M. Kapolyo, L'homme, Vision biblique et africaine, Farel/Emmaus, Paris/Saint Légier, 2007, p.31-32.

- **Relation de nature et d'origine** : cette relation s'explique par le fait que l'humain a été créé à partir de la terre. Dans le récit de Genèse 2, 7a, le Seigneur Dieu prit de la poussière du sol (Adam) et en façonna un être humain (adamah), le terme hébreu pour désigner le sol ou la terre. Dans ce verset, l'article qui précède le mot Adam nous montre que ce mot est employé comme un nom commun. Il désigne donc un être humain (et non un homme). Dieu forme l'humain à partir de la terre. Ce faisant, l'humain fait complètement partie de la terre, voire de la création.

- **Relation de protection et d'usage** : Le Seigneur Dieu créa l'homme et l'établit dans le jardin d'Éden pour le cultiver et le garder (Genèse 2,15). Dieu confia ainsi à l'humain non seulement une autorité sur la terre, mais surtout une responsabilité et une mission. Dave BOOKLESS dira que les mots «cultiver et garder» doivent être compris comme un commentaire sur ce que signifie refléter l'image de Dieu. « *Cultiver et garder* » *la terre* est équivalent de «*servir et préserver*» le reste de la création. La domination entre les mains de l'être humain est celle de rois - serviteurs et non pas de dictateurs arbitraires.[17] Du coup, le règne de l'être humain diffère d'une tyrannie égoïste. Partant du *cultiver*, qui se dit en hébreu, littéralement, *servir*, dans son rapport à l'humus, l'homme devra agir avec humilité.

Dieu veut maintenir dans l'existence ce qu'il a créé. Ainsi, planter un arbre, c'est vouloir maintenir dans l'existence ce que Dieu a créé. C'est faire «sa volonté." Non seulement, l'humain commandera à la nature en obéissant à ses lois, mais aussi, il le fera pour le bien de la création même, en sorte qu'elle accomplisse sa vocation : le jardin cultivé sera comme un chant de louange au Dieu de l'ordre, de la vie et de la paix. Le deuxième chapitre de Genèse s'accorde encore avec le premier à propos de l'imitation de Dieu dans le travail : si l'humain se consacre à l'horticulture, c'est le Seigneur qui a planté le jardin. En servant la terre, l'humain fera les œuvres de Dieu, après lui. Cette mission de service et de protection sera renouvelée même après le péché et l'expulsion du jardin d'Eden : le Seigneur Dieu renvoya donc l'homme du jardin d'Éden, pour qu'il aille cultiver le sol dont il avait été tiré (Genèse 3,23). L'entretien et la culture de la terre sont étroitement liés à la vie de l'être humain. Car toute la nourriture et le vêtement de l'humain lui viennent de la production de la terre.

- **Relation d'origine et de destination**

  Les récits bibliques précisent bel et bien que la terre est le lieu où retournera l'être humain après son séjour sur la terre : *car tu es poussière, et retourneras à la poussière* (Genèse 3, 19). N'est-ce pas ce qu'expose le symbolisme des rites de naissance

---

17   Dave Bookless, « Vers une théologie du changement climatique », dans Émile HOBBS, Jean-François Mouhot et Chris Walley, Évangile et Changement climatique, p. 25.

et d'inhumation qui s'observent dans quelques pays en Afrique et au Bénin en particulier? Dès, la naissance de l'être humain, son placenta est enfoui dans la terre, et à sa mort sa dépouille mortelle est enterrée dans la terre.

Conclusion

Dans un monde en mutation, où toute la terre est menacée, l'être humain, «clou» de la création est désorienté, perdu au milieu des multiples transformations voire dégradations. D'aucuns se posent la question de savoir si c'est Dieu qui change en tant que Créateur ou si ce sont les humains qui changent au gré des mouvements; tels que le réchauffement de la terre entraînant le changement climatique et la destruction de l'écosystème qui contribue à la destruction des sols. Or le développement humain n'est possible que par la protection de la terre et l'assurance de la souveraineté alimentaire. Le bien-être humain n'est pas assuré en dehors de son environnement et de son alimentation. Car l'être humain a été instruit, depuis sa création, à se nourrir à partir des produits du sol et de la création autour de lui tout en la protégeant (Genèse 1). La protection de la terre est bien plus qu'un impératif. Cette interpellation se résume dans les objectifs de l'ODD et constitue une des trois dimensions de la mission évangélique. Les Églises, elles-mêmes sont plus que jamais aux prises avec une plus grande insécurité. Un peu partout, des personnes sont en quête de chemins de spiritualité alternatifs, parce que les Églises n'apparaissent plus comme une référence pour ceux et celles qui ont faim et sont mal nourris. Cette réalité dans laquelle le monde est plongé, surtout avec la particularité des pays en développement, constitue un contre-témoignage à l'Évangile du Christ.

La terre nous porte, nous soutient et nous nourrit tout au long de notre existence. Elle nous accueille, nous enveloppe ou nous loge en son sein, après notre passage ici-bas. Nos aïeux, dans certaines traditions, n'ont-ils pas raison de faire de la terre, une divinité?

Le terme responsabilité sociétale semble être la formule magique réclamant une meilleure relation entre les humains et l'environnement dans lequel ils vivent. Le modèle de vie qui a pour fondement la surconsommation et la cupidité doit être corrigé et remplacé par celui du souci de la protection terre, et de ses composantes. Des mesures dynamiques et transformatrices doivent être prises à travers des programmes de développement visant à susciter des actions dans des domaines d'importance critique telle que la préservation de la biodiversité, le reboisement, l'éducation à l'écocitoyenneté, la lutte contre les sachets plastiques et l'accaparement des terres, etc. Il s'agit selon le pape Jean-Paul II[18] d'éduquer, d'un côté, l'être humain

---

18   Pape Jean-Paul II, Discours, à l'organisation des nations unies pour l'éducation, la science et la culture (Unesco), 2 juin 1980.

à ne pas «tyranniser» la nature et, de l'autre, à défendre la vie humaine. Prendre soin de la terre, c'est respecter le présent gratuit qu'elle constitue et c'est exercer la responsabilité individuelle et collective à son égard.

Pour la protection de la terre, chaque être humain est invité à prier ainsi :

Seigneur, garde moi humble dans l'abondance comme dans le manque

Aimant la terre que tu m'as confiée

Afin que je ne cherche pas tant

À récolter qu'à recevoir

À régner qu'à cultiver.

Références bibliographiques

Bibles et Livres

Bible. 2011. *ZeBible*, Société Biblique Française.

Bible d'Etude. 2005. *Version du Semeur 2000*, Excelis.

Bookless, D. 2017. «Vers une Théologie du Changement Climatique» in E. Hobbs, J.F Mouhot et C.H. Walley, C., Évangile et Changement Climatique, Vivre n° 40, Je Sème.

Dossou D. D. 2019. Pratique Ethique et Management Socialement Responsable, OBA.

Durokozoi G. et Roussel A. 1987. Dictionnaire de Philosophie, Paris, Nathan.

Ka M. et Kenmogne, J. B. 1997. Éthique Ecologique et Reconstruction de l'Afrique, Bafoussam/Yaoundé, Cipcre/ Clé.

Kapolyo J. M. 2007. L'Homme, Vision Biblique et Africaine, Paris/Saint Légier, Farel/Emmaus.

Thiaw-O-Une, L. (s/dir.). 2006. Questions d'Ethique Contemporaine, Stock.

Wittman, H., Desmarais, A. A. et Wiebe, N. 2010. *Food Sovereignty: Reconnecting Food, Nature and Community*. Fernwood Publishing, Food First, Pambuzuka Press.

Ziegler, P. 2008. Promotion and Protection of all Human Rights, Civil, Political, Economic, Social and Cultural Rights, Including the Right to Development, Report to the UNHRC.

Internet

FAO-Rapports 2011, 2012, www.fao.org /docrep/017/i3028f/i3028f.pdf

La Via Campesina 2009, www .viacampesina.net/downloads/PDF/FR -3.pdf

Zagore, D. 2016. Laudato Sì et la Mission en tant qu'Engagement en Faveur de la Création, www.fides.org/fr/news /67971, Agence Fides, 23/05/2020.

Global Food Policy Report, in International Food Policy Research Institute (IFPRI), www.ifpri.org /publication/2016-global-food-policy -report

Jean-Paul II. 29 Juin 2000. Message du Saint-Père à l'Occasion de l'Inauguration d'un Ermitage Franciscain sur la Colline des Croix, Vatican. http://www.vatican.va /content/john-paul-ii/fr/letters/2000 /documents/hf_jp-ii_let_20000711 _padre-bini.html

Saint-Père François. 24 Mai 2015. Lettre encyclique 'LAUDATO SI' sur la sauvegarde de la maison commune, Rome. http://www.vatican.va/content /francesco/fr/encyclicals/documents /papa-francesco_20150524_enciclica -laudato-si.html

web.unep.org/environmentassembly/fr /terres-et-sols.

Pape Jean-Paul II, Discours, à l'Organisation des Nations Unies pour l'Education, la Science et la Culture (Unesco), Paris ; 1980 in http://www .vatican.va/content/john-paul-ii/fr /speeches/1980/june/documents/hf_jp -ii_spe_19800602_unesco.html.

PART TWO

Re-imagining Women's Oppression and the Earth

THE MISSIONARY INITIATIVE
OF VEGETABLE GARDENS

Benefits and Shortcomings from
an Eco-centric Perspective

Esther Mombo[1]

Esther Mombo[1]

Abstract

Efforts to transform the lives of families through nutrition were an integral part of missionary work in most African communities. The decision came out of the realization that it was the duty of the woman to provide the food and drink for the household. Wood getting, water carrying, digging, weeding, harvesting, grinding, cooking and caring for children were all the tasks of women. These tasks were done in a communal way by the women as it was one way the women supported each other. The missionaries introduced Christianity to the communities but created separate villages for those who converted to Christianity. In the Christian village, each woman was encouraged to have her own vegetable garden as a source of food for her family. The vegetable garden for a woman was a symbol of discipline, commitment and hard work. While the woman was expected to work in the other portions of land, the vegetable garden was her main space around which her other activities were based. The education of women, which was for the domestic sphere, was inclusive of vegetable gardening. Through the vegetable gardens, new work ethics and social interaction between women were introduced. As well as this, the ideas of domesticity were reinforced about land such that women were disconnected from determining how land would be used. This paper seeks first to evaluate how the introduction of the individual vegetable gardens were associated with new ways of being women in the Christian community. The creation of vegetable gardens introduced and affirmed the ideas of domesticity that impacted on women's roles and place in society. Since there was no similar education and compulsion for men to work as hard or produce food for the family, this means that women were exploited for their labour in contrast to the men. Moreover, focus on vegetable gardens sidelined women from ownership of larger lands

---

1   Esther Mombo is an associate professor at St. Paul's University in the department of Church History, faculty of Theology. She obtained her PhD from the University of Edinburgh and her thesis Title was The Role of Women in the Development of the Quaker Church in Western Kenya. She was awarded an honorary doctorate by Virginia Theological Seminary in 2007 for her work in bringing to the fore issues of gender disparities and gender justice in church, especially in Theological Education. Her research and teaching interests span the fields of Church history, African women's theologies, Gender, HIV and AIDS. Among her publications is If You Have No Voice Just Sing: Narratives of Women in Search of Accessing Theological Education and Service in Church.

which in the future could become commercial. The entrenchment of domesticity created room for the domination of women, similar to the ways the land was also dominated by those who had power to own it. This chapter seeks to evaluate the process by which women were socialised into the new society through individual vegetable gardens. The chapter also seeks to show the shifts of land use and how they continue to be exploitative to women. Finally, the chapter shows ecocentrism as a way to embrace a new way of relationships that leads to the empowerment of women as part of the wider society in the use of land than being confined to the small space of vegetable gardening.

The chapter uses the critique of colonial and missionary modernizing theories to show the connection between the domination of women and the exploitation of land and offers a creative format for ways to avert the ecological crisis that is facing Africa today.

Introduction

Ecological degradation and the ensuing crisis has impacted all living and non-living things. It is no secret that this crisis has caught humanity's attention instantaneously, regardless of one's economic and or political class, nationality, age, race, literacy and spirituality among other dimensions. Sallie Mcfague observes that God as our Mother/Creator doesn't shape creation 'outside' herself, but gives birth within herself, so that the earth is God's own body.[2] Elizabeth Amoah points out that "at the present time there is tremendous awareness on the environment and the threat that humanity's use or misuse of it poses to human survival."[3] Degradation of the environment, therefore, affects humanity in relation to who they are and the roles they play in society.

There is a general agreement that due to the gender division of roles, women are affected more by the menace of climate change as they interact with the earth often than men. Mercedes Canas, in her chapter 'In us Life Grows: An Ecofeminist Point of View,' rightly points out that "the majority of women learn to protect that which they respect and recognise as vital to life: water, forests, soil, plants, animals and others."[4] In agreement, Wangari Maathai, the 2004 Nobel Laureate from Kenya noted that from food shortage to forest degradation and subsequent conflicts over meagre resources, the impact is directly felt by women and girls. For example, deforestation means that women walk twice as far to find water and firewood, and pollution means there is a greater struggle for clean water, and children in informal settlements sometimes die from unclean water. Thus, to address the menace of climate change and global warming that are impacting harshly on the ecosystem, the empowerment

---

2   McFague, S. 1993. *The Body of God: An Ecological Theology.* MN: Augsburg Press, 181.

3   Amoah, E. 1997. Where God Reigns: Reflections on Women in God's World. Accra: Sam-Woode, 3.

4   Canas, M. 1996. In Us Life Grows: An Ecofeminist Point of View. In: R. R. Reuther. *Women Healing Earth: Third World Women on Ecology, Feminism, and Religion Ecology & Justice.* 26.

of women cannot be wished away. Realizing the need for empowerment, embracing it and implementing measures towards women empowerment will contribute greatly towards reducing the impact of climate change.

Land in most African communities was owned by the whole clan or community rather than the individual. Individual land ownership with title deeds came with colonial and missionary movements of the 18th and 19th century. Like the men of their time, women did not own land or other immovable properties. The irony is that, in most parts of Africa, women are closely associated with the production of food and raw materials for the industrial sector.[5] In Africa, ownership of land and associated resources is very much anchored in patriarchy. The consequences for women not owning, controlling or accessing land are grave, given that the natural resources were the main sources of their livelihood. In Africa, it was a woman's role to provide food and drink for the household, a belief that has overtime contributed to their repression, lack of land, and further degradation of land.[6] This belief was adopted and replicated by the missionaries in their efforts to Christianise Africa through training women to keep vegetable gardens as a way of supplementing their family diet.

Land and Gender Roles in Pre-Christianised Africa

Gender is an important organizing category in the religious movements in Africa.[7] It is thus important to delve into gender roles that were evident in Africa before the arrival of missionaries. The oppression of women is centuries old, and is probably older than biblical history. Casimir et al (2014) traces the motivations of repression from the theological interpretation of man's relationship to woman, which is revered with the same unquestionable awe that the church upholds biblical canons with.[8] This negative theological interpretation was accepted by the church without genuine scrutiny and understanding. The highly regarded special group of men inspired by God's word misled the church with dictates. The inspired men as well as the populace failed to understand that the 'inspired men' were still human mortals and subject to

---

5 Mbote, K.P. 2005. The Land Has Its Owners. Gender Issues in Law Tenure Under Kenya Customary Law. *International Environmental Law Research Centre Working Paper*, 9.

6 Ibnouf, F. 2009. The Role of Women in Providing and Improving Household Food Security in Sudan: Implications for Reducing Hunger and Malnutrition. *Journal of International Women's Studies*, 10(4):144-167.

7 Mwaura, P. 2013. Gender and Power in African Christianity: African Instituted Churches and Pentecostal Churches. In: African Christianity: An African Story. Trenton, NJ: Africa. 413.

8 Casimir, A., Chukwuelobe, C.M. & Ugwu, C. 2014. The Church and Gender Equality in Africa: Questioning Culture and the Theological Paradigm on Women Oppression. *Open Journal of Philosophy*, 4(2):166.

human errors of faith, reasoning and understanding.[9] It is this mentality of biblical authority that the missionaries applied to support discriminatory practices against women and has been probably applied to date.

In her book, 'The Will to Arise: Women Tradition and the Church in Africa,' Oduyoye rejects the hermeneutical problem of misinterpretation, creditable as it may sound. She observes that in the traditional communities of the Yoruba (Nigeria) and Akan (Ghana) gender inequality was the norm, a concept that had distorted the equality of men and women. Oduyoye notes that sexism is a problem in Africa, and was in no way created ...'by the arrival of Islam and Christianity, but one that is an Integral part of our Africa world-view.[10] Women were socialised to internalise that they were born innately inferior to men, a norm that they embraced with ease. They relegated themselves to nurturing, gathering firewood, fetching water, building, weeding, harvesting, grinding, cooking and raising children.[11]

The discrimination of women cuts across many areas of society. It can be discerned in oral traditions (proverbs and taboos), sexual fidelity, morality, western education, widowhood practices and inheritance, among others.[12] Inheritance in Africa was a preserve for men – women had no right to inherit or own land. They could sometimes inherit it following the passing on of their husbands! Inheritance as a cultural practice among the Africans has not been friendly to women.

With regard to land inheritance, the promising concept of matriliny is devoid of hope. The word 'matriliny' comes from the Latin words *mater/matris*, translated to mean 'mother'. It implies kinship or descent along the mother or female line.[13] Thus, a kinship structure that traces its familial ancestry through the mother's line is matrilineal society. Scholarship ideologies on African kinship political economies allude that under matriliny, wealth flow would be biased towards a matrilineal line rather than their paternal relatives.[14] Surprisingly, however, in these types of societies, children are taken care of by the woman while the men have power over women and children.[15] This means that matriliny should never be considered as a cultural system

9   Ibid.

10 Oduyoye, M. 1990. Who Will Roll the Stone Away? The Ecumenical Decade of the Churches in Solidarity with Women. WCC Publications, 15.

11 Osha, S. 2004. A Postcolonial Scene: On Girls' Sexuality. In: *2nd Understanding Human Sexuality Seminar Series*. Africa Sexuality Resource Centre: Lagos.

12 Familusi, O.O. 2012. African Cultures and the Status of Women: The Yoruba Example. *The Journal of Pan-African Studies*, 5:1-15.

13 Matriliny. 2009. Oxford Dictionary of Sociology. 445.

14 Mtika, M.M. and Doctor, H.V. 2002. Matriliny, Patriliny and Wealth Flow Variations in Rural Malawi. *African Sociological Review*, 6(2):71-97; Kharkrang, R. 2012. *Matriliny on the March*. Shillong: Vendrame Institute Publications.

15 Schneider, D.M. and Gough, K. 1961. *Matrilineal Kinship*. University of California Press. Scott, J. and Marshall, G. 2009. *Oxford Dictionary of Sociology*. New York: Oxford University Press. S.

which empowers women. It only gives the impression of the structural dominance of women while power does not reside with the woman. Gender injustice and inequality in Africa manifest as constructs of patriarchal power and privilege.[16]

Oppressive cultural and socio-economic practices of inequality and injustice in Africa, coupled with theological misinterpretations of the Bible, have encouraged discrimination and marginalization of women, deterring the recognition of women's roles in development. Women are perceived as existing for men and children, not as human beings in their own right.

The missionary cultural context contributed to the perceptions they held about African women and even more so the practices they put in place to liberate the women. Mission agencies to Africa adopted an evangelical theology of mission which was consonant with the ideology of domesticity. This ideology defined woman as complementary to man, physically inferior but morally superior.[17] Woman, therefore, was supposed to be more affectionate, selfless, dependent and devout by nature. The woman's sphere was the home, which was a supposed refuge from the public realm in which men competed for money and power. Mission work among and for women was therefore influenced by the ideology of separate spheres and defined the notions of "space, work, gender and power."[18] Missionary wives, through home visitations, sewing lessons, childcare, cookery and prayer meetings, disseminated the ideology of separate spheres. As well as home visits, ideas of domesticity were carried over into the formal education of girls.[19] The courses on housewifery, nutrition, home nursing, sewing and farming became a part of the curriculum for the girls' education in order to prepare them to be wives and mothers. Missionary reports indicated the ways in which the women were being trained to be industrious. For instance, some reports from the 1930s read: "It is the duty of the woman to provide the food and drink for the household. Wood getting, water carrying, digging; weeding, harvesting, grinding, cooking and caring for numerous children were her share of business."[20] It is against this background that the quest for vegetable gardens became important for women's lives in the community.

16   Murphy, C.C. 1994. *An Introduction to Christian Feminism (No. 59)*. Dublin: Dominican Publications.

17   De Jong, M. 1991. Protestant and its Discontents in the Eighteenth and Nineteenth Centuries. *Women Studies*, 19:260.

18   Moore, H.L. 1996. Space, Text and Gender: An Anthropological Study of the Marakwet of Kenya. Cambridge. 147-152.

19   Musisi, B.N. 1992. Colonial Missionary Education: Women and Domesticity in Uganda, 1900-1945. In: K. T. Hansen (ed). *African Encounters with Domesticity*. New Jersey: Rutgers University Press. 192-194.

20   American Friends Board of Foreign Mission. 1938:7.

Women's Vegetable Gardens: A New Way of Being a Woman.

The advent of missions and missionary work to communities in most African communities was in the context of colonialism and the ideology of domesticity. Domesticity is a historically constructed notion with many layers of meaning. The term 'domestic' denoted a space, physical setting (home), a type of activity or work (home keeping) or preoccupation (domestic affairs). As a relationship, it implied power – controlling family, civilizing or organising – i.e. household management. In the context of mission, it governed the Church in setting up missions so that mission or missions was basically male. In this regard mission work among women was in line with the domestic sphere rather than the public sphere. Moreover, domesticity impacted on land use, control and ownership.

As far as land was concerned women were perceived as those who worked hard to fend for the families. These perceptions influenced the ways in which women's roles were created. The first Christian missionaries to Africa were charged with the zeal of spreading the gospel. While effecting their commission, the missionaries incorporated their cultural, political and commercial values to the nations/tribes they resided with.[21] Christian missionaries were keen to promote a new moral order based on their perception of a civilised society whose food and feeding habits mirrored their countries of origin.

One of the challenges that the missionaries had to contend with was on matters of food. The missionaries were not used to eating local indigenous foods. This made it difficult for them to stay in missionised countries for long. Determined to Christianise Africa, over time they brought some crops, which they cultivated and which sustained them. Notable for the incorporation of commercial and cultural value is Robert Moffat, a Scottish Congregationalist missionary to South Africa under the London Missionary Society.[22] During his teenage years, Moffat worked on farms for his upkeep before embarking on his missionary journey. According to Edwin, it is from these experiences that he developed a passion for farm produce. As a result, he introduced new methods of vegetable gardening and crop irrigation amongst the residents of Kuruman in South Africa, his mission field at the time.[23]

According to Keatinge and others, a vegetable garden is an area around the dwelling where different vegetables, fruit trees, and medicinal plants are grown throughout the year, potentially with small stock present, to meet household nutritional

---

21   Hastings, A. 1994. *The Church in Africa 1450-1950*. New York: Oxford University Press Inc.

22   Smith, E. 1925. *Robert Moffat: One of God's Gardeners*. Edinburgh: Turnbull and Spears. Retrieved from https://missiology.org.uk/pdf/e-books/smith-e-w/robert-moffat_smith.pdf, 24.

23   Ibid. 146.

requirements. They are 'enterprises that can usually be undertaken by most of the rural and even urban poor irrespective of their land resources, educational status, cash investment, capacity or gender.[24] As Hastings argues, civilization was understood by the missionaries as "the vegetable gardens and fruit trees, clean houses and water, ploughs and forges, reading and writing, hats and shoes," the items that were familiar to them back in England in supplementing their diet.[25] Upon the mention of 'civilization,' African women embraced the concept of keeping vegetable gardens since culturally, it was deemed a woman's duty to provide food for her household. As well as this, Hastings observed that women were important for mission work as important pillars for the Christian faith. The methods used to introduce the Christian faith was through reading, western methods of health, and farming. The creation of mission stations became a space for evangelism, and for women to train on domestic work including the creation of vegetable gardens.[26]

Quaker missionaries in western Kenya, similar to other mission agencies on the continent, observed the significance of women in regard to feeding their families. In 1922 Edna Chilson remarked that:

> It is the duty of the woman to provide the food and drink for the household. Wood getting, water carrying, digging; weeding, harvesting, grinding, cooking and caring for numerous children are her share of business.[27]

It was important, therefore, to train the women on the cultivation of vegetable gardens as individuals. While the male missionaries introduced new farming methods for the men, cash crops that were sold for money, the women missionaries introduced and stressed the significance of women having a garden in which to plant vegetables, fruits and flowers. In some mission stations women were taught how to care for the families by preparing nutritious meals. Thus the significance of the vegetable garden which would provide sufficient for the family and surplus to sell for money to also supplement the kitchen budget.

The vegetable gardens had both positive and negative implications for the woman. A vegetable garden was important, because it meant that each woman had food available for her family. But at the same time, the vegetable garden was used by the church to reduce the social interactions among women except when it was for

---

24   Keatinge, J.D.H. et al. 2013. Vegetable Gardens and their Impact on the Attainment of the Millennium Development Goals. *Biological Agriculture & Horticulture*, 28(2), June:71-85.

25   Hastings, A. 1994:285.

26   Modupe L. 1993. From Heathen Kraal to Christian Home: Anglican Mission Education and African Christian Girls, 1850-1900. In F. Bowie, D. Kirkwood & S. Ardener. *Women and Missions: Past and Present Anthropological and Historical Perceptions*. Berg. 126-142

27   *Mombo, E.M. 1999. Haramisi/Jumaa: The Story of the Women's Yearly Meeting in East Africa Yearly Meeting of Friends. Wood Brooke Journal, (5), Autumn:1-25.*

church meetings or doing church work. It was a symbol of hard work, discipline and the right moral behavior for the Christian women. For those women who did not have the discipline of creating and maintaining the vegetable gardens, they were perceived as lazy and busy bodies. Since a lack of a vegetable garden was seen as a symbol of laziness, women spent most of their time making sure that their vegetable gardens were up to standard. Thus, the vegetable garden was used to reinforce the work ethic among women and isolation from other women.[28]

Comparative histories of gender have shown that prior to the modern era, the majority of women, most often peasants, played a significant role in the productivity of the self-sufficient family unit.[29] They have also argued that vegetable gardening enables women to have greater authority over the quality of the family diet. However, this form of embrace of limited authority within kitchen-confines in a cultural tradition where women are not supposed to own/inherit land greatly disadvantages women. This situation is in itself a major detriment. Although home gardens were introduced to African women in good faith by the missionaries, it just reinforced the deep-seated culture that forbade women from owning big farmlands. Vegetable gardening has over the years become principally the responsibility of women in most of Africa and Latin America.[30]

Discriminative tendencies arise from this bias. This is because vegetable gardens are pro-poor. The practice is undertaken by most of the rural and even the urban poor irrespective of their land resources, educational status, cash investment capacity or gender. The land needed and input costs are small, and availability of family labour, which is often women and children, is usually sufficient. It should thus be noted that work in the home gardens is physically demanding and can add a substantive burden to women with household responsibilities and care of the young or elderly, since they themselves perceive and are perceived as full-time nurturers. The energy required to garden successfully has received little attention when considering the abilities of women to harmonise farming and household tasks and is particularly pertinent when trying to empower women, this has in turn resulted in their marginalization.[31]

Historical accounts indicate that mission ideology of domesticity introduced above impacted on women's use of land. This was equally true of women's roles

28   Mombo E.M. (1998): The Role of Woman in the Development of the Quaker Church in Kenya. PhD thesis Edinburgh, 161.

29   Rule, T.M. and Levin, C.E. 2001. Discussion Paper 92: Assessing the Potential for Food-based Strategies to Reduce Vitamin A and Iron Deficiencies: A Review of Recent Evidence. Food and Nutrition Bulletin, 22(1):94-95.

30   Talukder, A. et al. 2010. Homestead Food Production Model Contributes to Improved Household Food Security And Nutrition Status of Young Children and Women in Poor Populations.

31   Cheng M.H. 2010. Asia-Pacific Faces Diabetes Challenge. Lancet, 375:2207–2210.

in leadership.[32] According to Gaitskell, the missionaries' preferred a model of the family that was as follows: "male breadwinner, dependent housekeeping wife and mother, dependent school-going children." As a result, "this was the family model which female missionaries considered the Christian ideal in the early twentieth century and which they tried to inculcate among the women and girls of the rural-urban black churches.[33] While women in Africa looked up to the colonial church as 'savior' that would liberate and restore their tradition-denied human right of land ownership as an opportunity for human development, the Missionary Church supported the ancient and modern bearers of the culture to draw up and sustain a paternalist gender structure and constructs that perpetuated inequality and injustices against them. Propagated and reinforced by the male oriented colonial era, the trend was continued into the post-colonial era amidst the quest for emancipation. The churches that were founded by Christian missionaries were compounded by patriarchal ideologies that did not allow women to participate in the leadership but to do domestic chores in the church as well. This was justified by the way in which Scripture was read and interpreted. This kind of interpretation justified the roles of women as dependents of men both in the public and private spheres. The interpretation had implication on land in view of domination and alienation rather than the notions of being caretakers and cultivators of land.

Post-colonial Eco-shift

The word post-colonialism literary refers to the period of time after colonialism or after independence. It depicted an illusion of attainment of freedoms that had been repressed by the colonial masters.[34] The expected positive connotation of the word 'post-colonial' with regard to land ownership by women alluded to a presumed cultural freedom, namely that women could now own land. This has not been the case. In most of African nations, the right to own and or inherit land by women has not been commendably realised. The notion of colonialism as a reinforcer of this form of inequality, given the many years of independence, challenges the post-colonialist tendencies that have continued with the repressive behaviors. The word 'postcolonial' has been coined to describe modern history of imperialism, colonialism, the struggle for independence, the attainment of independence from the colonial domination and the present neocolonialist realities.[35] The prohibition

---

32 *Manala. M.J. 2013.* The Impact of Christianity on Sub-Saharan Africa. *Studia Historiae Ecclesiasticae, 39(2):285-302.*

33 *Gaitskell, D. 2003.* Rethinking Gender Roles: The Field Experience of Women Missionaries in South Africa. *The Imperial Horizons of British Protestant Missions, 1880-1914, 241.*

34 Ashcroft, B. Griffiths, Tiffin. H (Eds.). (1989), The Empire writes back: Theory and Practice in Post-colonial literature. New York, 2.

35 Ibid., 2

of women from owning land, is a good example of neo-colonialist domination, which has to be fought from within.

The challenge at hand is the understanding of 'post-colonialism' both as a situated time frame and as a notion of continued colonial repression by patriarchal regimes. Griffiths et al. broaden the notion of post-colonialism by defining it as "the study of the interactions between European nations and the societies they colonised in the modern period".[36] The continued interactions, probably as a result of treaties signed and economic agreements either on provision of market or supply of raw materials for their industries, prompted more definitions. For instance, Dukor notes that the term 'post-colonialism' remains a "fuzzy concept stretching from a strictly historical definition to the more encompassing and controversial sphere of contemporary key-terms such as post-structuralism, postmodernity and the like."[37]

To get a glimpse of the interactions and their subsequent impacts, colonial and missionary modernizing theories will be evaluated to solve the puzzle of women and land crisis. One of the 'claimed missions' of colonialism was its "civilizing mission," with the goal of importing Western Europe's highly developed society and culture.[38] The civilizing mission of the colonisers was in part motivated by aspirations to make Africa inhabitable for the Europeans. As Taiwo notes, "the African world had to be made livable for the European missionaries – humanised as it were – and those areas that were made livable needed to have a cordon sanitaire erected around them to make sure they were not infested, polluted, or otherwise muddied by the disease-carrying primitive savage."[39] As a result, the presumed 'upgrade' of the African lifestyles (such as a vegetable garden) legitimised the coloniser's relationship of domination and control. Agbali puts the whole scenario into perspective with his assertion that "the colonial process repressed traditional cultural epistemic and indigenous ontological paradigms of meaning almost to the point of absolute decimation."[40]

In spite of a rich ontological and cosmological system of values that have a healthy balance of respect and recognition of the mutual equality of the two sexes in 'African theistic humanism' the male guardians of the customs did not find it necessary to protect women from unnecessary harm and oppression in line with their gender.[41]

---

36 Ibid.

37 Dukor, M. 2010. Theistic Humanism of African Philosophy: The Great Debate and Substance of Philosophy. Saarbrucken: LAP Lambert Academic Publishing, 2.
Uchem, R. (Ed.). 2005. Gender Equality: From a Christian Perspective. Ifendu Pulications.

38 Johnson, R. 2003. *British Imperialism*. Hampshire: Palgrave Macmillan. 107-112.

39 Taiwo, O. 2010. *How Colonialism Preempted Modernity in Africa*. Indiana University Press.

40 Agbali, A.A. 2005. Ritualizing Identity, Santeria, and Globalisation: Yoruba Imageries and Creole Paradigms. *Orisa: Yoruba Gods and Spiritual Identity in Africa and the Diaspora*. 97.

41 Dukor, M. Ibid: 35.

This paradox of ontological values and raw custom sanctioned by selfish patriarchal lords has led to a vicious cycle of customary mistakes that continue to threaten the lives of women and treat them by the society as second class citizens. This position of cultural paradox was also pointed by Shonayin in her painful observation that "Africa has not deemed it necessary to protect its women and its land."[42] In Africa, the same mistakes are being repeated perpetually because the selfish patriarchal regimes hide these atrocities or justify them with unhelpful traditional beliefs.

A shift in frames of thought from colonialism and missionary modernizing theories has been advanced in postcolonial theory. Postcolonial theory is concerned with matters of race, ethnicity and gender with the challenges of formulating a postcolonial national identity. It tries to describe how a colonised people's knowledge was used against them in the service of the colonisers and how knowledge about the world is generated under specific relations between the powerful and the powerless.[43] Postcolonial theory also encourages the creative resistance of the colonised to the coloniser. The theory tries to provide a framework that destabilises dominant discourse in the developed world and challenges "inherent assumptions" and critiques the "material discursive legacies of colonialism."[44]

Critically understood, post-colonialism is a hopeful discourse in situating women in a position that they can engage with nature in a conservable manner. The word 'post' can be perceived to connote a propelled movement of looking forward to a world void of all that is associated with colonialism. It aims at decolonizing the future by destabilizing the way of thinking of the developed world in order to create space for the marginalised women and enable them to speak and produce alternatives to dominating discourses. This means a redress of the meanings of assistance, modernization and cooperation among others to an embrace of overcoming selfish habits of thinking and acting. This will open an avenue of learning to cultivate and act out of our sense of interconnectedness. It is a human call to an eco-shift from patriarchal dominance towards inter-relatedness.

There has been a gradual shift in orientation of these policy approaches towards women from 'welfare', to 'equity' to 'anti-poverty' to 'efficiency' and finally to 'empowerment.'[45] There is, however, a lack of scientific evidence that home gardens contribute to women empowerment. This is because it is premised mainly on subsistence upkeep without economic viability, which can translate to transverse

---

42   Shonayin, L. 2012. The African Report. Paris: Groupe Jeune Afrique, 44:98

43   Bahri, D. 1996, Introduction to Postcolonial Studies, accessed from, http://www. English.emory.edu /Bahri/Intro.htm.

44   Bahri, D. 1996:1

45   Dukor, D. 2010; Ibid.

farming. This is in spite of kitchen gardens being tended to supplement the health nutrients of all – children, men, elderly, rich and the poor. Hence, a need for a deeper shift reconnecting all humanity into ecology, where everyone will take a leading responsibility in sustainable co-existence.

The concept of eco-shift is anticipated to be a positive contribution into this change. It is driven by a self-realization of the plain truth that all humanity is taking part in ecological degradation. The resulting amount of suffering is not a preserve for a few, but for all. Human consciousness on ecology is now more evident and alert than ever. We are living in a time of great fear of worldwide consequence of running out of oil, food as a result of global warming and climate change. The rational inhabitants of the world are realizing that technologies, genetic modified food production, consumerism lifestyles and control of rising population do not only discriminate on women but are also not sustainable. They continue to strain the entirety of the eco-system. The realization, accuses and serves us with both guilt and responsibility. It is us, who will reverse the adverse effects.

It is thus not a feminist concern only, but everyone is involved regardless of their status, race, gender and religion. The eco-shift takes on this realization and impacts on our decision-making processes, alluding to one's sensitivity on personal behavior outcomes. A paradigm shift according to Kortens is "an optimistic culture that springs from an optimistic humanistic belief in the power of human reason and knowledge."[46] It is a shift from a culture controlled by consumerism tendencies to a culture which is guided by cooperation and sufficiency within an ecosphere. The paradigm shift must also aspire to draw human persons into a bonding interrelationship with all. This is ecocentrism.

Ecocentrism holds that "the earth and its systems are not here for humans to do with it as they will."[47] Ecocentrism removes human persons from the pinnacle as the final 'lords' of creation and replaces them back into the incredibly complex earth system in which they evolved and are a part.[48] Eco-centrist and eco-shift mind set places humans back into nature to live, to feed, to generate and to regenerate in interconnectedness with all that is in the ecosphere. The interrelatedness and inter-dependence alludes to a situated precolonial mind frame, where values of mutual interrelatedness would have been attained. The consumerist lifestyles impacted on our being as well as our careless uptake and internalization of it have compromised the notion of regeneration of the earth.

---

46   Korten, D. (2006). The Great Turning: From Empire to Earth Community. Bloomfield, CT. 2
47   Hettinger, N. & Throop, B. 1999. Refocusing Ecocentrism. *Environmental Ethics*, 21(1):3-21.
48   Ibid.

The double shifts of thought dialogue with the case at hand from a pre-colonial, colonial and to post-colonial perspective. The association of women with household chores and health nurturing of the family being a gendered construct may have been a welcome tradition in Africa before the coming of the missionaries. Colonialist mentality of consumerism with which was once a noble welfare activity may have aroused feelings of exploitation on the part of women and unwarranted gluttonous value for land by men. Sharing of land within an African setting was a natural parental duty and a right to their male children in keeping to their clan and tribe traditions. As the missionaries and colonies started exchanging land with monetary valuation, a detrimental insight settled in their mindset. Land became a commodity, and everything in it had to be exploited for money.

Postcolonialism aimed to combat colonial mentality and tendencies of exploitation as well as to safe guard what was left. Even though counter-fights ensued, the consumerist mindset and lifestyle had already impacted on African minds. The once held traditional concept of land being owned by men became deep seated even during the formalization of land ownership. Women would work on the land only for subsistence, and the extra was exchanged for money by men since it was from 'their' land. Men would own cattle and chicken, but only milk and eggs were at the disposal of women.[49] The tendencies of domination and control changed hands, from powerful 'white' elite on ignorant African men to consumerist 'black' men on vulnerable women.

The vegetable garden as a preserve of women was well intended for women to have a space that they would use to feed the family and one that they would own. But with modern economic systems, it has become a good example of domination because of commercialization that even what was sacred land is now a commodity. Even though they were meant for the well-being of all, the infiltration of the consumerist mind set has played against women as appertains land ownership. The consumerist lifestyle has become a point of departure for all repressions witnessed in the world, including those that attack the earth. The impoverishment of women and the impoverishment of the land means that women in rural settings walk twice as long to find water than before, and when they find it, it is worse polluted than before. Pollution means that there is a greater struggle for clean water for example. The fight for empowerment is women's retaliation to the selfish values that have been inculcated in African men. It is no longer cooperation and complementarity as it formerly was between the two sexes.

---

49   Arora, V.P.S. 2013. Agricultural Policies in India: Retrospect and Prospect. *Agricultural Economics Research Review*, 26(2):135; Njuki, J., Waithanji, E., Lyimo-Macha, J., Kariuki, J. & Mburu, S. (Eds.). *Women, Livestock Ownership and Markets: Bridging the Gender Gap in Eastern and Southern Africa*. Routledge.

Implications for Policy and Women Empowerment

It is clear that rewinding the earth's clock is impossible, but a change of attitude, inculcation and internalization of new values is possible. This is a call to a deeper evaluation, engagement, and an embraced implementation of policies that enhance sustainable change. While acknowledging the mission trail of the ideology of domesticity, a contextualised reconstruction of its principles is a promising endeavor. A genuine empowerment of women in Africa should start with the correct interpretation and reconstruction of the theological, cultural and traditional errors that are the roots of women discrimination and marginalization.

Women's association and closeness to nature ought to originate from a positive premise, since it encourages regeneration that has lacked on the earth. Hawkins argues that biological decomposition of waste is important. [50] In this case of women tending vegetable gardens, using recycled kitchen water as well as enhancing decomposition in vegetation rotation is a package that turns into dirt, decomposing and giving forth new life. Designing for decomposition rather than recycling is the way to go for a sustainable world around us. Thus, agroecology has been correctly described as:

> [...] the answer to how to transform and repair our material reality in a food system and rural world that has been devastated by industrial food production and its so-called Green and Blue Revolutions. We see Agroecology as a key form of resistance to an economic system that puts profit before life. Our diverse forms of small holder food production based on Agroecology generate local knowledge, promote social justice, nurture identity and culture, and strengthen the economic viability of rural areas. As smallholders, we defend our dignity when we choose to produce in an agro ecological way.[51]

Vegetable gardening done and embraced by women is not an activity of reproach attracting demeaning associations, but a step towards the well-being and sustenance of the earth. Agro-ecological practices are normally inexpensive, simple and effective; there is a minimal dependence on external inputs. The yields may be higher but can also be lower than those in conventional agriculture. 'What counts more for women is the total benefit they derive: enough diverse and healthy food to feed the family, a decent net income, fodder to feed the animals, and improved soil health.[52] For women, living in harmony with nature and choosing the agro-ecological path is ultimately a choice for autonomy. Women explicitly choose to follow a pathway with nature, not against it. In following this path, the women acknowledge that "the

---

50   Hawkins, L.G. 2010. Managing Fruit and Vegetable Waste. *University of Georgia Extension, Georgia.*
51   The International Forum for Agroecology, 2015, 1-2.
52   Declaration of the International Forum for Agroecology, 2015, 36.

Earth is God's and all that is in it" (Psalm 24:1). They also acknowledge that what comes out of the ground is meant to nourish all people who live on the land. When all the people have been fed from the land, they relate harmoniously with each other and with God. Food produced from the land is for sharing and not for creating inequities in the society. The insecurities of property ownership emanate from selfish tendencies impacted on African men by the missionary colonisers. The African men in turn grounded their learned selfishness on baseless cultural and traditional dictates, which were formerly mutual in ensuring co-existence. Land ownership by women in Africa calls for an economic policy that is based on mutual agreement and development of our common resources of nature and human skill- with the end focused on regeneration – not on ourselves.[53] The consumerist selfish attitude affected all, both men and women, and has all along become the foundation of negotiations towards equity and empowerment. The time that this attitude has been abhorred deep within peoples' hearts has caused considerable damage that will require lots of effort to demystify. It is thus necessary to shift our focus from domination and exploitation tendencies to all-inclusive regenerative values of respect, co-operation equity and contentment for an interconnected well-being of all.

Conclusion

This chapter has shown how the establishment of vegetable gardens was significant in affirming the role of women in the production of food but also as a training ground for the women who became Christians. One also sees how the concept of domesticity was inculcated in the whole program of creating Christin womanhood. As much as it was an important process, in it was an oppressive and hierarchical system of relationships through which women remained in the domestic sphere in as far as issues of land were concerned. While the men grew in the public sphere and influenced by capitalist and consumerist attitudes of missionised colonisers, the women remained in the domestic sphere on issues of land in particular. The colonial and post-colonial regulations denied women access to land inheritance and/ or ownership. When land was commercialised, it became a valuable commodity of the men that could be exploited to yield maximum profit. For instance the cutting of trees has led to some parts that were rich with bountiful rain become dust bowls. It is the women who are hit hard with land degradation at all fronts.

The embrace of positive values of respect, co-operation, equity and contentment would found a solid ground for change. It is in this spirit that this chapter argues for a paradigm shift: an Eco shift that sensitises us into a double responsibility; that is we have participated in ecological degradation, so it is our responsibility to work

---

53   Johnson, T. V. (2003). Diesel Emission Control in Review– The Last 12 Months. *SAE Transactions*, 1-14.

towards fixing it. The chapter has further argued for an embrace of ecocentrism that places us back as participants in the ecosphere – not as 'lords' of the ecosystem. The embrace of this shift opens the way to an agro-ecology that encourages regeneration. Selfish capitalistic tendencies have for a long time been used as foundations for efforts towards equality and empowerment, a reason that explains why it is still a challenge for women to own land. The empowerment of women challenges all forms of domination including human domination over creation.

References

Agbali, A.A. 2005. Ritualizing Identity, Santeria, and Globalization: Yoruba Imageries and Creole Paradigms. *Orisa: Yoruba Gods and Spiritual Identity in Africa and the Diaspora*, 259-319.

Arora, V.P.S. 2013. Agricultural Policies in India: Retrospect and Prospect. *Agricultural Economics Research Review*, 26(2):135.

Bahri, D. 1996. Introduction to Postcolonial Studies. Accessed from http://www. english.emory.edu/Bahri /Intro.htm

Casimir, A., Chukwuelobe, M.C. and Ugwu, C. 2014. The Church and Gender Equality in Africa: Questioning Culture and the Theological Paradigm on Women Oppression. *Open Journal of Philosophy*, 4(2):166. https://doi.org /10.4236/ojpp.2014.42024

Cheng, M.H. 2010. Asia-Pacific Faces Diabetes Challenge. *Lancet*, 375:2207-2210. https://doi.org/10.1016/S0140 -6736(10)61014-8

Declaration, N. 2015. Declaration of the international forum for agroecology. *Sélingué: International Forum for Agroecology*. Retrieved from http:// www.foodsovereignty.org/forum -agroecology-nyeleni-2019

Duggan, L. 1998. Introduction to Part 2: Women's Unpaid Work. In: N. Visvanathan, L. Duggan, L. Nisonoff and N. Wiegersma (eds). *The Women, Gender and Development Reader*. London and New Jersey: Zed books Ltd. 103-111.

Duncan, D. 2004. Postcolonial Theory. Accessed from http://www4.cord.edu/ projects/murphy/Postcolonial%20 Theory

Dukor, M. 2010. *Theistic Humanism of African Philosophy: The great debate and substance of philosophy*. Saarbrucken: LAP LAMBERT Academic Publishing.

Familusi, O. 2012. African Cultures and the Status of Women: The Yoruba Example. *The Journal of Pan-Africa Studies*, 5:1-15.

Gaitskell, D. 2003. Rethinking Gender Roles: The Field Experience of Women Missionaries in South Africa. *The Imperial Horizons of British Protestant Missions, 1880-1914*, 131.

Hawkins, G. 2010. *Managing Fruit and Vegetable Waste*. Georgia: University of Georgia Extension.

Hastings, A. 1994. *The Church in Africa 1450-1950*. New York: Oxford University Press Inc.

Hettinger, N. and Throop, B. 1999. Refocusing Ecocentrism. *Environmental Ethics*, 21(1):3-21. https://doi.org/10 .5840/enviroethics199921138

Hawkins, G. 2001. Plastic Bags: Living with Rubbish. *International Journal of Cultural Studies*, 4(1):5-23. https://doi .org/10.1177/136787790100400101

Ibnouf, F. 2009. The Role of Women in Providing and Improving Household Food Security in Sudan: Implications for Reducing Hunger and Malnutrition. *Journal of International Women's Studies*, 10(4):144-167.

Johnson, T.V. 2003. Diesel Emission Control in Review–the Last 12 Months. *SAE Transactions*, 1-14. https://doi.org/10.4271/2003-01-0039

Kalabamu, F. 2006. Patriarchy and Women's Land Rights in Botswana. *Land Use Policy*, 23:237–246. https:// doi.org/10.1016/j.landusepol.2004.11 .001

Kameri-Mbote, P. 2005. The Land Has its Owners: Gender Issues in Law Tenure Under Kenya Customary Law. *International Environmental Law Research Centre Working Paper*, 9.

Korten, D. 2006. The Great Turning: From Empire to Earth Community.

Bloomfield, CT. https://doi.org/10.1057/palgrave.development.1100286

Kharkrang, R. 2012. *Matriliny on the March*. Shillong: Vendrame Institute Publications.

Manala, M.J. 2013. The Impact of Christianity on Sub-Saharan Africa. *Studia Historiae Ecclesiasticae*, 39(2):285-302.

Maathai, W. 2004. Retrieved from http://www.wangarimaathai.org/ Retrieved June 2019.

Moffat, R. 1842. Missionary Labours and Scenes in Southern Africa. Retrieved from http://books.google.com/ebooks?id Moffat, R. (1876).

Mombo, M.E. *1999. Haramisi/Jumaa: The Story of the Women's Yearly Meeting in East Africa Yearly Meeting of Friends. Wood Brooke Journal, (5), Autumn:1-25.*

Mtika, M.M. and Doctor, H.V. 2002. Matriliny, Patriliny and Wealth Flow Variations in Rural Malawi. *African Sociological Review*, 6(2):71-97. https://doi.org/10.4314/asr.v6i2.23215

Murphy, C.C. 1994. An Introduction to Christian Feminism (No. 59). Dublin: Dominican Publications.

Musisi, B.N. 1992. Colonial Missionary Education: Women and Domesticity in Uganda, 1900-1945. In: K. T. Hansen (ed). *Africa Encounters with Domesticity*. New Jersey: Rutgers University Press. 192-194.

Mwaura, P.N. and Kalu, O. 2013. *African Christianity: An African Story*. Trenton, NJ: Africa.

Njuki, J., Waithanji, E., Lyimo-Macha, J., Kariuki, J. and Mburu, S. (eds). 2013. *Women, Livestock Ownership and Markets: Bridging the Gender Gap in Eastern and Southern Africa*. Routledge. https://doi.org/10.4324/9780203083604

Oduyoye, M.A. 1984. Violence against Women: A Challenge to Christian Theology. In: E. Fiorenza (ed). *In Memory of Her: A Feminist Theological Reconstruction of Christian Theology*.

Oduyoye, M. 1990. *Who Will Roll the Stone Away? The Ecumenical Decade of the Churches in Solidarity with Women*. WCC Publications.

Ruel, M.T., and Levin, C.E. 2001. Discussion Paper 92. Assessing the Potential for Ffood-based Strategies to Reduce Vitamin A and Iron Deficiencies: A Review of Recent Evidence. *Food and Nutrition Bulletin*, 22(1):94-95. https://doi.org/10.1177/156482650102200115

Shonayin, L. 2012. The African Report (No. 44, p. 98). Paris: Groupe Jeune Afrique.

Schneider, D.M. and Gough, K. 1961. *Matrilineal Kinship*. University of California Press.

Scott, J. and Marshall, G. 2009. *Oxford Dictionary of Sociology*. New York: Oxford University Press.

Smith, E. 1925. *Robert Moffat: One of God's Gardeners*. Edinburgh: Turnbull and Spears. Retrieved from https://missiology.org.uk/pdf/e-books/smith-e-w/robert-moffat_smith.pdf Retrieved June 2019.

Taiwo, O. 2010. *How Colonialism Preempted Modernity in Africa*. Indiana University Press.

Osha, S. 2004. A Postcolonial Scene: On Girls' Sexuality. In: *2nd Understanding Human Sexuality Seminar Series*. Africa Sexuality Resource Centre: Lagos.

Uchem, R. (ed). 2005. *Gender Equality: From a Christian Perspective*. Ifendu Pulications.

WOMEN AND THEIR RIGHT TO LAND OWNERSHIP

A Biblical and Holistic Approach

Master O. Matlhaope[1]

Abstract

The dualistic perspectives, where spirituality and materiality are regarded as asynchronous have deprived the world of a needed inclusive and holistic development. The Christian faith has in the past contributed positively to remedy some complex human challenges whilst secularism has often held religion accountable to some atrocities done supposedly in the name of God. These two entities need not work in antagonism. Today, more than ever before, the Christian faith is called forth to extricate relevant biblical precepts to address inequality and unfairness towards women, especially on their disempowered status on land ownership. The incarnation of Jesus brought spirituality and materiality into oneness. As Matsveru and Gillham[2] succinctly put it, "In a distinctly patriarchal context, Jesus uplifted women. He treated them with dignity and respect. Jesus upheld the dignity of women throughout His Earthly ministry." The redemptive purpose through Christ was to restore God's original plan of creation. Consequently, a Christocentric approach could be deployed to bring equity and justice to the issue of women and land. There is therefore, need to extrapolate normative principles based on pre-fall biblical narratives to form a per-locution or an informed action. This ought to be done in order to untangle some of the deeply ingrained cultural stereotypes that negatively impact women.

---

1   Master Oboletswe Matlhaope is a holistic Human Practitioner and a Lecturer at the Assembly Bible College. He is a member of the Advisory and Arbitration Council under the Ministry of Nationality, Gender and Immigration. Matlhaope obtained his PhD on practical theology from North West University (NWU) – Potchefstroom Campus (South Africa), in 2018, having completed part of his doctoral research at Cambridge University (United Kingdom) under Tyndale House. His thesis focused on the role of Evangelical theology on the socio-economic and political space in the context of Botswana. Over the years, and as part of his service to the nation of Botswana, he impacted the community of Francistown and was recognised and certificated by the Department of Women Affairs and also certificated as one of the Builders of the City of Francistown. He was one of the 30 selected persons for the Presidential Task Team (PTT) in 2015 to design, develop, draw and document a long-term vision for the country (Botswana- Vision 2036).

2   Matsveru, F. and Simon Gillham. 2015. A Biblical Survey of the Dignity of Women and Men. In Mouton, E.; Gertrude Kapuma, 45

Introduction and Rationale

The marginalisation of women with regard to land ownership is an eye-sore on the global attempt for inclusive development. Land is an economic resource, and denying women its ownership is a serious setback to inclusive socio-economic development. Women are the backbone of society; their economic status is a critical yardstick for gauging the socio-economic growth of a society as a whole. Empowerment of women-socially and economically does not only increase their self-worth, but positions them as critical players in wealth creation and also creates a more just and fairer socio-economic and political order. Attempts of poverty eradication that neglect women and their access to land are a futile exercise. Current disparities between the rich and the poor, subjugation of women and many other flaws in our societies, are results of flawed socio-economic human development approaches. These flawed approaches have been employed throughout human history along cultural and geopolitical lines. They are characterised by a disconnect between the creature and its Creator. What then obtains are ideologies devoid of original intentions of the Creator.

In the context of the discourse related to the marginalisation of women in the acquisition of land, this chapter argues that proper understanding by the public, transformation development agencies and governments, can serve as conduits for furtherance of equity, justice, and flourishing of all irrespective of gender or race. The chapter is divided into small sections, namely, hypothesis, methodology, contextualisation, synchronization, holistic approach and rhetorical summary. The chapter submits that the withdrawal of Christian principles from the socio-economic space leaves a moral vacuum, and humanity becomes susceptible to pressures that are antagonistic to a purview designated by God. The chapter will extrapolate normative principles that are based on the pre-fall narratives to inform a per-locution or an informed action. Such a per-locution calls for what Carson[3] calls distantiation, where the interpreter stands back from the text to study it critically. Such an approach should properly articulate a biblical view and inform proper biblical paradigms.

Hypothesis

This chapter argues that if we could integrate principles of equity and equal access to land by both men and women, we will have a better society. The advent of the fall of humanity has affected the holistic sphere of human existence, and both religion and secularism were affected. All human efforts thereafter always fell short of God's original intention and consequently short of the ideal standard. The creation of

---

3   Carson, D.A. 1996. Exegetical Fallacies, 2nd ed. Grand Rapids, MI: Baker Academic, 23-24.

difference, tension and dichotomy between religion and non-religion (or religion and secularism) have not helped the situation out. It is a product of the 18th century European enlightenment, when the world was dominated by human philosophies. The dichotomy should have its share of blame in the current disparities, not only involving women and land but also between the rich and the poor, and the disadvantages of the minorities of the world. Nonetheless, while this chapter argues that God, particularly in reference to the Christian religion, is the answer to the world's problems, it neither claims that human religion is flawless nor denies that secularism has occasionally outdone religion in empowerment through deconstruction, re-construction and activism, especially in the postcolonial era. Thus, the theoretical framework of this chapter acknowledges that while the colonial-era project of the evangelization of the two thirds world was carried out by missionaries with mostly good and compassionate motives, they could not be absolutely separated from the blemishes of fallen human nature. Patriarchy and discrimination are traceable in both religion and culture, and could be better combatted by eliminating the largely aesthetic division between religion and secularism.

The dichotomy of religion versus secularism contributed to socio-economic models devoid of godly principles of equality, justice, fairness, love for all, honesty, goodness and critical illumination. Religion that overlaps into the non-religious world could aid governments, as Schmidt[4] documents, in the outlawing of infanticide, child abandonment and gladiatorial games in ancient Rome, ending the practice of human sacrifice among European cultures, banning paedophilia and polygamy, and prohibiting the burning of widows in India. Schmidt further states that: William Wilberforce, a committed Christian, was the force behind the successful effort to abolish the slave trade in England. In the United States, two-thirds of abolitionists were Christian pastors. In the 1960's, Martin Luther King Jr., a Christian pastor, helped lead the civil rights movement against racial segregation and discrimination. In this time, we have the need and opportunity to change the status of women based on sound theological principle. Thus, the church has generally defended the oppressed and aided in develoment, as elaborated above, although there have been times when it took an ambiguous or outrigtly oppressive position.

Methodology

To realise the objective of formulating a normative base, the chapter used a holistic socio-economic and political development approach in dialogue with both socio-rhetoric and synchronic methodologies. These were based on the pre-fall text of Genesis to argue for a theo-centric socio-economic and equitable land distribution.

4   Schmidt, A. 2004. How Christianity Changed the World. Zondervan.

The synchronic methodology especially, focused on the genre of equality of being and privileges in the creation account of both man and woman. This led to the extrapolation of basal pre-fall imperatives for both man and woman that resonate with the contemporary world. The relevant biblical data obtained through this method made plausible conclusions on a biblical socio-economic and political paradigm that is inclusive, just and potentially remedial to the question of justice for women and women and land discourse. The chapter, however, is not exhaustive but shall serve the purpose of stimulating further discussion on the subject matter.

Contextualization

As Myers,[5] rightly observes: "no process of human and social transformation can be entirely defined locally. Every community is part of social systems that are regional, national, and finally globally." Patriarchy, which is a gendered power system, has become part of the global world. It has been used positively and negatively and continues to be scrutinised. In Botswana and like in other African countries, patriarchy has been used negatively against women in the area of land control by men. Kalabamu has sufficiently covered the negative scope of its adverse use in his article of 2006. He succinctly summarises the status of women and land in Sothern Africa when he points that:

> Although women in most parts of Southern Africa have traditionally been responsible for growing food crops and, in some communities, building houses, they never owned the land on which they carried out those activities. Land ownership was vested on respective jural communities or tribes but administered by chiefs, and headmen or tribal male elders. (Kalabamu, 2006:1)[6]

Indeed, land ownership in Southern African countries was only for women through their husbands and their male sons. The Lesotho Council of women as quoted by Kalabamu (2006)[7] buttresses the point well when they state; "Before marriage, women were the children of their fathers; after marriage, they were children of their husbands, and during their widowhood they were children of their heirs or sons." Moyo[8] in her chapter that deals with *An Examination of the Dignity of Women in a Zambian Context*, buttresses this point when she states;

Under a patrilineal system, succession is traced through the father's lineage, and often the eldest son of the senior wife inherits, or if there is more than one wife, the

---

5   Myers, L. B. 2011. Walking with the Poor: Principles and Practices of Transformational Development. New York: Orbis Books.

6   Kalabamu, F. 2006: Patriarchy and Women's Land Rights in Botswana (University of Botswana), 1.

7   Kalabamu. 2006. Patriarchy and Women's Land Rights in Botswana (University of Botswana).

8   Moyo, N. 2015. An Examination of Dignity of Women in Zambian Context. In E. Mouton; G. Kapuma, L. Hansen and T. Togom, *African Perspectives on Gender Equality*. Cape Town: Sun Press, 182.

eldest son of the senior wife inherits the property of the deceased. In the event that there are no male heirs, the eldest brother of the deceased inherits, and if there are no brothers, then the eldest sister inherits. In the event of having no siblings, the parents will inherit.

The scenarios given by both Kalabamu and Nolipher cuts across Africa and denied women equal privileges. Under such systems, names, property, titles, and other valuables were passed on through a male line. In most of the times, females did not inherit, unless there were no male heirs. This included matters relating to land ownership and inheritance.

In the context of Botswana, traditionally, *dikgosi* (tribal authorities) held land in trust for their communities. With such a responsibility, the tribal authorities ensured that all members of the society have a piece of land for residence and for subsistence pastoral or arable purposes. The land would be in the name of the male figure of the family, holding it in trust for the family. This was essentially because husbands or males were heads of households and female headed households were a rarity.

The tradition was such that a female gets married, and then through marriage, she changes her surname and domicile. She would then be entitled albeit without direct ownership, to what her husband owned. Land was associated with a household name and as such, in anticipation of marriage and the change that comes with it to the females, it was preserved through the male householder. This in a way preserved element of social justice in favour of children in the event their mother got married by another man. Notwithstanding the aforesaid, women were left with limited privileges to land. They could use land to build their houses and produce food for their families but they could not own the land.

There is need to further understand and appreciate some of the historical context for such patriarchal structures in order to peacefully transit to a more accommodative and inclusive arrangement. The Judaeo patriarchal tradition, which has lots of similarities to African tradition, associated land ownership to war conquests. The Jewish lands were acquired through wars, such as, for example: the conquest of Jericho in Joshua 6; the conquest of Ai in Joshua 8; the conquest of territories beyond Jordan; the acquisitions of the lands of Judah, Hebron, Manasseh, Benjamin, Simeon, Naphtali, Dan etc. in Chapters 13-19. In these contexts, land was acquired and maintained through war and in general, men led in those wars and defended the land.

It is noteworthy to mention that, notwithstanding the foregoing traditional narrative, the Bible generally notes that the land belonged to God. For example; Exodus 19:5 declares that "all the Earth is mine." Leviticus 25:23 also says; "the land is mine." God is the ultimate owner but has delegated stewardship to his image bearers, which according to Genesis 1:26-28 include both male and female. The advent of Western ideas on civilization has changed the traditional set-up. Now a civil authority services the land and thereafter allocates it on a first come first served basis regardless of gender. The scenario of first come first served creates and environment of survival of the fittest as Botswana, with a Gini-Co-efficient of 60.5[9] is the third most unequal country in the world. The Gini index measures income or wealth inequality and was originally developed by an Italian statistician Corrado Gini in 1912. A Gini index of 0 represents perfect equality while an index of 100 represents perfect inequality.[10] It may not be farfetched that the Gini-Co-efficiency among women, may even be worse.

Earlier research by the United Nations Development Programme[11] indicated that the economic growth process in Botswana has not been pro-poor. The conclusion of that report[12] is that:

> ... the proportion of individuals living below the Poverty Datum Line (PDL) declined from 46.1% in 1985-1986 to 32.9% in 1993-1994. Whereas it only decreased from 32.9% in 1993-1994 to 30.2 in 2002-2003.[13]

In other words, the head count index reduced at the annual rates of 4.2 and 0.9 percent in 1985-1994 and 1993-2003 periods respectively. This scenario presents a problem of negative equality score and a huge gap between the rich and the poor which shows uneven distribution of national resources among the citizens. Under the circumstances, those with financial muscles would likely buy and in most cases, would buy as much as their financial muscles enable them. Consequently, they end up having more while the poor, the majority of whom are women, remain with little or with nothing as it is in most cases. This ultimately increases inequality and women marginalisation.

Over and above the disparity in land ownership, women are grappling with other socio-economic challenges. The Third Botswana National Strategic Framework (NSF) for HIV& AIDS 2019-2023 (65)[14] states that:

> maternal mortality 156.6 deaths per 100,000 live births in 2016 is not yet under control, and Botswana did not attain the millennium Development Goal target of 82 deaths per 100,000 live births. The country is still striving towards

---

9   Monageng, M. & Fancis Nyamnjoh. 2015. Botswana at 50: Democratic Deficit, Elite Corruption and Poverty in the Midst of Plenty. *In Sunday Standard News Paper.*

10   Monageng and Nyamnjoh, 2015, 2.

11   United Nations Development Programme (UNDP). 2005. Human Development Report: International Cooperation at a Crossroads: Aid, Trade and Security in an Unequal World. New York: United Nations, 5.

12   UNDP, 5.

13   Ibid.

14   The Third Botswana National Strategic Framework (NSF) for HIV& AIDS 2019-2023 (65).

achieving the set Sustainable Development target of 54 deaths per 100,000 live births by 2030.

Further to that, according to NSF for 2019-2023 (17), 210,887 women aged 25-49, which is 57% of all women of that same age, are living with HIV compared to 158,289 men. The reasons could rightly be social and economic, yet of course not ruling out physiological reasons. The statistics should however, be taken with caution, reason being males generally have poor health seeking behaviour than females. As it is observed (NSF, 2019-2023, 17) only 74% of boys aged 20-24 know their HIV status.

That being said, it is noteworthy to acknowledge and state that unfair discrimination against women was outlawed in Botswana through the epochal case of the Attorney General Vs Dow in 1992. According to Kirby et al.[15] since that judgement, "the government has taken steps to progressively eliminate this wherever it occurs." He gave examples of Abolition of Marital Power Act Cap 29:07,[16] the Amendment of Married Persons Property Act Cap 29:03[17] and the Constitution Amendment Act No. 9/2005.[18] These quintessential amendments, emphasise the need for the society as a whole, to reject any form of discrimination against any person on the base of gender.

On another seminal judgement at the Court of Appeal, Kirby *et al.* inhumed inadmissible customs that underprivileged women. Among other things, the judgement stated that,

> It need hardly to be said that any customary law or rule which discriminates in any case against woman unfairly solely on the bases of her gender would not be in accordance with humanity, morality or natural justice. Nor would it be in accordance with the principles of justice, equity and good conscience.[19]

The referenced case was with regard to a yard that belonged to Silabo Ramatebele which he occupied with his wife Thwesane. The husband passed on in 1952 and his wife remained in the yard. Her daughters assisted her to further develop the yard but the sons never assisted her. However, she also later died and one of the daughters, who at the time of the case was 80 years old, stayed in the yard. One of the grandsons from one of the sons, who had not assisted in the development of the yard, was now laying a claim to the yard. This he did, on the bases of cultural norms

---

15 Kirby, I., Seth, T., Foxcroft, J.G., Legwaila, E.W.M.J. & Lesetedi, I.B.K. 2013. Court of Appeal (Republic of Botswana). Civil Appeal No. CA-GB-104-12. High Court Civil Case No. MAHLB-000836-10, 7.

16 Abolition of Marital Power Act Cap 29:07.

17 Amendment of Married Persons Property Act Cap 29:03.

18 Constitution Amendment Act No. 9/2005.

19 Kirby et al., 24-25.

and the case ended up at the Court of Appeal. The Court then ruled in favour of the 80-year-old daughter and declared the tribal custom unfair and unjust. This in essence was paradigmatic and implied that all customs and traditions ought to comply with justice, fairness and good conscience. The Court also emphasised that "Customary law must adapt to accommodate evolving society, (2013:25).

The dispensation of equal access to land in Botswana therefore provides women with an opportunity to turn the tide against the historical pervasive denial of women to own land. Every woman now is entitled to the same rights and privileges of applying for and owning land irrespective of marital status provided she has attained the age of 21. Here in Botswana and elsewhere in Africa, legal changes have come to change traditional gender biased perspectives.

In Nigeria, On April 14, 2014, the Nigerian Supreme Court, in an unanimous decision, confirmed decisions of two lower courts, which had found unconstitutional an Igbo customary law of succession excluding female offspring from eligibility to inherit the property of their fathers (Goitom, 2014).[20] Among other things, the Supreme Court ruled that: No matter the circumstances of the birth of a female child, such a child is entitled to an inheritance from her later father's estate. Consequently, the Igbo Customary Law, which disentitles a female child from partaking in the sharing of her deceased father's estate is in breach of Section 42(1) and (2) of the Constitution, a fundamental rights provision guaranteed to every Nigerian.[21] This judgement has presumably positively affected the plight of women in Africa's most populous country and has helped set the tone for the rest of the continent.

The Nigerian judgement alluded to above and other positive developments in Botswana and elsewhere are welcome but will require a paradigm shift of whole societies. This is because one of the problems in Africa is that there are de facto, two legal systems in operation. The Nigerian high court may well hand down a judgment consistent with the national constitution, but in the local village, customary law holds sway and rural peasants may have no idea as to their constitutional rights. That is why other transformational development agencies such as churches and other non-state actors should collaborate in efforts to educate the general populace.

That said, western influences have also brought both the positive and the negative changes. The positive change is on the advent of equal access to land by both male and female. The negative includes the disparity between those who have and those who have not. There is need of a dialogue between the traditional dispensation

---

20   Goitom, H. 2014. Customary law, Discrimination, Inheritance and succession, Women's rights. (https://www.loc.gov/law/foreign-news/article/nigeria-supreme-court-invalidates-igbo-customary -law-denying-female-descendants-the-right-to-inherit/ Jurisdiction: Nigeria

21   Goitom, 2014.

which puts strong emphasis on the family and modernity which has emphasis on equality. Both family and equality are desirable.

The Synchronization

In general, the purview of theology places humanity before God while at the same time locates them in the society and in the gifts of governments. In such a locale, there is a consistent juxtaposition of good governance and poor governance. The former being a replica of righteousness where God reigns and the latter being synonymous with God's absence and consequent revulsion towards God. Humanity's revulsion is primarily evident in the catastrophes of the fall, the flood, and the flop of the tower of Babel. Attempts of human development or civilization apart from God and the consequences thereof are evident throughout Scripture. In addition, it is possible for religion to misinterpret God and instead take an oppressive route.

In church history, records of colonial-era missionaries reveal them often racially discriminating against the indigenous, denigrating them and sometimes supporting the looting of their land.[22] In South Africa, much evidence has been put forth of the racial discrimination of the Dutch Reformed Church.[23] Retracing history from as recently as the colonial era, this racial ideology is widely indicted as foundational to the current political and economic inequalities between Europe and the two thirds world. Not only did the missionaries occasionally subscribe to a racial dichotomy, but also laid a foundation in the church for gender inequality, which has kept women under the domination of men for many centuries. This happened through obedience and perpetuation of the Scriptures that forbid a woman to be a leader or be active in public (Cf. 1 Timothy 2:12). From such and similar biblical texts, interpretations have been made by church fathers, missionaries and some contemporary churches that subject women to dualistic disadvantages in many areas of life.[24] For example, the church has traditionally reinforced the system that restrains the woman to the subsistent domestic sphere, thereby subduing her participation in the socio-economic

---

22 Schulze, F. 2013. German Missionaries, Race, and Othering Entanglements and Comparisons between German Southwest Africa, Indonesia, and Brazil. *Itinerario*, 37(1); Rey, M. 2012. Intersectionality in the Book of Ruth: Constructing Ruth's Identity in Ancient Israel. A dissertation submitted in partial fulfillment of the requirements for the degree of Master of Sacred Theology. Boston University: Boston, 71.

23 Cf. Tshaka, R.S. 2015. The Black Church Is the Womb of Black Lliberation theology? Why the Uniting Reformed Church in Southern Africa (URCSA) Is not a genuine Black church? *HTS Teologiese Studies/ Theological Studies*, 71(3).

24 Berman, S.K. 2015. Of God's Image, Violence against Women and Feminist Reflections. *Studia Historiae Ecclesiasticae*, 41(1), 128. https://dx.doi.org/10.17159/2412-4265/2015/v41n1a9

and political affairs of the nation.[25] It is an ideological system that impacts on land ownership, inheritance, participation in commerce, and others.

Genesis Text Background

According to Jamieson et al. (1985:1)[26] its title in English, 'Genesis' comes from the Greek of Genesis 2:4 which literally mean "the book of the generations (*genesis*) of the heavens and Earth." Its title in the Jewish Scriptures is the opening Hebrew word, *Bereshit*, 'in the beginning.' There are different views to its authorship although the majority of Evangelicals believe that Moses wrote the book. They hold that he wrote it while in the wilderness journey from Egypt to Canaan, after he had been in the mountain with God at which he probably received full instruction for its writing.[27]

The Good God

On the onset, Genesis 1:1 paints a dateless past called the beginning. The epitome of this past is that God is the creator of the heavens and the Earth. Hence the whole frame of the universe owes its origin to God. This, notwithstanding subsequent evolution of that which was created, implies that all the natural endowments are the works of God. Within the created heaven and Earth are all the discovered and undiscovered replenishments for the well-being of mankind.

It is noteworthy that the Bible begins with "God created" and does not attempt to discuss how and when God began. The character of the God of creation is best enunciated by what He did. He created the heavens with all splendour and glory of galaxies, and the Earth with all the wonder and grandeur. In reference to the name 'God,' Jamieson et al. (1985:1)[28] state:

> As to the word itself, it is pure Anglo-Saxon, and among our ancestors signified, not only the Divine Being, now commonly designated by the word, but also 'good.' As in their apprehensions, it appeared that 'God' and 'good' were correlative terms.

What this means is that, 'God' and 'goodness' are inseparable. God is a good Being of absolute benevolence and beneficence towards all His creation. It is not wrong therefore to restate the creation verse as "in the beginning the Good Being" created

---

25 Osha, S. 2004. A Postcolonial Scene: On Girls' Sexuality. In: *2nd Understanding Human Sexuality Seminar Series*. Africa Sexuality Resource Centre: Lagos.

26 Jamieson, F.B., Matthew Henry & Adam Clarke. 1985. Condensed Edition. Minneapolis: Bethany House Publishers.

27 Lin, T. (1997). The Genuineness and Mosaic Authorship of Genesis. Lin T. *Genesis: A Biblical Theology: PhD. – Biblical Studies Ministries International*, 18-24; Bradlaugh, C. 1882. *Genesis: Its Authorship and Authenticity*, London: Freethought Publishing Company, 2.

28 Jamieson, F.B., Matthew Henry & Adam Clarke. 1985. Condensed Edition. Minneapolis: Bethany House Publishers.

the heavens and the Earth. It is no wonder at the end of the creation narrative that the Bible would say: "God saw all that He had made, and it was very good" (Genesis 1:31). This good being has no beginning; He is eternal, independent and self-existent. As Jamieson would further state: "The Being whose purposes and actions spring from himself."[29] He created the heavens and the Earth without foreign influence and with a good motive.

The second verse of the creation account is equally intentional and very important; "Now the Earth was formless and empty, darkness was over the surface of the deep, and the Spirit of God was hovering over the waters." With this verse, the Holy Spirit intended to show the background from which the 'good' creation emanated. From the watery waste and chaos was the beautiful garden crafted. All for the good and comfort of humanity and finally to the glory of God. The uneventful but progressive nature of the creation story from Genesis 1: 3-25 is meant to show God's providence and grace. As Henry points out: There was nothing at the beginning which was desirable "for it was without form and void – *Tohu* and *Bohu* – meaning confusion and emptiness" as the words are rendered in the Hebrew.[30] God is the architect of and rightful owner of the Earth's resources. From the very beginning, it was God alone who decided on the resources that human beings would depend on. The Bible records ten communications (Genesis 1:3, 6, 9, 11, 14, 20, 24, 26, 29, 2:18) that show God directly putting creation in a fruitful order that favours the well-being of humankind.

The theocratic works enunciated in the mentioned ten communications includes Gen 1:11 which says "Let the Earth bring forth vegetation: plants yielding seed and fruit trees yielding fruit whose seed is in itself, each according to its kind upon the Earth," Gen 1:20 further states: "Let the waters bring forth abundantly and swarm with living creatures…" and Genesis 1:24 which says: "Let the Earth bring forth living creatures according to their kinds: livestock, creeping things, and wild beasts of the Earth according to their kinds." These verses attribute the source of terrestrial, aquatic and aerial creatures to God. In other words, God freely endowed the universe with resources which were beneficial to humans. Essentially therefore, it is the will of God that all people must have some degree of access to the Earth's riches. Over and above that, the ownership of the Earth and all that is in it, belong to God. Psalm 24 verse 1 corroborates this as it says: "The Earth is the Lord's, and all the fullness of it, the world and they who dwell in it." All the Earth's property rights should be subject to the requirements of stewardship of God's resources.

---

29   Jamieson et al. 1995, 1.
30   Henry, M. Matthew Henry's Concise Commentary. London: Marshall, 37.

The Genre of Genesis 1:26-29

The Bible declares that God created a man and a woman in His image. Gen 1:26-27 says, "Let us make humankind in our image ... male and female He created them..." What is deducible from this is that:

1. Human beings are different from every other part of God's creation because they are made in God's image. They therefore enjoy uniqueness, dignity and value that no other creature has.

2. The image of God – *the imago Dei* – is in both male and female. Verse 27 states, "So God created humankind in His image, in the image of God He created He them-male and female.

3. Verse 26 states, "Let them have dominion over fish of the sea, over birds of the air, and over the cattle, over all the Earth..." both male and female were originally given ruler-ship over the whole creation, land included.

4. Equality of being and privilege is intricate to both male and female.

A Holistic Approach

Although the Genesis narrative cannot give a complete picture of Christian thought on socio-economics and political issues, it however provides a reference point on how God originally intended things to be. As such it gives a reference standard by which current economic theories, institutions, and policies can be evaluated. It is in this light that the three levels of relationships proposed by Richard Corker-Caulker resonate. According to him (2012:43), holistic socio-economic development is dependent on three levels of relationship:

1. A relationship with God, who created humankind as living beings in His image and likeness (Gen 2:7, 18, 28) whose act and behaviour exhibited a blue print for socio-economic development and social entrepreneurship.

2. Relationship between male and female (Gen 2:18-24) and the reproduction of human resources to interact with created existential resources.

3. Relationship with created things (Gen 1:28). Male and female were created for dominion over the Earth and its resources. Individuals have to be taught the value of socio-economic relationships and development.

Each of the three relationship areas is necessary for holistic development and success. Further to this, as Matsveru and Gillham[31] succinctly observes, " ... for Christians-human dignity transcends any human policies, conventions, charters, acts or any

---

31 Matsveru, F. and Simon Gillham. 2015. A Biblical Survey of the Dignity of Women and Men. In E. Mouton and G. Kapuma.

other such legislative instruments." The dignity of a woman is God given and not a human invention. If any nation fails to integrate God, humanity and environment in the socio-economic development agendas, such a nation's effort will be futile. The created things offer opportunities for research, development, manufacturing, explorations, job opportunities, innovations, industries etc. for both male and female. Consequently, both male and female should act together to sustain creation.

A socio-economic development approach that recognises God in the formula of development will facilitate not only spiritual fulfilment in worship, obedience and service to God, but will also enhance accountability in the execution of the stewardship mandate of God's resources. Such an approach is also in line with the original perfect plan. God freely endowed the universe with resources which were beneficial to humans. Essentially therefore, it is the will of God that all people must have some degree of access to the Earth's riches. Over and above that, the ownership of the Earth and all that is in it, belong to God. Psalm 24:1' corroborates this as it says: "The Earth is the Lord's, and all the fullness of it, the world and they who dwell in it." All the Earth's property rights should be subject to the requirements of stewardship of God's resources.

Rhetorical Summary

In summary, what is deducible from the creation narrative is that:

1. God independently and without any external influence created the heavens and the Earth with all their natural endowments
2. God, out of His omniscience and power created and made sufficient resources for enjoyment and comfort of both male and female.
3. God has absolute entitlement and ownership of all resources in the universe
4. God as the creator knows better than the creature. Therefore, there cannot be any better administration of natural resources without God.
5. God and goodness are inseparable; He created both man and woman good and for good.

The power play and subjugation of women are consequences of sin and were never the intention of the Creator from the beginning. The evolvement of society after the fall of humanity has led to families without male figures. This notwithstanding, the significance of family cannot be substituted. Family is the bedrock of society. It is the economic base and security of individuals. Denying women equity and equality is counter-productive to the society as a whole.

References

Berman, Sidney K. 2015. Of God's image, violence against women and feminist reflections. *Studia Historiae Ecclesiasticae*, 41(1), 122-137. https://dx.doi.org/10.17159/2412-4265/2015/v41n1a9

Carson, D.A. 1996. Exegetical fallacies, 2nd ed. Grand Rapids, MI: Baker Academic.

Casimir, A., Chukwuelobe, C.M. & Ugwu, C. 2014. The Church and Gender Equality in Africa: Questioning Culture and the Theological Paradigm on Women Oppression. *Open Journal of Philosophy*, 4(2):166. https://doi.org/10.4236/ojpp.2014.42024

Corker-Caulker, R. 2012. 21st Century foundation and principles for socio-economic development and social entrepreneurship. Bloomington, IN.: Trafford Publishing.

Goitom, H. 2014. Customary law, Discrimination, Inheritance and succession, Women's rights (https://www.loc.gov/law/foreign-news/article/nigeria-supreme-court-invalidates-igbo-customary-law-denying-female-descendants-the-right-to-inherit/ Jurisdiction: Nigeria

Henry, M. s.a. Matthew Henry's Concise Commentary. London: Marshall. http://biblehub.com/commentaries/genesis/2-8.htm Date of access: 26 October 2016.

Jamieson, F.B., Matthew Henry & Adam Clarke. 1985. Condensed Edition. Minneapolis: Bethany House Publishers.

Kalabamu. 2006, Patriarchy and women's land rights in Botswana (University of Botswana). https://doi.org/10.1016/j.landusepol.2004.11.001

Kirby, I, Seth Twum, J. G. Foxcroft, E.W.M. J. Legwaila, I.B.K. Lesetedi. 2013. Court of Appeal (Republic of Botswana). Civil Appeal No. CA-GB-104-12. High Court Civil Case No. MAHLB-000836-10.

Len Hansen and Thomas Togom. 2015. African Perspectives on Gender Equality. Cape town: Sun Press

Lin, T. (1997). The Genuineness and Mosaic Authorship of Genesis. *Lin T. Genesis: A Biblical Theology: PhD.—Biblical Studies Ministries International*, 18-24.

Matsveru, F and Simon Gillham. 2015. A biblical survey of the dignity of women and men, in Mouton, E., Gertrude Kapuma,

Ministry of Health and Wellness; Botswana. The Third Botswana National Strategic Framework for HIV& AIDS, 2019-2023. Ministry of Presidential Affairs, Governance and Public Administration.

Monageng, M. & Fancis Nyamnjoh. 2015. Botswana at 50: democratic deficit, elite corruption and poverty in the midst of plenty (In Sunday Standard News Paper; 2015).

Moyo, N. 2015. An Examination of dignity of women in Zambian context, in Mouton, E., Gertrude Kapuma, Len Hansen and Thomas Togom. 2015. African Perspectives on Gender Equality. Cape town: Sun Press.

Myers, L. B. 2011. Walking with the poor: Principles and Practices of Transformational Development. New York: Orbis Books.

Osha, S. 2004. A Postcolonial Scene: On Girls' Sexuality. In: *2nd Understanding Human Sexuality Seminar Series*. Africa Sexuality Resource Centre: Lagos.

Rey, M. 2012. Intersectionality in the Book of Ruth: Constructing Ruth's Identity in Ancient Israel. A dissertation submitted in partial fulfillment of the requirements for the degree of Master of Sacred Theology. Boston University: Boston.

Schmidt, A. 2004. How Christianity Changed the World, (https://en.wikipedia.org/wiki/Secularity).

Schulze Frederik. 2013. German Missionaries, Race, and Othering Entanglements and Comparisons between German Southwest Africa, Indonesia, and Brazil. *Itinerario*, 37 (1). https://doi.org/10.1017/S0165115313000235

United Nations Development Programme (UNDP). 2005. Human development report: International cooperation at a crossroads: aid, trade and security in an unequal world. New York: United Nations.

FEMALE HEADSHIP AS A PARADIGM SHIFT TO A HARMONIOUS SUSTAINABLE ECOSYSTEM

Angeline Savala[1]

Abstract

A large knowledge gap exists in how the female gender has a key impact in the study of ecology. This is because headship is a concept generally understood as power from a masculine lens that silences the female from taking up an active decision-making role in life. Thus, there is a call for re-addressing the meaning of 'headship' from a religious and theological forum. This is explicit in the history of the Church. Despite both males and females being active in various Mother Earth activities, the early church depicts males at the forefront as the think tank while females participated in silence. The missionary era echoes the early church where publicly men were the decision makers, while women obeyed or privately served as personal assistants or administrators. The contemporary church (the traditional churches) have men taking the top leadership roles while women deputise them, although this position is being challenged by new religious movements and Pentecostal ministry movements where women are taking over the top leadership positions.[2] Looking at Christianity, gender and ecology, this chapter introduces the theory of feminist headship as an important concept in shaping the development and management of a harmonious sustainable ecosystem. The premise of the chapter is to incorporate gender dimensions into all programs, especially regarding the women who make up a proportionate number of the marginalised, yet very functional, women in environment[3] conservation activities. This would involve gender capacity building in Christian Ethics, as well as understanding the Christian shepherding principles and theocentric approach to ecology, gender and Christianity. Theological analysis and theorizing on the concept of 'headship' is a typical research topic, since gender plays a major role in any given cultural context. The chapter submits that re-considering the concept of gender 'headship' as servant leadership that cares, provides and protects is part of the solution we

---

1   Lecturer, School of Arts and Social sciences, Department of Social Science, Education-Religion Division, Masinde Muliro University of Science and Technology (MMUST), Kenya. yanzamasitsa@gmail.com +254 722575010

2   Savala, A.M. and Nandi, J.O.M. 2015. Women and Church Headship: A Focus on Selected Churches in Kakamega County, Kenya. Eldoret: Utafiti Publisher, 146.

3   The concept of nature or environments used here has the same meaning as creation.

are looking for in regard to the subject under the study. This is applicable to many, if not all, institutions, such as social, political, educational, religious and family areas, from an economic and biblical perspective.

"Then the Lord God took the man and put him in the garden of Eden to tend and keep it"[4]

Introduction

Ever since the creation of the planet, creatures have lived and depended on each other as well as on Mother Earth and her rich environment for sustenance and material gains. God's creation has existed as an organism community interacting well with each other and its physical surroundings. In other words, creation has had harmonious interrelations. It has depended on one another, humanity was loved by the environment, and Mother Earth was cared for and viewed as a core part of life. This is to say, mutual benefit marked the relationship that existed between the ecosystems, as is informed by the creation account (Genesis 1-2) where Adam and Eve received their livelihood from the environment and they in turn tended it for continuity.

In support of harmonious living and sustainable creation, cultures and traditions around the world, including Africa, viewed the universe as sacred and respected the environment which sustained their livelihood. In the African context, nature was part of worship and had healing elements. Mountains, rivers, lakes, forests, deserts, land, sun, moon and others were part of the sacred sanctuaries which were treasured and respected by all. Interestingly, women were not left behind. They fully participated in the function of the wholeness of the ecosystem. Men acquired property and the title deeds of land, but women owned and managed them, resulting in peaceful co-existence.

With the account of the fall of mankind as recorded in Genesis chapter three, things changed and the ecosystem experienced violence, isolation, oppression and depression. The incident might be seen as the beginning of domestic violence where the woman (Eve) was blamed for all the negative happenings (Gen. 3:12). "Then the man said, 'The woman whom You gave to be with me, she gave me of the tree, and I ate'."[5] As Mugambi and Vahakangas rightly put it, today population growth and technology development in Kenya, for instance, have led to the abuse of the environment in many ways[6]. This is evidenced in deforestation, family violence, civil disobedience, corruption and abuse of the universe in general. In my

---

4   Genesis 2:15. *New King James Version*, PV Study Bible Version 5.

5   Genesis 3:9-13.

6   Mugambi, J.N.K. and Vahakangas, M. 2001. *Christian Theology and Environmental Responsibility*. Nairobi: Ancton. 2.

experience of overseeing Nyayo Tea Zones Development Corporation as one of the Kenyan government parastatals for a period of six years, I encountered endangered ecosystems where people were wreaking havoc on the environment and squandering vital resources, such as the grazing of animals in the forests, the felling of natural trees in the forest, and the destruction of rivers due to unwanted activities around them. Greed has led to the depletion of natural resources. Participating in fieldwork of the Tea Zones where we were raising the buffer around the Kenyan forests, it was painful to witness the destruction of the forests, pollution of the waters, land overgrazing, climate change from soil carbon, and gender abuse. The majority of workers were females working hard to provide for their families, and yet culturally they had no voice in the decision making about what was best to protect the environment. We cannot ignore the ecosystem crisis, because many people's livelihood has been affected largely by unbalanced usage due to lack of proper management, which this chapter refers to as 'headship.'[7]

This correlates with some words that Mariya shouted at an innocent nine-year-old girl when she saw her planting trees in her parents' homestead: "Young girl, what are you doing? Don't you know that a woman is not supposed to plant a tree, otherwise she cannot give birth because her children will stick on her back?"[8] One can imagine the fear and confusion that befell the girl at that tender age as she was growing up. At school they were forced to carry seedlings for planting, while at home she was told she will be barren if she planted trees.

The perplexity of the matter was the privilege of being a trainer of church ministers, yet the same girl, now a young adult, could not be licensed to perform some religious duties because once again the power of man through a religious lens said that it is only men who should lead, thus silencing the women. Interestingly, during her father's funeral, a then Member of Parliament made a statement referring to her in relation to the ailment of her late father, who had succumbed to liver cancer: "… this homestead has a strong lady, actually not just a lady but this homestead has a brave man."[9] The usual belief is that men are strong and that they provide leadership, not women, but in this case a woman has done what men usually do. This implication sparked the writer's curiosity on the nexus between Christianity, gender and ecology. Therefore, from a gendered headship perspective and through the lens of theology, the chapter seeks to paint a seemingly more balanced view of gender roles that would benefit the ecosystem. It does this by theorizing on 'female headship' as a paradigm shift to a sustainable harmonious ecosystem.

---

7   Savala, A.M. 2015. Life Experience at Nyayo Tea Zones, Kenya from 2009-2015. Unpublished.

8   Musaba, M. 1972. *Musaabas Words*. Mukomari Village, Shanjetsao-kakamega-Kenya.

9   Were, D.A. 2004. *During the Late Mzee MushirasFfuneral*. Eregi, Kakamega-Kenya.

According to Parkinson, "headship" figuratively refers to the source of something.[10] It appears this is what Paul referred to in his writings that "the head of the woman is man" and went further to explain what he meant by saying, "but I want you to know that the head of every man is Christ, the head of woman is man, and the head of Christ is God ... for man is not from woman, but woman from man."[11] This has nothing to do with masculine power but rather the idea of source.

Conceptualizing the mandate of creation care, the Bible has a lot to say about human responsibility and a balanced utilization of our natural resources that enhances the quality of life. The scriptures begin by underscoring what headship is through the example of Christ portrayed as the head of the Church in Ephesians 5:21-33. The exegesis of the passage clarifies the ingredients of headship to be servanthood, love and protective measure. Can the female gender exhibit such elements of serving, protecting and loving? A critical analysis of the biblical roots of creation gives a better understanding of the nature of leadership that this chapter refers to as 'headship.' One might want to raise the question of whether the female gender was mandated with the issue of headship according to our definition. The scriptures (Genesis 1: 26-28) declare that both male and female were assigned the task of managing the planet, that is tending to Mother Earth and not exploiting her. Adam was not called to destroy what surrounded him in the garden of Eden, abuse Eve, cut down trees, and use unwanted chemical products, but rather to serve Mother Earth lovingly, respectfully, sacrificially and protectively. There is nothing about 'power' – lording over other people as well as mismanaging the environment. The Gender approach is used to underscore the concept of headship from the creation account, where mankind was instructed to take care of Mother Earth. Hence 'headship' has to do with service, protection and provision.

In summary, the chapter will survey eco-feminism and the Christian response to ecological issues. It will do this by looking at Christian ethical foundations of the ecosystem, Christian shepherd-hood towards God's creation, and a theocentric approach to Ecology. The central theme is on the fair utilization of resources in the context of biblical headship and the mandate to humanity anchored in the writings of the creation account, according to the book of Genesis and the Bible at large. Eco-feminist theory asserts that a feminist perspective of ecology does not place women in the dominant position of power, but rather calls for an egalitarian society in which there is no dominant group.[12] Specific attention is given to Christian participation in the mutual relationship with Mother Earth, where the female is encouraged

10   Glenn, P. 2002. *Biblical Headship: Marriage as God Intended*. Pasadena: Severena Park Evangelical Presbyterian, 1.

11   I Corinthians 11:2, 8.

12   Merchant, C. 2005. Ecofeminism. In: *Radical Ecology*. Routledge, 193–221.

to take the lead since, she is more involved with the environment than her male counterpart. It also discusses contemporary actions to be considered to restore the dignity of gender, the beauty of the environment and finally to join other voices in suggesting some theological models in gender and environment conservation for the Church and Christianity today.

Christian Ethical Foundations for Ecology

Globally, most environmental conservation conferences held or research done have at the top of their agenda the issue of ecology. Closer to home, that is in Kenya, a cautionary note is posted in every town by the environmental officers, reproving citizens about disposal of garbage. This calls for some critical questions and answers. In view of environmental pollution, what is the Christian ethical responsibility to gender and the ecosystem? Can the issue of environment and gender be adequately handled in some exclusive boardroom at local, regional, national or international conferences? Is there any wisdom that we can glean from Christianity and even from traditional African societies that can inform our attitudes towards the ecosystem? Particularly for theologians and religious leaders, is there a role religious institutions can play beyond the 'normal' spiritual issues, by formulating an eco-theological response to address the issue of a balanced utilization of our natural resources, which will in turn enhance the quality of life for all? Where is the place of women here?

In the context of Christianity, Christian Ethics deals with what is morally right and ought to be done, and what is wrong and should be avoided. Theologically, such an ethic finds its basis in God's character. Due to the belief that moral norms come from God's nature and essence, Christian believers find themselves committed to a specific moral order revealed to them through both special and general revelation, as seen in Paul's writings that say, "for since the creation of the world, His invisible attributes are clearly seen, being understood by the things that are made, even His eternal power and Godhead, so that they are without excuse."[13] In this case, Christian Ethics is viewed as a moral heritage, since there is a universal basic similarity in the moral code within diverse cultures based on God's character, which materialism and naturalism cannot explain. Furthermore, St. Paul, in his epistle to the Romans, confirms that moral right is the work of the Law in man's heart (conscience).[14] Therefore, Christian Ethics sets the standards in which duties and obligations are defined.

---

13 Romans 1:20.
14 Romans 2:15.

The deep-seated conviction of Christians is the presupposition that God exists and that He has revealed Himself. The revelation contains the absolute set of standards rooted in God's character and defines human duty (Exodus 20:1-7). The mandate and command constitute a supernatural window into which the choice of what is good, right, just and perfect is emphasised in contrast to what is evil, wrong, unjust and imperfect. This is to say, Christian Ethics goes beyond the range of conduct and includes all acts for which gender can be held responsible. That said, the chapter argues that the nature of ethical questions on environment and gender need to be considered. Is it morally right for females to have a voice concerning the environment around them? Is it right for females to be abused just because they were created female? What is the Christian ethical responsibility to the physical surroundings in which women live? As said earlier, the mandate for the Mother Earth mission is anchored in the creation account where God summons humanity to serve Mother Earth as a sacred habitat. It points man to ecological theology that regards female 'headship,' which responds well to this quest since females are closer to nature. Thus, the connectedness of women and nature and the roles of women in nature are inseparable.

The chapter submits that most, if not all, female activities are geared around the environment which, if taken good care of, lead to life and good health. Women being given a voice in such matters, being freed and allowed to participate in decision making, will be very productive compared to denying them the opportunity to take the lead in protecting Mother Earth. Naturally, women have a special grace of a tender heart and as such lean to be more caring to Mother Earth. In turn, Mother Earth takes care of the rest of God's creation. This aspect of caring, loving, protecting and providing is what the chapter is referring to as 'headship.' Trying to remove these ingredients is gender oppressive, depletes the environment, poisons nature, shatters the entire ecosystem and affects both the environment and mankind. Mankind's obligation (both female and male) is to take care of Mother Earth by serving and preserving the environment. For this to happen well, a call on empowering women by redefining what is meant by 'headship' is necessary. Mother Earth can only keep mankind and their surroundings if she is well kept.

Gender as an approach emphasises that women do play an important, yet largely unrecognised, role in the upkeep of Mother Earth. Understanding women's contributions is the paradigm shift veiled in headship that is being theorised here. It is not about women taking men's position but rather women being given the opportunity in decision making on how to take care of the environment, since they are the ones fetching water and firewood, tilling the land, and producing the food that they serve the family. Parkinson explains it better by alluding that the nature of Adam's headship stemmed from one simple fact: not that he was superior, not that he was male, but simply that he was first – first in the sense that he was the source. Adam was not created to rule over Eve, but to lead her in submitting to God's rule[15] so that both may have dominion and tend God's creation. This raises the concern of whether patriarchy can engage women well in regard to the welfare of Mother Earth. Is it in order for male to dominate over female? Can females have a say in matters relating to the environment? Can a female exercise headship by serving Mother Earth? Those who conceptualise power as a resource understand it as a positive social good that is currently unequally distributed amongst women and men. For feminists who understand power in this way, the goal is to redistribute this resource so that women will have power equal to men. Implicit in this view is the assumption that power is "a kind of stuff that can be possessed by individuals in greater or lesser amounts."[16] Women who are empowered have the upper hand in positively overseeing the environment as the major source of the family, community and society.

It is on this basis that I submit that the scriptures declare the necessity for Christians to be true to the mandate of taking care of God's creation according to the creation account given in Genesis 1 and 2. The female is not left behind. She deserves to be taken care of if she is to do the same. Contrary to this, society looks at the planet through a lens of hostility based on the fall account (Genesis 3), emphasizing the failure of mankind and especially blaming the female. Christianity asserts that with the entrance of sin, humanity became spiritually separated from God and lost the benefits that flow from living under theocratic rule. Sin changed the nature of the ecosystem from harmonious living to enmity, and the concept of leadership from biblical headship to patriarchy (the rule of men). Biblical headship and patriarchy are not the same thing. Biblical headship strives for God's rule while patriarchy strives for male rule. The account in the book of Genesis, the third chapter, describes pain and patriarchy as the default condition of creation in the fallen world. In other words, headship was a responsibility entrusted to Adam and he failed.[17]

In general, the notion of headship as the source is echoed in the traditional African worldview that God is the source of all life. This life is seen in the physical world. It was the responsibility then of everyone to preserve this life. The power and glory of God was being revealed in the world through nature. The harmony of life was paramount in most traditional cultures, if not all. All living things lived well in

---

15 Glenn, P. 2002. Biblical Headship: Marriage as God intended. 4.

16 Young, I. M. 1990a. *Justice and the Politics of Difference*. Princeton: Princeton University Press. 31.

17 Glenn, P. 2002. Biblical Headship: Marriage as God intended. 5.

harmony with the whole creation because God penetrates all creatures with His presence.[18]

Several feminists make the distinction that it is not *because* women are female or 'feminine' that they relate to nature, but is because of their similar states of oppression by the same male-dominant forces. The marginalization is evident in the gendered language used to describe nature and the animalised language used to describe women. Some discourses link women specifically to the environment because of their traditional social role as a nurturer and caregiver.[19] This gives a woman better opportunity to care for nature, thus exercising her 'headship' evidenced in servanthood, caring motherly spirit and providing to her family. When the family is healthy, the community too will be healthy, and this health will extend to the entire world. Understanding the meaning of headship as service will allow the tending of Mother Earth in a respectable manner.

Considering the ecological perspective among many African societies, natural objects and phenomena are seen as God's revelation of Himself to humanity. This lays a level ground where Africans see themselves as partners rather than masters of nature.[20] Abundant life, therefore, means that human beings live in harmony and respect with all creatures, carrying out acts that sustain life. In other words, a materialistic view results in a disintegrated world. A fallen world embraces technological exploitation based on man's power. A materialistic view sees the environment as a limitless source of energy. Over time this view has produced humans who, by virtue of being supposedly in charge of the world around them, influence it negatively. Through technology they can change their environment in ways desirable for their own ends. Their philosophical view grows out of a secular humanist worldview. The existence of nature with all of its resources is taken for granted. As a result, the environment suffers oppression, depression, malnutrition and maldistribution of resources. This does not leave out gender. Males socialised to be powerful influence females negatively, evidenced by domestic violence, and as a result the environment suffers.

It is intriguing that African traditional religion and its spiritual wisdom upholds the work in the created Mother Earth. Every life in the created order is sacred and important to all since there is divine presence everywhere. Thus, nature in its broader sense is filled with religious significance where every creature has a spiritual and physical significance. If not for worship, then it is for food and/or medicinal purposes. Worship, food and medicine are administered in the world of feminism,

---

18   Mugabi and Vahakangas. Christian Theology and Environmental Responsibility, 58.
19   Shiva, V. 1988. Staying Alive: Women, Ecology and Development. London: Zed Books.
20   Gitau, S.K. 2002. The Environmental Crisis: A Challenge for African Christianity. Nairobi: Action, 4.

which gives the female the upper hand in decision making compared to approaching the same issues from the context of masculinity.

African religious heritage links mankind with creation because rivers, stars, sun, clouds, rain, animals and plants are all manifesting the presence of God with us.[21] Preservation and conservation of both nature and living things was one of the values in the African life in relation to ecology as a whole. They lived in harmony as is expressed in poems, symbols and beliefs. Myths that were told in various African tribes taught respect for nature. From a young age one was made to understand the value and sanctity of life and its interdependence on creation. For example, there were and still are holy trees, forests and water bodies that you could not do anything with to destroy, e.g. Mugumo among the Kikuyu; Mutoto, Mukhuyu or Mukumu trees among the Luhya; and rocks like Kit-Mikai in Luo Nyanza. Gender was also respected.

Gitau has noted in his writing, *The Environmental Crisis*, that in some traditions, their gods did not allow them to destroy trees or kill certain animals. He observes that this is because some animals and trees were associated with the presence of God.[22] The Maasai, for example, agree that God gave them animals to take care of. The stories surrounding the animals assist significantly in their preservation. Some animals and plants are used for food while others are used for medicine. In retrospect, the collapse of the subsistence system and the adoption of an extensive and highly extractive cash-crop production marked a turning point in the environmental histories of the African. For the African this "tended to emphasise the decline of their culture, population, autonomy and ways of living in the environment." What we viewed as innovation was in essence the onset of environmental degradation.[23]

The philosophical basis of the theology of environment, therefore, is the fact that humanity and nature are but one thing. This fact that the world is sustained and operated by God is well expounded in scriptures (Hebrews 1:3, Colossians 1:17). The Psalmist clearly declares that the world is the reflection of God (Psalm 91:1, 139:7-12). Nature is not totally outside but also within human beings. Human beings are a product of nature and form part of it. There is interdependence of nature and human beings, so that if nature is affected, the life of humanity is also affected. For example, humanity gets its food from the ground and if anything like erosion happens because forest was cleared, we will not have good soil for food to grow. The growth of the plants also depends on what humanity does with

---

21 Mugambi and Vahakangas. 2001. Christian Theology and Environmental Responsibility. 17.

22 Gitau, 2002. The Environmental Crisis: A Challenge for African Christianity. 34.

23 Jacobs, N.J. 2003. *Environment, Power, and Injustice.* Cambridge: Cambridge University Press, 206-207.

the environment. The solution, then, that has been offered through the African traditional wisdom and philosophy is to love, care and have respect for nature and mankind. Humankind should utilise nature and environment with a good purpose in mind and for the conservation of life.

Christian Shepherdhood over God's Creation

The narrator in Genesis 2:5-15 expounds on the purpose for which man was created. He ascertains that:

> before any plant of the field was in the earth and before any herb of the field had grown, there was no rain on the earth, and there was no man to cultivate the ground; ...and the Lord God formed man of the dust of the ground, and breathed into his nostrils the breath of life; and man became a living being. The Lord God planted a garden eastward in Eden, and there He put the man whom He had formed. And out of the ground, the Lord God made every tree grow ... *Then the Lord God took the man and put him in the garden of Eden to tend and keep it.*[24]

It is within the divine plan of God that there is peaceful co-existence between God's creations. Before the creation of man, God did not allow anything to appear on Mother Earth. Even the rain was withheld because there was no one to work the ground. Upon the creation of man, he was placed on the earth to work it and take care of it. The implication is that the existence of human beings is first and foremost to manage the creator's property. More specifically, Christians are duty bound to speak to all issues that threaten the realization of abundant ecological life, including gender violence. The female gender was created as suitable helper, one responsible in guiding, advising, and contributing to the well-being of the ecology. This, to a greater extent, is in harmony with the creation account as clearly stated in the first two chapters of Genesis, as well as what the African traditional wisdom and philosophy captures from time immemorial. Traditionally, although women did not own title deeds, they managed the land and that which surrounded them, supporting what God created for them. There is value in every creature of God and therefore a call to respect, love, care for and utilise it responsibly and with accountability.

The Chapter is in agreement with Mugambi and Vahakangas, alluding to the book of Genesis, that God created everything good. Nothing was created without value and nothing that was to be of value was left out of creation. Our Christian faith tells us to be good stewards.[25] From the narrations of creation and the dealings of God with man and creation, it is important to note that all creatures

24   New King James Version.
25   Mugambi and Vahakangas. 2001. Christian Theology and Environmental Responsibility, 65.

belong to God.[26] Amos 5:21-24 confirms that God continued to be active in creation. Also, in Deuteronomy we read that "to the Lord belongs all, heavens and the earth with all in it."[27] Another point is that God has placed man on Earth to take care of the planet.[28] The creation account suggests that gender, both female and male, was given full dominion over nature to take care of, provide and protect it. God was proud of His creation, even declaring how good it was. God placed man in the garden and gave him the ability to tend it (Gen. 2:15). That is to say that they were placed in the garden to serve and protect it.[29]

In the New Testament, all life is sacred because it has its origin in God through Christ. "All things were made through Him, and without Him nothing was made that has been made."[30] This could suggest the fact that life does not belong to us, but that we are just stewards of it (Col. 1:15-17). The whole concept in the gospels as we look at the parables, such as the wicked tenants, is the notion that Christians are servants who take over responsibility for their master's property while he is away. They are expected to use that property in a profitable way, and at the end a good steward will receive his/her reward, but the wicked will be punished as depicted in Matt. 21:33-41; 24:45-51; Lk. 19:12-16).[31] The Bible is clear that creation is God-given to be taken care of by human beings. This is philosophically implied in the book of Romans, where Paul argues theologically that humanity should appreciate the idea of general revelation of God in nature "because what may be known of God is manifest in them, for God has shown it to them. For since the creation of the world His invisible attributes are clearly seen, being understood by the things that are made, even His eternal power and Godhead, so that they are without excuse."[32] To me this is exactly what God has revealed in African traditional wisdom and philosophy, mentioned in the paragraphs above. The environment is given to humanity, who is also part of the environment, that they may live in harmony and mutual respect. Humanity has no excuse but to cherish God's property and to tend it, and in this case, the female gender is well placed in a partnership to help the male gender in realizing this goal. Theorizing on female headship calls on allowing the female gender to exercise her God-given special endowment of grace to work the environment and take care of it.

---

26   Ps. 24; Gen. 14; Ex. 9:29; Deut. 10:14; Job 35:7; 41:11; Rom. 11:35.

27   Deuteronomy 10:14.

28   Genesis 2:5-15, Ps. 24:1-2; 33:6-9; 74:12-14; 104:5-9.

29   Mugambi and Vahakangas. 2001. Christian Theology and Environmental Responsibility. 92.

30   John 1:3.

31   - Gitau. 2002. The Environmental Crisis: A Challenge for African Christianity, 73.

32   Romans 1:19-20.

However, when all is said and done, it should be noted that man disobeying God and assuming that he can do anything to satisfy his ego in the third chapter of Genesis, caused disharmony in the relationship between man and the entire creation (Genesis 3:14-19). In the strife between genders the creation would suffer, as in the Kiswahili saying that "*Ndovu wawili wakipigana nyasi huumia,*" meaning that 'when two elephants fight it is the grass that suffers.' Creation that had yielded readily to man would in time become 'an enemy' yielding thorns and thistles. "So it is inevitable that man should lose the sense of purpose and meaning with respect to the physical world ... increased food production is achieved at the price of rural poverty, domestic violence, environmental pollution (pesticides) and increased energy output."[33] Humankind would struggle to cause it to produce fruit for a lifetime until he would return to dust (Gen. 3:19), except that Christ came to replace Adam for a new humanity that believes in Him, as Glenn elucidates. As the new source of eternal life, Jesus demonstrated everything Adam's headship was designed to be. He has all authority in heaven and on Earth, but it is *the authority of a Head, not a Patriarch*. He does not focus on his own will, but on the will of God. The goal of Jesus's lordship is to lead men and women to affirm God's sole right as the Creator to determine good and evil. This new model of authority is a headship patterned after Christ. The church is called to practise it, where ecclesiastical authority is considered ministerial and declarative.[34]

In support of eco-feminism, there is need to shift from a hierarchal view and a culture that dominates over women and nature, to God's view where all creation is good and important. This will lead to a harmonious ecosystem, a creation-care perspective. Eco-feminism addresses the parallels between the oppression of nature and the oppression of women to emphasise the idea that both must be understood in order to properly recognise how they are connected. These parallels include but are not limited to seeing women and nature as property, seeing men as the curators of culture and women as the curators of nature, and how men dominate women and humans dominate nature.[35]

A Theocentric Approach to Ecology, Gender and Christianity

Without sin, there was no need to govern in any coercive fashion. Adam was not created to rule over other human beings as a master. God was the ruler, and God alone was the master. For Adam, his obligation and authority was to lead Eve to

---

33   Elsdon, R. 1981. Bent World: Science, the Bible, and the Environment. Leicester: InterVarsity. 112.

34   Glenn. Biblical Headship: Marriage as God Intended, 5-6.

35   Spretnak, C. 1990. Ecofeminism: Our Roots and Flowering. In: I. Diamond and G. Ornstein. *Reweaving the World: The Emergence of Feminism*. Sierra Club Books, 3-14.

God in submission, which Glenn refers to as headship. Headship is a ceremonial relationship designed to help every Christian practise the Lordship of Christ. When headship is embraced, neither male nor female will rule over the other. Neither will they find a compromise between their personal desires. Instead, they will find unity in submitting themselves to the will of God.[36]

Christian attitudes towards gender and ecology should be based on the fact that God is the creator of the universe and man is the manager of this magnificent and glorious world. As the manager, man's duty is to protect, provide, respect and preserve, and not to corrupt or pollute. While the scripture supports the assertion that the physical universe is good and that it reflects the glory of its creator (Psalm 19:1, I Tim 4:4), sustained and operated by God (Hebrews 1:3, Colossians 1:17), mankind on the other hand is the keeper of the environment (Gen 1:28, 2:15). To the contrary, Mugambi and Vahakangas observe that "we have realised the impact of humanity on the environment and how all stakeholders including theologians have tried to address transformation of our values which contribute to our disregard of the environment."[37] Acknowledging this problem calls on Christians to be on the forefront to fix it. The male gender need not feel threatened by female headship from the context of ecology, but should rather embrace this kind of 'headship' as leadership that zeroes in on servanthood; leadership that seeks the welfare of God's creation. This is to say, women should be acknowledged for sustainable development in their areas of jurisdiction. The voice of women should be heard as they participate in their environmental activities. They should be listened to the way Jesus would do. They should be allowed to live their lives to the fullest.

From the perspective of gender, within the environment, we all depend on one another for our livelihood. We belong to one another and are part of one life. God created us all for mutually beneficial relationships. Although some read dominion over nature as warranting exploitation of nature and the resources we have in our world, God did not intend it that way. We need to live in harmony with everything in the world and remember our responsibility towards it. Unfortunately, modern man with his technological advancements can do things without limitation. "Everything he can do he does, he kills the world, he kills mankind, and he kills himself."[38]

Many have acted as if the whole world is theirs and they can just decide what to do with it, without consulting the owner. God still reigns and is concerned with the environment. He still sees it as good and as something that has value. Every life

---

36   Ibid. 10.

37   Mugambi and Vahakangas, Christian Theology and Environmental Responsibility, 96.

38   Schaeffer, F.A. 1970. Pollution and the Death of Man: A Christian View on Ecology. London: Hodder & Stoughton, 66.

and all creation is useful to God because He created it. While in human analysis some things are dispensable, we need to go back to the author and understand that all things were created good. If the present controversy over women's role in the church can not result in the eradication of some of the following failure to recognise that God often gives women equal or greater spiritual gifts than men, failure to encourage women to have full and free participation in the various ministries of the church, and, failure to take full account of the wisdom that God has given to women with respect to important decisions in the life of the church, then the church as a whole was never fit greatly.[39]

Eco-feminists following this line of thought believe that these connections are illustrated through the coherence of socially labeled values associated with 'femininity', such as nurturing, which are present both among women and in nature. Women have a special connection to the environment through their daily interactions and this connection has been ignored. According to Shiva, women in subsistence economies who produce "wealth in partnership with nature, have been experts in their own right of holistic and ecological knowledge of nature's processes."[40] This is what this chapter is emphasizing: that the female gender is endowed with special gifts, which if tapped into are the backbone for the basic needs from the environment in terms of food security, clean water and a healthy family. Once we have a healthy family, we automatically have a healthy community, society and of course a healthy environment, thus female headship taking care of God's creation.

From the worldview of ecology, we must be concerned with a harmonious sustainable environment, because lives would be in grave danger if the ecology were disturbed. Rampant deforestation, overgrazing and careless farming all lead to massive erosion and is the cause of an unhappy Mother Earth. Mugambi and Vahakangas add to this that the pollution of water and air by industrialization, over-mining and over-fishing are among the many causes of a distressed environment.[41] The problem we must address is that of attitude and an understanding of our role in the world – if we treat Mother Earth well, she will in turn treat humanity and our surroundings well. If we mismanage her, then natural calamity will befall us, such as famine, global warming and sickness. We are not at liberty to do with the world whatever we want to do. It has its owner, and we are required to work it and utilise it according to the lease agreement with the owner.

39   Grudem, W. 1994. *Systematic Theology: An Introduction to Biblical Doctrine.* Grand Rapids: Zondervan Publishing House, 77.

40   Shiva, V. 1990. Development as a New Project of Western Patriarchy. *Reweaving the World: The Emergence of Feminism,* edited by Irene Diamond and Gloria Ornstein, Sierra Club Books, 189-200.

41   Mugambi and Vahakangas. Christian Theology and Environmental Responsibility, 97.

God has called us to be stewards of His creation. This is understood as a spiritual principle and a biblical teaching. "It is the biblical view of nature that gives nature a value *in itself*… because God made it."[42] Christians are not called to dominate the universe for our ego but to serve the world in humility and self-sacrifice. This is the 'headship' referred to in this chapter. In this relationship there is a great deal of dependence, and all creation is inseparable from one another. The creation is important because it is good, and man was created to manage it for his survival by taking good care of it. God has given life to all living things. Moltman, in his theology of the Spirit, captured the biblical view of the spirit as the Spirit of life, and this life penetrates all living things.[43] Mother Earth belongs to God and so must be protected. Out of this attitude grows reverence for life. The earth is also valuable because it is the place where redemption happened.

In view of this, I would submit to Christian believers that, first, humanity has been given a mandate to care for and till the land. The mandate here is to serve Mother Earth. Careful attention should be given to how the environment is cared for, so as to sustain life. Air and water pollution, like what is happening to our rivers and forests, is doing harm to the living creatures in the air and sea, and ultimately destroying even human life. Second, humanity should live with the mindset that they are responsible for how they deal with the environment. The parable of the talents declares that God will judge us at the end for how we have used the charge given to us. This is written in the gospel according to Saint Matthew as follows:

> There was a certain landowner who planted a vineyard and set a hedge around it, dug a winepress in it and built a tower. And he leased it to vinedressers and went into a far country. Now when vintage-time drew near, he sent his servants to the vinedressers, that they might receive its fruit. And the vinedressers took his servants, beat one, killed one, and stoned another. Again, he sent other servants, more than the first, and they did likewise to them. Then last of all he sent his son to them, saying, "They will respect my son." But when the vinedressers saw the son, they said among themselves, "This is the heir. Come, let us kill him and seize his inheritance." So, they took him and cast him out of the vineyard and killed him. "Therefore, when the owner of the vineyard comes, what will he do to those vinedressers?" They said to Him, "He will destroy those wicked men miserably, and lease his vineyard to other vinedressers who will render to him the fruits in their seasons."[44]

Christian foundations are anchored in God's word, where God in his cabinet meeting agreed to make man in God's own image, according to God's likeness, for them to have dominion over the fish of the sea, over the birds of the air, over the cattle, over

---

42 Schaeffer. Pollution and the Death of Man: A Christian View on Ecology, 34.

43 Karkkainen, V. *An Introduction to Ecclesiology*. InterVarsity, 133.

44 Matthew 21:33-41.

all the earth and over every creeping thing that creeps on the earth. "So, God created man in His own image; in the image of God, He created him; male and female He created them."[45] Their responsibility was to manage the universe. Mismanagement, such as over-mining, over-fishing, deforestation, pollution, and violating women's rights, has detrimental consequences to the well-being of ecology.

Conclusion

The chapter proposed that Christianity, gender and ecology trace their history to the creation account. They have their basis in God's nature and complement each other for harmonious sustainable development. They are not mutually exclusive, but rather they are one and need each other in order to reach a harmonious ecosystem through a moral basis of tending to Mother Earth, protecting and providing for her. This ecosystem is the kind of leadership the chapter theorises as 'headship,' where each gender is empowered to nurture the planet. It has nothing to do with power or masculinity but rather the spirit of servanthood, in which case women are better placed to serve and to lead, thus 'headship.'

We can agree that addressing gender issues culturally is very challenging. I must admit, together with my theological ancestors, that the word 'nature' is not readily available in the understanding of our modern man. "We must rethink and re-feel our nature and destiny."[46] The word used is 'creature,' which includes all that was created by God. Just as we have noted the significance of nature to African traditional religions, so it was in the history of the Israelites in ancient times. There were sacred trees, mountains, stones, and even water that was treasured as holy and that no one would tamper with. Both African traditional lifestyles and the ancient Jews had a theology of nature. It is a theology that enhances a peaceful co-existence between humanity and the rest of creation. Such theology assures smooth harmony in the relationship between man and nature.[47] The theology of creation gives no room for human beings to mismanage nature. Man is bound to love and take care of it. He needs to think of it as a friend and not an enemy from which he must "wrest by force and ingenuity what little he can for his own use … the major sources of our ecological disasters are greed and short sightedness, which amount to much the same thing."[48]

Science and technology should be used to bring harmony to the ecosystem. We can use the environment for construction and irrigation for good that will allow

---

45   Genesis 1:26-27.

46   Schaeffer. Pollution and the Death of Man: A Christian View on Ecology, 85.

47   Gitau, 2002. The Environmental Crisis: A Challenge for African Christianity, 143.

48   Passmore, J. 1974. Man's Responsibility for Nature. Surrey: Gresham Press, 186-187.

God to bless the work of our hands. We cannot profess to be Christians and yet be involved in the destruction of our environment. In my own traditional backyard, the Kakamega forest, reputably the last of the traditional rainforests with some of the most unique flora and fauna: columbus monkeys, hornbills, snakes, orchids, and medicinal herbs, is under threat from deforestation. We need to preserve it. At the same time, we cannot profess to be Christians and yet relegate Eve to be second-class material when she is the mother of all living things (Genesis 3:20). Gendered environmental responsibilities provide case studies that call on us to research and provide the way forward. In Eve's case, this chapter supports the Eco-feminism theory that women have a more natural role in the environment. By upholding feminist, 'headship,' the environment will be at ease, since females are naturally closer to nature as evidenced in everyday life. There is need to read Bible stories positively, especially those considered to present a false perception of women as victims of curses, by redefining the 'headship' concept from the creation perspective. At the same time, we should be careful not to abandon our biblical and cultural heritage in living in harmony with our environment. The mandate is to preserve and enhance life, which women do naturally.

The role of the church should be notable in the protection of women and our environment. As Christians, we should work towards a well-balanced life where justice for ecology becomes a living testimony in revealing God's love for both humanity and nature. It has been shown that the dominion God gave to Adam and Eve, and subsequently to all humankind, was delegated for responsibility and co-operative work. Humanity is to use the environment in such a way that he is accountable to God. We need to have regard for God's creation, which includes women, and treat the creation with due respect. Nature may be used for food and other beneficial uses, with accountability to God as good stewards. Disrespect for women is harmful, for the social status of women affects the scarcity of resources. Human vulnerabilities must be considered as priority over social structures.

This chapter discussed two models for the Church in Kenya and even beyond to use in enhancing the theory of female 'headship' and creation care. First, understanding that 'headship' has to do with servanthood and not power, and on that basis, women are better placed to serve the creation, based on the nurturing instincts they possess. Borrowing from the African traditional wisdom of collective good and sacredness of life, one can have a proper understanding of our relationship with nature – as partners with one another and not as competitors. Mary Mellor, in her chapter *Ecofeminism: Linking Gender and Ecology*, claims that there is a connection between the exploitation and degradation of nature, and the subordination and oppression of women.[49] Reconciling the two will provide an ethical foundation of respect for gender and the environment. It is true that mankind may not be capable of preventing natural calamities, but they are able to lessen the damage from potential destruction. Man may not be able to recreate gender into what he desires her or him to be, but he can stop violence and lessen the damage from potential destruction like divorce or death.

Secondly, in the biblical observations the ethics of good stewardship, when embraced, will ensure respect for gender and the environment. In Christian Ethics the absolute basis of morality is the love of God and one's neighbours. The concept is still prevalent that whatever Christians do with creation should be directed to God's glory as the owner of the universe. This is summed up well in God's commandment: love for God and love for your neighbour as yourself (Mark 12:30-31). All having been said and done, African traditional wisdom and biblical teachings on ecology tell us that all creation comes from the single source of life, wisdom and compassion. Life and its continuation are only possible in the warmth of sharing it with one another. All creation is interdependent for its survival and abundant life,[50] and therefore it is of the essence that we take care of it well, based on the mandate given by God to treasure his creation – humankind.

Theorizing on headship as a paradigm shift for harmonious sustainable ecosystem, we are considering gender headship and stewardship as the two vital factors the Church should embrace if we are to implement ecology conservation projects. Female gender is the backbone of family, community and society at large. Positively release her for the sake of the ecosystem. She was created as a suitable helper to tend and keep Mother Earth together with man. According to Adam she is the mother of all life (Genesis 3:20).

49   Mellor, M. 2007. *SAGE Handbook of Environment and Society*. London: SAGE publication, 66-67.
50   Boff, L. and Elizondo, V. 1995. *Ecology and Poverty*. London: SCM, 65.

References

Boff, L. and Elizondo, V. (eds). 1995. *Ecology and Poverty*. London: SCM.

Elsdon, R. 1981. *Bent World: Science, the Bible, and the Environment*. Leicester: InterVarsity.

Gitau, S.K. 2000. *The Environmental Crisis: A Challenge for African Christianity*. Nairobi: Action.

Glenn, P. 2002. *Biblical Headship: Marriage as God Intended*. Pasadena: Severena Park Evangelical Presbyterian.

Grudem, W. 1994. *Systematic Theology: An Introduction to Biblical Doctrine* Grand Rapids: Zondervan Publishing House.

Jacobs, N. J. 2003. *Environment, Power, and Injustice*. Cambridge: Cambridge University Press. https://doi.org/10.1017/CBO9780511511981

Karkkainen, V-M. 2002. *An Introduction to Ecclesiology*. Downers Grove: InterVarsity Press.

Merchant, C. 2005. Ecofeminism. In: *Radical Ecology*. New York: Routledge.

Mugambi, J.N.K and Vahakangas, M. (eds). 2001. *Christian Theology and Environmental Responsibility*. Nairobi: Action.

Passmore, J. 1974. *Man's Responsibility for Nature*. Surrey: Gresham Press.

Savala, A.M. and Nandi, J.O.M. 2015. *Women and Church Headship: A Focus on Selected Churches in Kakamega County, Kenya*. Eldoret: Utafiti Publisher.

Schaeffer, F.A. 1970. *Pollution and the Death of Man: A Christian View on Ecology*. London: Hodder & Stoughton.

Shiva, V. 1990. Development as a New Project of Western Patriarchy. In: I. Diamond and G. Ornstein. *Reweaving the World: The Emergence of Feminism*. Sierra Club Books.

Shiva, V. 1988. *Staying Alive: Women, Ecology and Development*. London: Zed Book.

Spretnak, C. 1990. Ecofeminism: Our Roots and Flowering. In: I. Diamond and G. Ornstein. *Reweaving the World: The Emergence of Feminism*. Sierra Club Books.

Young, I. M. 1990. *Justice and the Politics of Difference*. Princeton: Princeton University Press.

PART THREE

Re-imagining Women as Change Agents Who
Care for the Earth

GENDERED BODIES AND THE FORGOTTEN MOTHERS OF NATURE

An African Woman's Rethinking of the Ngbokondems and Forest Preservation among the Ejagham of Cameroon

Jennet Tabe[1]

Abstract

This chapter uses an African women's narrative method of enquiry to retell the story of the Ngbokondems[2] as powerful women ancestors of the Ejagham of Cameroon, who impacted life by the careful usage and preservation of the natural environment. These women were gifted with special supernatural knowledge that enabled them to communicate with the Ndem spirit and perform religious rites and rituals for the living community. Mbiti calls them 'human specialists,' 'sacred personages,' or 'sacred specialists.' They used forests, trees, water, animals, and birds not for demonic manifestations as claimed by early missionaries; but as spaces to commune with the Ndem[3] for the well-being of the land. Their methods ensured the preservation of nature. African women's storytelling methodology traces the paths of these efficient and powerful women who championed religio-spiritual leadership in the community from the pre-colonial to the modern era. However, colonialists and missionaries labelled them witches, and the sacred abode of the Ndem spirit became an evil forest. This forest was then invaded, and its products sold to foreign markets. Patriarchy also infringed on Ngbokondem's

---

1. Jennet Tabe is Registrar and Lecturer at Presbyterian Theological Seminary in the department of Systematic Theology and Christian Ethics. She obtained her PhD in Systematic Theology and Christian Ethics at the University of Pretoria, South Africa in 2018 with a dissertation focusing on women, gender and sexism and culture in the Cameroonian rural contexts. Over the years, Jennet Tabe has been involved in various initiatives serving women on national and continental levels. She published academic articles in peer-reviewed journals.

2. These were priestesses who, up to the early 2000s, were prominent in Ejagham for their special knowledge of the spiritual universe. They ministered for the spirit being called Ndem through usage of the natural environment to ensure the welfare of the living community. There are various appellations for the same women by different authors; for instance, Niger-Thomas (2009:171) uses *ngboko-ndem*, while for Ruel (1969:203) it is *ngboko-ndem* or *Mbokondem*. Talbot (1926:130) gives more appellations as *Ngbokondem, Mbok-ndemm, Mbokkndamm, and NenkaiNimm*. The study will use Ngbokondem throughout according to the local dialect, except when citing an author's usage.

3. Pa Atopako reports that before Christianity and colonisation arrived, Ndem was known as the Spirit (female Being) that protected the land through prophetic prediction of impending evil, and ensured fertility and procreation. The name of God Almighty in the Kenyang language used by the Ejagham clan is called *Mandem* from two words: *Ma*, meaning Mother, and *Ndem*, meaning God. God is Mother God. But when the missionaries came, they insisted that this 'Ma' is a He and not a She. So they changed the gender of God, while the language still stipulates Him as Mother God.

sexual norm, an invaluable zone for their survival.[4] The Ngbokondems association has phased out, but the consequences of their demise refuse to leave the land; Mother Earth is still weeping in degradation. I undertook an empirical study for this initiation practice along with four other researchers.[5] The chapter comes to the conclusion that, had the Ngbokondems not been stigmatised and demonised to their demise, the ecosystem of the Ejagham might have been better than the waste it is today.

Introduction

The Ngbokondems among the Ejagham people of the South-West Region of Cameroon are women with special knowledge of the spiritual universe who lived, thrived and sustained the living community from the pre-colonial era. They became one of the prominent women's associations of the land, amongst which were Moninkim, Ekpa, Nenwa and others. Niger-Thomas[6] traces the origin of the first *ngboko-ndem* from the sky. Her description aligns with local and oral history that is transmitted from generation to generation in the Ejagham. The first Ngbokondem fell from the sky into a large *Boma* tree; she wore strange dancing attire and spoke to awed spectators in a queer language. She taught some women her secrets and was married in the area. Thereafter, parents started initiating their first-born daughters and the association developed. Trees, forests, the sky, grass and the natural order became crucial for the Ngbokondem's survival since then. These features are also known to be vital in most African religious beliefs and practices.[7]

It is now well established that African traditional beliefs and practices, primal religions and cultures, though considered 'primitive,' uncivilised, heathen and backward by colonialists and western explorers,[8] made an immense contribution to the conservation of the Earth because these beliefs saw imprints of God in nature.[9] In

---

4   These priestesses had strong norms guiding their sexuality; they were not supposed to marry or have sex, as this would cause their visionary eyes to be closed.

5   We interviewed 18 people: 5 men and 13 women. Eight of the respondents were surviving Ngbokondems and obales, i.e. six and two respectively, while the rest are relatives of Ngbokondems. Their ages ranged between 72 and 86. Five different initiation practices were studied with 182 respondents in all.The paper is written for the 2019 conference of Circle for Concerned African Women Theologians, titled Mother Earth and Mother Africa in Theological/Religious/Cultural/ Philosophical Imagination. The study falls under the subtheme: Environmental Imagination in African Rituals and Taboos. It is drafted from the Doctoral thesis: Tabe, J. 2018. Women Initiation Practices among Ejagham Women of Cameroon and Patriarchy: A Womanist Perspective. Unpublished Thesis University of Pretoria.

6   Niger-Thomas, M. 2009. Commemorating Women in Patrilineal Society. In: I. FowlerandV, Fanso (eds). *Encounter, Transformation and Identity.Peoples of the Western Cameroon Borderlands 1891-2000.* USA: Berghahn Books, 169-184. Cf also Ruel, M. 1969. *Leopards and Leaders: Constitutional Politics among a Cross River People.* London: Tavistock Publications, 203.

7   Mbiti, J.S. 1969. *African Traditional Religions and Philosophy.* USA: Heinemann Educational Publishers.

8   John Mbiti's book *African Religions and Philosophy* of 1969 is in response to this colonial mindset. We are using the second edition of 1989.

9   Mbiti. 1969. African Traditional Religions, 48-57.

recent times, these views are making an impact in eco-theological questions that arise from the natural crises that plague our environment. African religions and cultures in whatever settings they were found, used trees, forests, animals (totems), birds, streams and rivers as vital meeting as well as dwelling places for the spirits. These natural features, embellished with the presence of the divine, could not be destroyed or defiled carelessly. The sky, or the atmosphere, was/is sacred, as it was considered the place for the Almighty Creator and Supreme Being of all things and spirits.[10] Moreover, this Creator God created the universe and endowed some humans with spiritual insights to properly handle the natural environment for its conservation for the benefit of the living community; Mbiti[11] calls these humans specialists. The Ngbokondems of the Ejagham were such humans, such 'sacred personages' or 'sacred specialists,' so referred to because of their specialised office, knowledge, and skill in religious matters. These priestesses performed ritual sacrifices to cleanse the land and ward off diseases. They are described by many today in Ejagham land as the custodians of nature; a notion that was never imagined until the final demise[12] of the association in this early 21st century.

Ngbokondems mediated between the 'Ndem spirit,'[13] the Supreme Being and the living community, and used solely nature as their meeting place with the divine. As such, trees, rocks, forests, hills, rivers, lakes, reptiles, birdsand leaves were jealously preserved as places of encounter with the divine for the protection of the living community. However, their spiritual prowess became a threat to the patriarchal status quo of the day, chiefly Christian missionaries. Soon, colonialists arrived in Ejagham land with their gendered mentality and stigmatised Ngbokondems as witches. They condemned the association and its activities as demonic, while using male associations such as Ngbe with almost similar activities as Ngbokondem.[14] Their practicing forests were labelled as evil forests and its trees brought down with impunity. Today, many are pondering if the Ngbokondems and their 'evil forests'

---

10   Mbiti. 1969. African Traditional Religions, 52; local Ejagham people address God as *Atah Obasi k'ossoyansi*, meaning 'Papa God of up and down,' which means of sky and ground or heaven and Earth.

11   Mbiti. 1969. African Traditional Religions, 162.

12   We use demise here because the association no longer exists as a traditional cultic body in the land. Some respondents in Eyumojock report that the last *Arem* gathering took place in 2014. Many of the younger generation Ngbokondems claim that they have repented and now believe in Jesus. Now they claim that they prophesy for Jesus in some churches at the border with Nigeria. However, some respondents declare that they are still using the Ndem power in these churches.

13   While some consider this spirit as a malevolent spirit, others in Ejagham believe that this spirit had direct encounters with the Supreme Being, *Atah Obasi K'Osoh* (Father God Above) and related issues from Him to the village.

14   Hamilton, A. 2013. A General Overview of Kenyang Language. princehamilton.blogspot.com. Hamilton notes matter-of-factly that while Ngbe, the male mystical political status achievement association of the land was used by missionaries to summon people to church, Ngbokondems were seen only as witches to be accepted in church when they stopped all encounters with the spiritual universe.

were not more a blessing to the Ejagham than the curse that ruthless exploitation has brought on the land. The indigenes have watched over the years how the same 'evil' trees were carried along the deplorable roads of the Ejagham by heavy vehicles to foreign markets in Europe, leaving the land plagued with bad roads, deforestation, poverty, marginalization and the broken statues/bodies of these powerful women ancestors of the Ejagham in their tattered graves.

This chapter is organised in three sub-divisions. First, the presentation of the research context and methodology with which the work is realised, as well as the research problem, objectives and hypothesis. Second, presentation of Ngbokondem priestesses as agents of spirituality and eco-conservation, prominent religious leaders whose cultic observations paved the way for Christianity to take root in the land. Third, the presentation of Ngbokondems as gendered bodies whom colonial and home-based patriarchy succeeded to infiltrate, puncture, and silence their existence. The study concludes by advocating a return to traditional spirituality and habits of nature conservation as true worship that sustains Mother Earth as God's creation.

Context of Study and Methodology

The Ejagham community is situated in the South-West region of Cameroon in the present-day Manyu division. The Manyu division is unique in the country for housing some of Cameroon's best rivers, parks and forest reserves. A vast virgin forest in the country, which supplies wood to the rest of Africa and the world, comes from the Ejagham area. Cultural affiliations remain strong among the Ejagham, as the area is replete with associations that are largely gendered. Women have the 'Moninkim,' 'Ngbokondem,' 'Ekpa' and others, while men have the 'Angbu' for young boys, and 'Ngbe' and 'Ekpe,' which is the leopard society for adult men who often perform during funerals and other rites.[15] These are all ancestral associations with complicated rituals that have endured from the pre-colonial period. The Ngbokondem as religio-spiritual space occupied an important place in this community's associations. It became one of the most powerful in the land because of its use of nature to transmit and/or implant the spiritual.

The chapter employs African women's storytelling methodology, which "shapes and reshapes our identity, recasting the images we have of ourselves as women."[16] Storytelling methodology becomes the vital 'principle of hermeneutics' for the

---

15   Bayen, B.P. 2016. The Effects of Female Genital Mutilation in Cameroon: Case Study of the Ejagham Community of Eyumojock Sub-division. Masters in Peace and Development Work, Department of Social Studies (4FU42E); Otob, T.J. 2018. Initiation Practices among Ejagham Women of Cameroon and Patriarchy: a Womanist Perspective. Unpublished Doctoral Thesis. Pretoria: University of Pretoria.

16   Phiri, I.A; Govinden, D. B and Nadar, S. 2002. *Her-Stories: Hidden Histories of Women of Faith in Africa.* Pietermaritzburg: Cluster Publications, 6.

chapter in that it is used to rethink and retell the lives of Ngbokondems as African women heroines who shaped their society, but who like many African women became subject to multiple degrading patriarchal labels.[17] Emphasis on storytelling methodology as the starting point is not accidental; it takes into consideration the fact that this sector of Ejagham society, who ought to have been lauded for the formidable contribution they made to the ecosystem and humanity through their special spiritual understanding of the universe, instead earned the labels of witches. Such labels exposed them to culture, class and gender oppression, which gradually moved them from their positions of head in the pre-colonial era, to occupy the margins of society.[18] This chapter takes on a liberation perspective that attacks the nonacquiescence to reduce these special women of nature to be defined only according to the limited cultural lens of patriarchy, coloniality and uncritical religiosity as forces of dehumanisation.

The storytelling methodology can comfortably be situated within the ranks of Black theology of liberation in that in re-imaging, re-imagining, re-shaping, and re-telling the lives of these powerful yet marginalised women, the methodology aims to recreate a lasting legacy for them. It hopes with Mosala to take seriously the historical, cultural and ideological challenges the Ngbokondem and all black people have been subjected to.[19] It uses myriads of stories to challenges oppression in all forms, be they sexist, racist, class, cultural or others. The African storytelling methodology therefore becomes a useful tool to better portray the lives of Ngbokondems and the hermeneutical framework to understand Ngbokondems by peering again into the lives of these 'great women leaders' who impacted society through their genius in traditional cosmology, spirituality and epistemology. While their association was labelled and limited by missionaries and colonial administration, and exploited by home-based male domination, literature and oral history transmitted from generation to generation furnishes African women's storytelling with enough tools to rethink the Ngbokondems. First, as protectors of the Earth and its inhabitants, and second, also as gendered entities who endured the brunt of patriarchy right to the breaking of their bodies. This chapter advocates that the Ejagham society should officially commemorate these women and lament their demise.

We carried out visits to the Ejagham clan of the Eyumojock sub division in the periods between 8 December 2015 and 9 March 2017. Here we engaged five women initiation practices with sexual implications that shape women's lives. For the practice of Ngbokondem, we interviewed 18 people, 5 men and 13 women, in

---

17   Oduyoye, M.A. 2001. *Introducing African Women's Theology*. Britain: Sheffield Academic Press. 12; Otob, Initiation Practices, 27.

18   Otob, T.J. 2018. Initiation Practices, 28.

19   Otob, T.J. 2018. Initiation Practices, 27.

8 different villages, 8 of whom are former Ngbokondems. We did both group and individual interviews.

Research Problem and Objectives

The chapter attempts a re-thinking and re-imaging of the Ngbokondem beyond the perception of their being witches and demoniacs to seeing them as custodians of Ejagham culture and protectors of Mother Earth. It therefore poses the question:

Could the same Ngbokondems who were labelled, demonised and stigmatised, have been the solution to the deforestation and environmental degradation that plagues the Ejagham today?

The chapter is driven by two objectives. The first objective is to show that traditional African women have played major roles in the preservation of the natural environment through their mastery of the spiritual universe. The second objective is to use the spiritual ingenuity of these strong women of the Ejagham to propose measures to preserve the environment.

Hypothesis

The chapter is rooted in the hypothetical assertion that Ejagham land would have been a better geographical entity today with beautiful, touristic and spiritual sites, had the Ngbokondems been allowed to thrive with their religio-spiritual association that was purely pro-nature, pro-life and pro-forest preservation. Their contact with the ecosystem made it a 'no-go' zone to the Ejagham except at their permission. Disrespect for the Ngbokondems based on their gender, culture and epistemology caused the mass destruction and exploitation of the Ejagham's forest and natural environment.

Understanding the Ngbokondems

Up until today, the identity of the Ngbokondems remains a dilemma. Their descriptions by some Ejagham people are outlined below:

"That woman them wey they bi di fall that their thing" (Those women who fall and become unconscious)

"When they fall that their nonsense"

"Woman them for mamiwata" (Wives of mermaid)

"Early prophets them for Ejagham tribe" (Early prophetesses of the Ejagham tribe)

"We early mami them wey Papa God bi di make them see road di tell we weti for do for make contry be peace" (Our foremothers who used to have revelations from Father God and tell our village how to be peaceful).

"Very strong big mami them for old days" (Very powerful grandmothers of old)

"Na wa own church before Whiteman church for wacontry"

"We fit tok say mami them wey them bi get eye. Whether na for God oooh!, or for Satan oooh! Ooooh! But they bi di do both good and bad, so they be they for God and for Satan the same time." (We can say they are mothers who foresaw. Whether they did it for God, I cannot tell! Whether they did it for Satan, I cannot tell. However, they did both good and evil)

"Some wonderful powerful mysterious women. They had super (spiritual) powers and people respected them and were afraid of them."

These descriptions depend on where the respondent is standing. If they are Christians, they describe them as sorcerers and fortune tellers, while traditionalists describe them as invaluably powerful. The last two responses, however, are curious as they place both good and ugly in the Ngbokondems at the same time.

From the above descriptions, one comes to the understanding that the Ngbokondems manifested the earliest form of religious expression, consciousness and interaction within the cultural spiritual universe of Ejaghjam. They handled the spiritual needs of the people long before the arrival of colonial Christianity. The association which mirrors ancient Ejagham society is an indication that women in the pre-colonial society stood at the head of spiritual leadership and by implication political leadership.[20] Their involvement in the association gave them considerable power and control since most communities are directed through interaction with the spiritual[21] for life and well-being. A people's religious ethos and their philosophical perception could be properly comprehended when their view of the spiritual universe around them is pro-life. The survival of this powerful association signifies that women from pre-colonial times dispensed their spiritual authority with honesty and vigour. The

---

20 They that control the spiritual/religious in Ejagham are consulted in all crucial political issues concerning the land. Again, as we shall notice, the Ngbokondem priestesses marry most of the chiefs of the villages and notables of the land because of their beauty and spiritual ingenuity (cf Ruel, 1969); thus, they had direct access to influence political decisions. Moreover, they were the only women to sit with men and dignitaries in all important gatherings.

21 In Ejagham cosmology, there is no real demarcation between the spiritual and the physical universe. People are attached to both and pay allegiance to all those who have access to the spiritual universe. A purely physical and natural phenomenon, such as rainfall or the overflow of a river, could be spiritualised to demand spiritual intervention, be it from a religious official or from a medium – whoever will be more effective to address the issue.

association therefore assured the community's religious and spiritual well-being through women's interactions with nature and the paranormal.

The Association as an Early Expression of Religion in Ejagham

Some people have rightly noted that Africans are "notoriously" and "incurably" religious.[22] Religion forms the backbone of African ontological consciousness. African cosmology is endowed with rich religious expressions and experiences. Religion penetrates every sphere, both physical and spiritual. Women often take religion seriously or are taken seriously by religion. Oduyoye[23] calls them "religion's chief clients;" especially those that are bonded to culture and have the spiritual and psychological prowess to use religious knowledge "to make life meaningful, liveable, even desirable and enjoyable."[24] These were the skills of the Ngbokondem.

In the Ejagham villages of Ossing, Ndekwai, Ntenako and myriads of others, one comes across graves that lie in front of compounds with statues of women on top of them, and Baeta's[25] words immediately come alive: "Africans live with their dead." The statues were built in honour of some prominent women known as *ngboko-ndem* or *Mbokondem* as Ruel[26] calls them. Ruel Pemunta et al[27] point out that these effigies – formerly in mud within a protective hut and later in cement – were built in commemoration of a dead member of the *Ndem* association.

The Ngbokondem and other associations with an extramundane worldview are described by some Ejagham indigenes as, "we own church before Whiteman hi church for we contry," signifying pre-colonial expressions of religious consciousness in the Ejagham before the arrival of missionaries.[28] Through its cultic orientations, the association is thought to have made it easy for subsequent religions like Christianity and Islam to reach out to an already spirit-minded people. Bediako[29] suggests that through the religio-cultural commitments of agents like the Ngbokondem, the

---

22 Mbiti, J.S. 1969. *African Traditional Religions and Philosophy.* USA: Heinemann Educational Publishers. 1; Oduyoye, 1995. *Daughters of Anowa: African Women and Patriarchy.* Maryknoll, New York: Orbis Books. 109; Otob, T.J. 2018. Initiation Practices, 119.

23 Oduyoye, 1995. *Daughters of Anowa,* 109, 110.

24 Oduyoye, 1995. *Daughters of Anowa,* 109.

25 Bediako, K. 1996. *Christianity in Africa: The Renewal of a Non-Western Religion.* Maryknoll, New York: Orbis Books. 216; Otob, Initiation Practices, 120.

26 Ruel, 1969. Leopards and Leaders, 203.

27 Ruel, Leopards and Leaders, 204. Pemunta, N.V., Tabi, C.T. and Mathias, F.A. Communitarianism and the Obasinjom Mask Performance as Ritual Healing among the Bayang and Ejagham of Southwest Cameroon, 11. In: A. Parish (ed). 2014, *Ritual Practices, Ethnic and Cultural Aspects and Role in Emotional Healing.* New York: Nova Science Publishers, Inc.

28 Bediako, Christianity in Africa, 212; Otob, Initiation Practices, 120.

29 Bediako, Christianity in Africa, 212.

salvific activity of the 'Supreme Being' was already available in Africa. Human agents, such as the Ngbokondems, who represented the Supreme Being were already present in African communities "prior to the historic proclamation and reception of the gospel."[30] They were then used to prepare the ground for the gospel through their cultic orientations. Bediako[31] describes their cultic interventions in the community as the first expression of 'African primal religions'; they were "the womb out of which Christianity was born" in Ejagham and Africa as a whole, as Maluleke[32] puts it.

The Ngbokondems and their association were not just "passive traditional cosmologies" but were dynamic institutions that were able to adapt as well as respond to new situations as they grappled with human needs in society.[33] Bediako[34] states that they, like the Biblical ancestors, at critical points in their lives and careers, made choices which contributed to shaping the destinies of our traditions until the fullness of time, when our histories became merged in Christ with the history of the people of God.

Moreover, their cultic interventions could be seen more as prefiguration and anticipations among Africans and the Ejaghams of the coming Christ brought through the gospel by Christian missionaries.[35] Hence, not only missionaries made Christianity possible in Africa as most have thought. Cultic participations and interventions such as those of the Ngbokondems strongly support the many-sided manner in which the ancestors have been part of the making of Christian Africa.[36]

The skill and mastery of indigenous knowledge that the Ngbokondems had in blending the supernatural and natural as well asthe stigma they suffered, could be compared to the powerful medieval women in European lands who were burnt alive as witches in the 16th/17th century because they threatened the androcentric authority of the Christian church at the time.[37] The Ngbokondems, like these women, were empowered with the possession of ancestral knowledge and they played leading roles in the communities where they were accorded high status.[38] Their effective supernatural knowledge is what the Ejagham indigenes marvel about.

---

30   Bediako, Christianity in Africa, 224.

31   Bediako, Christianity in Africa, 212.

32   Maluleke, T. 1997. Half a century of African Christian Theology.Elements of the emerging agenda for the twenty-first century. *Journal of Theology for Southern Africa* 10; Otob, Initiation Practices, 121.

33   Bediako, Christianity in Africa, 212.

34   Bediako, Christianity in Africa, 227-228.

35   Bediako, Christianity in Africa 225.

36   Bediako, Christianity in Africa, 228; Otob, Initiation Practices, 121.

37   Grosfoguel, R. 2013. The Structure of Knowledge in Westernised Universities: epistemic racism, sexism and the four Genocides epistemicides of the 5th long 16th Century. *Human Architecture: Journal of Sociology of Self-Knowledge*, 11(1): 85; Otob, Initiation Practices, 121.

38   Grosfoguel, The Structure of Knowledge, 85

It is believed to come from the sky[39] where the Ejagham believe the Supreme Being resides. Among both the male and female associations that operated in Ejagham land, the Ngbokondem association grew into prominence as a result of its religious affiliations.

The Ngbokondem and the Natural Environment

Nature in all its splendour was the sole sustenance for this association. The forest, trees, grass, rivers, reptiles, rocks, and the sky therefore became crucial for the Ngbokondem's survival. Talbot[40] reports that several seven-day trips were made into the bush throughout the Ngbokondem's life where she went to seek knowledge and power. In a group interview with four women of the Eyumojock, Mbenyan, Agborkem and Ossing villages, Ma Obenemblar and Ebanghachu[41] describe these trips as some of the most mystical undertakings of the Ngbokondem. She will not pack a bag to leave for these trips but sometimes will just disappear from sight and enter bushes and trees. Suddenly, she will reappear again after seven days anywhere she pleases with her wares. She will then begin to recount all the things that were said and done in her absence, stating that she was just nearby. Other times she will actually carry people along to the forest when she has to collect herbs or something kept for the village. This happens after she was unconscious in a trance and awakes again. *Ndem* priestesses foretold the future and cured mystical illnesses; they averted misfortunes and even prevented defeat in war by alerting the entire village beforehand.[42]

Membership and Initiation

A young girl of between 12 and 18, often a firstborn daughter of the family, was initiated while she was young. Ngbokondem was such a great honour that most parents enrolled the girls. Membership was by initiation through special rites of *Nkim e Nkim* (clitoris fixing)[43] and herbal procedures. Only firstborn daughters who accepted to undergo the fixing process were allowed into the *Ndem* association. Families willingly offered their girls to go through fixing. Based on the ages of the girls, one can hardly imagine that they will voluntarily go though the fixing process as they are not at decision making ages. The Ngbokondems are expected

---

39 Niger-Thomas, 2009. Commemorating Women, 171
40 Talbot, P.A. 1926. *Life in Southern Nigeria*, 130.
41 Interviewed as group on 6 March 2017.
42 Talbot, P.A. 1926. *Life in Southern Nigeria*, 132.
43 What is known internationally as female genital mutilation. The local language designates fixing the clitoris to make it smooth and beautiful.

to manifest strength and vigour during the fixing process by not crying or being afraid, to show that they are able to embrace the elaborate and complicated mystical process of ritual activities. It is after the fixing that the priestesses are kept in a special house and initiated fully with herbal concoctions. These cause them to go into brief unconscious seizures where it is declared that they have been caught by *Ndem* spirit, 'bhagboNdem.' At this point of dead (unconsciousness), they are translated to the spiritual realm where they connect with the *Ndem*.

They are then revived or "woken up"[44] after a while by other members of the association through a medicinal/herbal process to deliver messages for the community. Herbal concoctions and plants that have been shown during their 'dead' experience are delivered for the community's healing and welfare. This phenomenon is the origin of the 'die wake up' phenomenon labelled on Ejagham daughters as stigma.[45] This religio-mystical affiliation of the association's priestess prompts her description by Margaret Niger-Thomas[46] as "mami water" (mermaid spirit).[47] Some Ejagham people contest Niger-Thomas' description because the 'mami water' appellation has a negative connotation. It is a beautiful but malevolent female spirit that is feared for her vengeance when disobeyed. However, if one deciphers Pa Dickoben's[48] report of the *Ndem* as a jealous spirit who punishes rivalry or disempowers the Ngbokondem after disobedience, then Niger-Thomas could have a point. Nonetheless, the Ngbokondems are more revered than feared in Ejagham society. With all these, they earn the title "leaders among women."[49] The fixing and initiation all invest the priestesses with supernatural potentials for religio-cultic services to the community. They handle this position until they die or become too old to serve. Yet they are consistently consulted for advice on community or clan issues.[50]

When the *Ngbokondems* die, elaborate funeral rites are conducted for them and a statue built over their graves. The statue is decorated with feathers from a cock. These feathers are worn on the head by priestesses to show their traditional rank in the association and community. The number of feathers signify the level of and strength in leadership. During ceremonies, she sits among dignitaries and male leaders. As it is today, the association has declined all over Ejagham with barely a few of its members still alive, and even fewer still involved in Ngbokondem activities. Yet the

---

44   Ruel, Leopards and leaders, 203.

45   It is common locally in most settings in Cameroon to describe Ejagham women as dying and rising again as haunting ghosts (*benem*). It all resonated from the *Ndem* experience.

46   Niger-Thomas 2009. Commemorating Women, 171.

47   Mermaid spirits are commonly believed to live in water spaces and mystically penetrate the physical realm to influence human activities, especially the sexual, through fertility and procreation.

48   Interviewed 18 February 2017.

49   Ruel, Leopards and leaders, 204.

50   Otob, Initiation Practices, 125.

strong status and personality it accorded women in a solely male-dominated society is a mark that never departs. Even today, women bearing Ngbokondem names are still believed to be special in some way, bold and assertive in their interactions with people. This potential is a liberating factor in a context where women are subject to varied patriarchal challenges. Their graves and dilapidated statues still survive as monuments to lament their declining status and memory.[51]

The Ngbokondem and Women's Empowerment in the Priestly Prophetic

The association is being hailed within and outside of Ejagham land for the uplifting of women's status. It concentrated on the very essence of the clan's survival as it ensured procreation and multiplication of society, where the *Ndem* priestess mediated between the community and the *Ndem* spirit to ensure fertility and procreation in the land. This action of filling the Earth sets her apart in the pre-colonial African religious mindset as a 'messenger' of the "Supreme Being who is the ultimate Source and Sustainer of life and the universe."[52] Moreover, Ma Eyere of Ayukaba[53] describes her prophetic role that is her ability to predict events that affected the community negatively and positively. This happened after her unconscious and spectacular spiritual experiences. Her prophetic utterances were taken seriously because of their eventual fulfilment. This supports the testimony that in pre-colonial Africa, God did speak to our foreparents through prophets and prophetesses at many times and in various ways.[54]

Their mediations brought good things into the land, such as children, food, health and prosperity. It is for this reason that the current living community still accords her the same spiritual status as Biblical priests. Their priestly prophetic role has caused Ma AtopOben of Mbakang,[55] who revealed that she has a similar gift, to revere them as God's agents in the land, as she reveals in the following words:

> Ngbokondem is a gift that you are born with; the gift is given by God. Just like this people who carry Obasinjom, not anybody can carry it … It is those people whom God has given them gift originally, a gift to see. And that is because God had originally given you the powers. That is why some people see their dreams and they become real, even the Bible talks about it…Ngbokondem is that kind of a person…They give birth to you with a gift … When she falls, immediately they know something is wrong in the village. So then they will take precaution

---

51   Otob, Initiation Practices, 126.

52   Oduyoye, Daughters of Anowa, 111.

53   Interviewed 8 March 2017.

54   Bediako, Christianity in Africa, 225.

55   Interviewed 6 March 2017. She revealed that she is a Christian Manyi, meaning she has spiritual abilities to predict things, and she uses the Bible and herbs to cure people.

> on what to be done. She is like an announcer, she prophesies, like a seer... You will be prophesying, they will show you medicines and you will cure people. None of these people are evil. They do it according to their own life how they could see it from God. All these gifts are given by God.

In her opinion, Ngbokondems were powerful messengers of 'AtahObassiK'osohyaNsi' who mediated for the living community. Their prophetic gift of seeing comes from God only, for no one is able to bestow such a gift on human beings except God Almighty. In her opinion, God chose prophets and priests in Africa and Ejagham land even before the introduction of Biblical prophets to the community.[56]

Gendered Bodies and Forgotten Mothers of Nature

In her collection of poems titled, *A Basket of flaming ashes*, Joyce Ashuntantang[57] dedicates a section on the Ngbokondems. Here she laments the demise of this prestigious association in Ejagham land. Citing the dilapidating state of the statues, she blames brutal Western imperialism that ravages not only *Ndem* but all Ejagham land and forest. She states the following:

> The absence of your hands tells the story of your rape, the rape of your land, the rape of your people. But your beauty is legend... This morning the mist cleared, your right leg was gone too and that pretty face has lost an ear... Maybe when I return you will be gone completely.

In Ashuntantang's[58] opinion, the broken statues in front of the houses and inside the bushes tell the same story: the rape of culture and land by a Western imperialistic enterprise that manifests itself religiously, politically and economically in Ejagham land. Religiously, we have stated that Ngbokondem was considered the first religious expression of the people, with the priestess as an intermediary between the people and the supernatural being. However, Talbot,[59] who is one of the earliest European sources to report on the association, could describe it only as 'juju' or a minor deity, together with *Mfam, Obasi Njom* (God medicine) and *Ngbe*.[60] Maluleke's[61] insight could be used to question how much "privilege, interest, control and knowledge" researchers such as Talbot, Ruel, and the early missionaries had over the researched, as they describe their religio-cultural world in such simplistic terms. Considering,

56   Otob, Initiation Practices, 121.
57   Ashuntantang, J.B. 2010. *A Basket Of Flaming Ashes*. Makon, Bamenda: Langaa Research and Publishing CIG. 36.
58   Ashuntantang, J.B. 2010. *A Basket of Flaming Ashes*, 36.
59   Talbot, Life in Southern Cameroon, 117-138.
60   Talbot, Life in Southern Cameroon, 126-128; Otob, "Initiation Practices," 128.
61   Maluleke, T. 1996. Theological Interests in AICs and Other Grass-root Communities in South Africa: A Review on Methodology. *Journal of Black Theology in South Africa,* 10(1):41-43; Otob, "Initiation Practices," 129.

that the 'juju' appellation carries with it negative connotations in the Ejagham mindset, it should not fit the description of their associations. If colonial Christianity saw these associations only in such light, then their stigmatization and subsequent ostracization are understood, for the 'jujus' had to be destroyed to implant the more 'civilised' God.[62] Comparing their situation with the burning of women with special knowledge as witches in Europe, Grosfoguel[63] thinks that this was a strategy to consolidate Christian-centric patriarchy, as the "autonomy, leadership and knowledge of these women threatened Christian theology, church authority and the power of aristocracy [...] in the colonies."[64] The prestigious association that sustained the living community throughout the pre-colonial period suddenly became a source of evil, witchcraft and stigma and was labelled by Western Christianity as malevolent.

Ashuntantang[65] mentions the operation of the colonial political economy through the exploitation of forests and vegetation, which are vital features for *Ndem* activities. From the reports above, Ngbokondems made several trips into the forest during their lifetime to increase their power. MoninkimElisOben and Ma Ayuk of Mbenyan confirm this report. They state that a Ngbokondem could see her own way through a dense forest without the guidance of anyone. This happened when she went to collect whatever was kept there by *Ndem* spirit who lives in Boma trees, water, Earth and on reptiles.[66] Creation and nature lavished this on this area with a beautiful resting place where God walks in the fresh evening breeze to have communion with humanity (Genesis 3). Here *Ndem* priestesses could penetrate nature's womb to get instructions from the 'Supreme Being' for the welfare of the community.[67]

All this was destroyed by the colonial political economy and exploitation. The continuous pulling down of forests for timber exportation to foreign markets is an example of the ruthless exploitation of Western imperialistic patriarchy. Even though dwelling in the land, the people have become landless through marginalization. They are powerless to question the heavy French vehicles with foreign labels ploughing the bad roads directly to the sources of wood without noticing the dilapidated villages and graves of the Ngbokondems along the roads. They pull down everything along their path, even dragging along the legs, ears and arms of the Ngbokondems to foreign markets.[68]

62   Otob, "Initiation Practices," 129.
63   Grosfoguel, The Structure of Knowledge, 87-88; Otob, "Initiation Practices," 130.
64   Grosfoguel, The Structure of Knowledge, 87-88.
65   Ashuntantang, J.B. 2010. *A Basket of Flaming Ashes*, 36.
66   Niger-Thomas, Commemorating Women, 171; Otob, "Initiation Practices," 130.
67   Otob, Initiation Practices, 130.
68   Otob, Initiation Practices, 131.

Male domination also had a gendered grip on this association in the following ways:

A gendered cultural divide produced such a deep gulf between the two sexes that it became an almost natural phenomenon. On the contrary, men succeeded in penetrating the most sacred realm of the *Ndem* association. Through introduction and initiation of Obales, firstborn sons were gradually introduced as initiates to become members of this female only association. Their role was to play the drums for the women to dance. The introduction of Obales placed men's presence at the heart of women's space and activities; some respondents think it was a ploy to regulate women.

Patriarchy ensured that it was only the father of the girl who could register her into the association by paying her fees as a young woman.[69] No woman could enrol herself or enrol another woman. As such, though founded and led by women, its survival and thriving rested in men's hands.

Moreover, father and husband of the Ngbokondem gained some advantages from her membership in that "small fines" were often paid to them in cases where anyone in the community broke the rules against their daughter or wife.[70] In addition, "bridewealth for a Ngbokondem was higher than for other women; and a heavier fine could also be demanded in the case of adultery."[71] This father/husband benefit played more to the advantage of the men rather than the Ngbokondem.

Similarly, the fact that almost all traces of this prestigious women's association are disappearing while male cults such as *Ngbe (Ekpe)* and *Njom* that existed at the same pre-colonial period are still thriving today, could be an indication of a patriarchal society that exalts the male. It is claimed that the last *arem* in the area took place at Eyumojock two years ago.[72] One of our respondents only referred to their activities now as "when they fall that their nonsense." This description is a result of continuous labelling from the worshipping communities. Ma ObenOjong from Ekok town claims to have been delivered from that "demon cult" by "Jesus and prayer." She revealed that she used to fall into unconsciousness and get up again in another spirit, speaking strange languages; while dancing, seeing mystical things that came to be. Now she no longer connects with that realm. She has the Spirit of Christ now.

Contrarily, her view is directly refuted by Pa EkambaNtui of Nkpot village.[73] He disagrees with these "Jesus deliverance" exclamations by stating that churches chased

---

69   Ruel, Leopards and Leaders, 203.

70   Ruel, Leopards and Leaders, 204.

71   Ruel, Leopards and Leaders, 204.

72   That is 2014, from the date of the first interviews for empirical data collection for the study.

73   Interviewed 6 March 2017 at Eyumojock.

their own prophetesses from their villages. He laments the demise of this powerful association when he explains that "we, in Ejagham, have made a huge error by outlawing our *Ndem* gatherings. This is because neighbouring Nigerians are making great use of theirs today by using them as prophetesses in almost all the churches you see thriving in Nigeria." In his opinion, these women are the ones making the churches in Nigeria prominent as they are using their foretelling powers inside most churches to solve people's mystical problems. Hence, while Nigeria has situated its Ngbokondems inside the church, Ejagham has used its own churches to destroy the powerful association.

As Sexualised Bodies

Associations of the magnitude of the Ngbokondem survive by vital and sometimes secret rules and regulations that have to be strictly adhered to. One such rule that Talbot[74] states as a precautionary measure was the code that guarded the sexuality of the Ngbokondem. MbuyBeya[75] has rightly noted that most early African communities usually set apart certain special individuals to perform particular religious and social functions for the community. One of these criteria for the survival of such individuals was a form of ritual celibacy that upheld sexual purity through leading a single life void of marriage or sex. The idea is that sex or the sensual hinders concentration and distracts the individual from the spiritual realm.[76]

Hence, for the Ndem priestess to stay powerful and the association to survive, she was not to have sexual intercourse with any man "else the *Nimm (Ndem)* in the bush will close her eyes and she will not see the road again."[77] However, because of their high status, popularity and peculiarity, some power-hungry men of the land took advantage to defy the rule and preyed on their celibacy status through marriage and eventually, sexual intercourse. This then impinged on the sacred non-intercourse code and contributed to the weakening of the association to its demise. Exactly forty-three years later when Ruel[78]wrote about the same association after Talbot, he stated:

> The association came in this way to reflect indirectly the system of status achievement and competition among men of the community: community

---

74   Talbot, P.A. 1926. *Life in Southern Nigeria*, 132; Otob. Initiation Practices, 131.

75   MbuyBeya, B. 2005. Human Sexuality, Marriage and Prostitution. In: A.M. Oduyoye and R.A.M. Kanyoro.*The Will to Arise. Women, Tradition and the Church in Africa.* New York: Orbis Books, 162-163.

76   Otob, Initiation Practices, 131.

77   Talbot, Life in Northern Nigeria, 132; Otob Initiation Practices, 132.

78   That is from when Talbot last reported about the practice; Ruel, 1969; Leopards and Leaders, 204; Otob, Initiation Practices, 132.

leaders bought status for their daughters (and thus indirectly for themselves) through the association; while in turn those men seeking community status sought also to marry these 'leaders among women.' It was not a matter of chance that in both Tali and Besongabang when I inquired about Ndem, I was sent to the senior wife of the village leader.

With the above explanation, male domination in the form of status acquisition, a quest for power, prestige, influence and sexual control had a direct hand in the demise of the *Ndem* association, as men broke the sexual norm.[79]

Conclusion and Recommendations

In conclusion, in this work we have used an African women's storytelling methodology to retrace and retell the story of the Ngbokondem of the Ejagham, the great mothers of nature in Ejagham land. They are fast being forgotten today, save for their tattered graves with broken effigies. The study holds that they should be hailed for their efforts to use their spiritual prowess to conserve nature in Ejagham. One can state that although they were demonised and stigmatised as witches, their presence in Ejagham could have preserved nature and especially the forest better than they are today. Their association had the potential to protect the land from the deforestation and environmental degradation she experiences today. The study showed that the existence of the Ngbokondem priestesses and the association was a blessing rather than a curse, as it was propagated by the Christian missionaries and converts. They were pro-nature and pro-life, as they accorded nature the spiritual dignity it deserved. In contrast, their demise has exposed the land to exploitation through deforestation, erosion, drought and other phenomena. While it will not be possible to recreate the association, the chapter advocates a return to some of the Ngbokondems' activities, such as considering the rest of nature as a spiritual universe for whosepreservation one needs to fight ceaselessly. African women of this generation become Ngbokondems in their various settings as they spiritualise nature and fight to preserve the Earth.

---

79 Otob, Initiation Practices, 132.

References

Ashuntantang, J.B. 2010. *A Basket of Flaming Ashes*. Makon, Bamenda: Langaa Research and Publishing CIG.

Bayen, B.P. 2016. The Effects of Female Genital Mutilation in Cameroon: Case Study: Ejagham Community of Eyumojock sub-division. Masters in Peace and Development Work, Department of Social Studies (4FU42E). Linnaeus University.

Bediako, K. 1996. Christianity in Africa: The Renewal of a Non-Western Religion. Maryknoll, New York: Orbis Books.

Grosfoguel, R. 2013. The Structure of Knowledge in Westernised Universities: epistemic racism, sexism and the four Genocides epistemicides of the 5th long 16th Century. *Human Architecture: Journal of Sociology of Self-Knowledge,* 11(1):85.

Hamilton, A. 2013. A General Overview of Kenyang Language. http://princehamilton.blogspot.com/2013/03/a-general-overview-of-kenyang-language.html[Accessed 10 August 10 2020]

Maluleke, T. 1997. Half a century of African Christian Theology.Elements of the emerging agenda for the twenty-first century. *Journal of Theology for Southern Africa,* 99:10.

Maluleke, T. 1996. Theological interests in AICs and Other Grass-root Communities in South Africa: A Review on Methodology. *Journal of Black Theology in South Africa,* 10(1):41-43.

Mbiti, J.S. 1969. *African Traditional Religions and Philosophy.* USA: Heinemann Educational Publishers.

MbuyBeya, B. 2005. Human Sexuality, Marriage, and Prostitution. In: M.A. Oduyoyeand and M.R.A. Kanyoro. *The Will to Arise. Women, Tradition and the Church in Africa.* New York: Orbis Books 162-163.

Niger-Thomas, M. 2009. Commemorating Women in Patrilineal Society. In: I. Fowler and V. Fanso (eds). *Encounter, Transformation and Identity. Peoples of the Western Cameroon Borderlands 1891-2000.* USA: Berghahn Books. 169-184.

Oduyoye, M.A. 2001. *Introducing African Women's Theology*. Britain: Sheffield Academic Press.

Oduyoye, M.A.1995. *Daughters of Anowa: African Women and Patriarchy*. Maryknoll, New York: Orbis Books.

Otob, TJ. 2018. Initiation Practices among Ejagham Women of Cameroon and Patriarchy: a Womanist Perspective. Unpublished Doctoral Thesis. South Africa: University of Pretoria.

Phiri, I.A. Govinden, D.B and Nadar, S. 2002. *Her-Stories: Hidden Histories of Women of Faith in Africa.* Pietermaritzburg: Cluster Publications.

Pemunta, N.V., Tabi, C.T. and Mathias, F.A. 2014. Communitarianism and the Obasinjom Mask Performance as Ritual Healing among the Bayang and Ejagham of Southwest Cameroon. In: A. Parish (ed). *Ritual Practices, Ethnic and Cultural Aspects and Role in Emotional Healing.* New York: Nova Science Publishers, Inc.

Ruel, M. 1969. *Leopards and Leaders: Constitutional Politics among a Cross River People.* London: Tavistock Publications.

Talbot, P.A. 1926. *Life in Southern Nigeria.* London: Routledge, Taylor & Francis Group.

WOMEN AND SUSTAINABLE AGRICULTURE IN THE CONTEXT OF THE KASISI AGRICULTURAL TRAINING CENTRE

A Catholic Initiative in Zambia

Nelly Mwale[1]

Abstract

While the worldwide Christian community has accepted that women's rights are part of social justice, and ecology has particularly become a priority for the Jesuit religious order as seen through their initiative at Kasisi Agriculture Training Centre in Zambia, the voices of women's experiences and contributions in this initiative remain unheard. Thus, this chapter is a reaction to this silence, as well as an exploration of the mission of the Church to the Earth through the contributions of rural women towards the care of our common home. The chapter uses two women's trajectories in sustainable agriculture. Informed by narrative research, data was collected through recorded interviews. Literature analysis was also done and thematically analysed. The chapter reveals that the Kasisi Agriculture Training Centre as part of the Jesuit initiative in Zambia since the 1970s, was informed by Catholic social teachings and driven by a concern for social justice, including justice for the environment and women's rights. Women's well-being was at the centre of the initiative. Women were empowered in sustainable agriculture and their welfare improved.

The narratives of two women who had received training at the centre and whose trajectories were trailed, reflected how their lives had transformed into being entrepreneurs using sustainable agriculture techniques in a Zambian rural format. Their narratives also demonstrated their involvement in organising women's agriculture clubs in their local communities. From a gendered ecological mission perspective, the chapter argues that when given the right opportunities and when religion was used constructively, rural women were making a contribution not only towards the care of the Earth through sustainable agriculture, but also through improved livelihoods in their communities and beyond through commercial agricultural production. Most importantly, the chapter advocates the celebration and

---

1   Nelly Mwale is a lecturer at the University of Zambia in the department of Religious Studies. She is also a research fellow at the Research Institute for Theology and Religion, University of South Africa. She has published several scholarly articles and book chapters in referred journals and edited book volumes. Mwale is also a member of the Circle of Concerned African Women Theologians, the African association for the study of religions (AASR), and the Association for the Study of Religion in Southern Africa (ASRSA).

recognition in Zambian scholarship of such women, who were making a difference towards the care of the Earth, lest their contributions remain only as part of the Jesuits' initiative at Kasisi but unknown to the broader ecological success story.

Introduction

This chapter explores the mission of the Church to the Earth through women's contributions towards the care of the Common home as exemplified in their narratives in sustainable agriculture and the encounter with the Jesuit ecological mission in rural Zambia. The chapter is anchored in the long-standing relationship between religion and agriculture in which agriculture is a religious act. Agriculture's potential to contribute to economic development is underscored by religion,[2] by a long-established link between women and nature in the African context as affirmed by African women theologians,[3] and by an engendered sustainable agriculture discourse. Theologians such as Banks and Stevens noted that the aspects of agriculture that are built into biblical teachings include those concerned with land distribution, soil care, agronomic practices, the production of healthy agricultural produce, minimal interference with the natural environment and off-farm community responsibilities.[4] This signifies that the Church is God's principally ordained agency for agricultural development.

In contemporary times, the link between agriculture and religiosity is often demonstrated through the blessing of the seeds before planting in the field and thanksgiving after harvest as well as through other rituals related to the rain and soil fertility. At the same time, the injustice to the Earth cannot be detached from agriculture. In the face of the ecological crisis, the interconnectedness of the mission of the Church and the Earth has been revisited through notions like the third mission of the Church,[5] the eco-mission[6] and the care for our Common home.[7] This reawakening of the mission to the Earth has not only been manifested through the commentaries of Church institutions such as the Lutheran World Federation

---

2   Lang, M.K. 2018. The Role of religion in agriculture: reflections from the Bamenda Grassfields of Cameroon since Pre-colonial times. *Mgbakoigba: Journal of African Studies*, 7(2):54-73.

3   Siwila, L.C. 2014. Tracing the Ecological Footprints of Our Foremothers. Towards an African Feminist Approach to Women's Connectedness with Nature. *Studia Historiae Ecclesiasticae*, 40(2):131-147; Chirongoma, S. 2005. Motherhood and Ecological Conversion of Mother Earth. *Women in God's Image*, 10 & 11:8-12.

4   Banks, R. & Stevens, P. 1997. The Complete Book of Everyday Christianity: An A-Z Guide to Following Christ in Every Aspect of Life. Illinois: Intervarsity Press, 401-404.

5   Habel, N. 2010. Earth Mission: The Third Mission of the Church. *Currents in Theology and Mission*, 37(2):116.

6   Ayre, C.W. 2010. Eco-salvation: The redemption of all creation. *Worldviews*, 240.

7   Pope, F. 2015. Laudato Si: Our Care for our Common Home. 24 May.

and World Council of Churches[8] among others, but also through programmes with a concern for the environment. In the case of the Catholic Church, the care of the Earth has been embodied in the social teachings of the common good and caring for God's creation.[9] Concern for the Earth has also been part of the encyclicals, including the provocative encyclical on the environment[10] and the consequent launch of the Catholic Church's World Day of Prayer for the Care of Creation in 2015, as reported in the Guardian Newspaper.[11]

In Zambia, one avenue that exemplified the mission of the Church in the care of the Earth was the Jesuit engagement in agriculture through the establishment of the Kasisi Agriculture Farming Centre (KATC). Modeled on the principles of the Catholic social teachings with a special emphasis on women's rights as part of social justice and ecology, KATC was largely renowned as a faith-based initiative in sustainable agriculture in Zambia. For example, the Catholic Register reported that KATC was renowned for, among other things, the active advocacy role in organic farming and the stance against Genetically Modified Organisms (GMOs).[12] KATC was also chosen by the United Nations Development Programme as one of the 25 outstanding sustainable development initiatives around the globe.[13] According to the *Lusaka Voice* newspaper, the UNDP's Equator initiative singled out Kasisi for its practical steps to preserve Zambia's rural environment by training more than 10,000 small-scale farmers in sustainable farming techniques.[14]

Despite the recognitions, the success stories of the Centre, and the Jesuit acceptance that women's rights are part of social justice, and ecology a priority for the religious order, as observed through their initiative at the Centre, the voices, experiences and contributions of women as part of the mission of the Church to care for the common home remained undocumented. This was because the academic engagement with the Centre has been preoccupied with aspects such as the evaluation of the programmes offered,[15] the role of the centre in providing information to small-scale farmers in

8   Habel, Earth Mission, 120.

9   Compendium of the Social Doctrine of the Church. 2005. Pontifical Council for Justice and Peace. Rome, Italy, 470. Accessed on 24 May 2019.

10   Laudato si, 2015.

11   Mckenna, J. 2016. Pope Francis says Destroying the Environment Is a Sin. *The Guardian*, 1 September.

12   Swan, M. 2015. Br. Paul Desmarais, SJ: Reaping the Benefits of Organic Farming in Zambia. *The Guardian*, 22 April.

13   United Nations Development Programme. 2015. Kasisi Agricultural Training Centre. Equator Initiative Case Study Series. New York: UNDP.

14   Canadian Jesuit Favours Oxen over Tractors in Helping Zambian Farmers. 2014. *Lusaka Voice*, 6 September.

15   Johansson, K. 2003. Tiyeseko: A Study on Small-Scale Farming Women in Sustainable Agriculture in Zambia. Unpublished Advanced Paper. Stockholm, Sweden: Sodertorns Hosgkola University College.

Chongwe[16] and empowerment of small-scale farmers through technological skills,[17] among others. This chapter therefore interrogates the mission of the Church, as exemplified in the strides towards sustainable agriculture, through the contributions of women who were trained at KATC in Zambia's rural context.

The focus is on women not only because they constitute 64 per cent of the rural population and approximately 80 per cent of food producers in Zambia,[18] but also because scholarship on religion, gender and environment has been devoid of the connectedness between women's contributions and the mission of the Church in the Zambian context from a Catholic perspective. In addition, the focus on women was motivated by Chirongoma, a theologian who advocates for the need to embrace contributions made by indigenous communities in caring for the Earth, lest women and other excluded communities of the world remain nameless entities who are often pushed into oblivion in the fundamental discussions on issues of rights and existence.[19] Therefore, the chapter seeks to bring out the contributions of the women as part of the Jesuit ecological success story in the Zambian context.

By focusing on women in a rural context, the chapter does not suggest that women are merely vulnerable, but that they are powerful agents of change in their families and communities. This is through their engagement in sustainable agriculture that is underpinned by the mission of the Church in the care of the Earth. Similarly, by focusing on the women and the Jesuit mission at Kasisi, the chapter does not suggest that this was the only initiative by the Church, as other examples of mission and sustainable agriculture existed. For example, the Comboni Missionary Sisters opened the Mother Earth Centre in 2011 in western Zambia to promote sustainable agriculture and enhance rural livelihoods, food security and nutrition for farmers and their families. They also mitigate climate change impacts and care for the environment and spirituality, among other aims. To this end, the Comboni Missionary Sisters were organically cultivating and processing *moringa*, and using renewable energy, such as windmills, solar power, biogas and Earth bags to sustain their project. Other Christian churches were also involved in the care of the

---

16 Mtanga, N., Mulauzi, F. & Mwale, I. 2014. The Role of Kasisi Agricultural Training Centre in Providing Information on Organic Farming to the Small-Scale Farmers in Kasisi Area of Chongwe District, Zambia. Proceedings of the 21st Standing Conference for Eastern, Central and Southern African Library and Information Association (SCECSAL), 305-312.

17 Phakati, J. 2000. Participatory Rural Development and Technology Transfer: Empowering Small-Scale Farmers with Appropriate Technology Skills. Proceedings of the Workshop of the Animal Traction Network for Eastern and Southern Africa, 344.

18 Food and Agriculture Organisation. 2018. National Gender Profile of Agriculture and Rural Livelihoods-Zambia. Country Gender assessment Series. Lusaka: FAO, xi.

19 Chirongoma, S. 2018. Gleaning for Gender Justice in Laudato Si: Envisioning a Radial Eco-Feminist Conversion. Conference on the Radical Ecological Conversion after Laudato Si: Discovering the Intrinsic Value of all Creatures, Human and Non-human. Rome: Pontifical Gregorian University, 2.

environment. As such, the intent of this chapter is to exemplify and document the women's narratives on the care of the Earth by exploring the missing narratives at a popular eco-mission station in Zambia.

The chapter is informed by findings from a narrative research in which data were collected through recorded interviews and document analysis and thematically analysed through a gendered lens. It argues that, given the right opportunities, rural women were making a contribution not only towards the care of the Earth through sustainable agriculture, but also through improved livelihoods in their communities and beyond. It therefore advocates the celebration and recognition in the Zambian scholarship of women in rural areas who make a difference towards the care of the common home. The chapter unfolds by conceptualising the notion of 'Our Common home' and the mission of the Church, and provides a context in which the contributions of the women are situated. Thereafter, the narratives of the women's contributions are presented in light of the care of the common home, the Earth, and the third mission of the Church, or Earth mission, through a gendered lens.

Conceptualising 'Our Common Home' and the Mission of the Church to the Earth

The chapter is framed around the notion of our common home as implied in the Catholic social teachings, in particular, Pope Francis's Encyclical on the care for our common home in reference to the Earth. This is because the Earth mission at the KATC is grounded in social teachings of the Church. The chapter acknowledges that the encyclical does not explicitly deal with the interconnectedness of ecological destruction and domination and exploitation of women due to patriarchal and anthropocentric attitudes towards the universe. Nonetheless, the concept of the common home is employed because the Jesuit initiative has embraced social justice, which includes women's rights and ecology in their mission to the Earth as part of the common good.

The notion of the common home in this chapter is also closely related to Habel's third mission of the Church, envisioned to bring good news to the Earth and therefore framed around the discourse of the Earth mission. According to Habel, a theologian, the Earth mission encompassed a call to worship leaders, a call for advocacy, wisdom recognition and a call to faith.[20] With the call to worship leaders and a call for advocacy, Habel pointed to the sanctity and sacredness of the Earth that deserved celebration and protection, and empathy with the domains of the planet as they suffer injustices caused by humans, through enabling the voice of

---

20   Habel, Earth Mission, 114.

the Earth to be heard.[21] While the principle of recognition of wisdom was linked to exploring the ecosystem of the Earth in order to discern just ways of balancing the needs of all people and habitats of a planet in crisis, the call to faith emphasised affirmation that the ultimate motivation of healing the Earth was grounded in the act of God becoming incarnate to reconcile and heal all things.[22]

In the context of KATC, the call to worship leaders is reflected in strides to protect the Earth through sustainable agriculture. The call for advocacy was exhibited through not only siding with the poor farmers, but also with nature that had been exploited in unsustainable ways, by advocating for sustainable agricultural practices. The emphasis on practices informed by research affirmed the quest to link wisdom and the ecosystem in ways that demonstrated the sacredness of the Earth. The notion of the Earth mission and the care of the common home therefore had in common the acknowledgement that the Earth, or common home, was in an ecological crisis as well as a call for action through the ecological conversion of all. It is within this perspective that the chapter situates the contributions of women towards the care of our common home through sustainable agriculture. According to the Regional Emergency of Office for Southern African, sustainable agriculture is a resource saving agricultural crop production concept that strives to achieve acceptable profits together with high and sustained productivity levels, while concurrently conserving the environment.[23]

The chapter uses gender as an approach to understanding women's contributions that entail (en)gendering the environmental crisis and Earth mission, because perceptions and approaches differ according to one's gender.[24] Therefore, gender as an approach orientation emphasises that women do play an important, though largely unrecognised role (in this case in the Earth mission). Engendering the care of the Earth ought to be anchored in mainstreaming gender equality, which in practice calls for bringing the important voices and activities of women with the goal of sustainable agriculture and the care of the Earth.

By uncovering the contributions of women to the care of the Earth in the Zambian context, as exemplified by narratives of women farmers, the chapter builds on women's studies on the environment in the region that agreed on the connectedness of women and nature, as well as the roles of women in nature. For instance, Siwila,

---

21 Habel, Earth Mission, 114.

22 Habel, Earth Mission, 114.

23 Food and Agricultural Organisation of the United Nations-Regional Emergency Office for Southern Africa. 2010. Farming for the Future: An Introduction to Conservative Agriculture. Regional Emergency Office for Southern Africa Technical Brief 01. Johannesburg.

24 Munro, J. 2000. Gender and Peacebuilding. Prepared for Canadian International Development Agency, 2.

a theologian who traced the ecological footprints of our foremothers, argued that if ecofeminism was to be effective in responding to issues on ecology, discourses around African women's embedded ecological spirituality needed to be retrieved and transformed for the liberation of both women and nature. [25] In addition, Phiri, a theologian, in her analysis of the role of women in the preservation of the environment through the example of the Chisumphi cult, revealed that women were linked to the environment as providers for their homes and families (interaction with nature for domestic production of medicines, relish, firewood, herbs) and for purposes of income, ecological preservation and agricultural activities.[26] While both these studies addressed the indigenous roles of women in the Zambian and Malawian contexts, this chapter complements these perspectives by bringing to the fore the contributions of women to ecological care through agriculture.

Other studies that the chapter hopes to complement are those that have been framed around African Traditional Religion and climate change. For example, Kanene explored the measures that had been undertaken by the Tonga people of southern Zambia to sustain their local biophysical environment and revealed that selective harvesting, totemism and taboos, organic farming, crop rotation and intercropping, sacredness of water sources and traditional authority were the main instruments of environmental conservation.[27] Mwale examined African traditional religion in the context of climate change and argued that the environmental crisis had threatened the religious practices anchored on nature in Zambia, and hence called for tapping into indigenous knowledge systems to address the crisis.[28] These perspectives highlight that the care of our common home and the Earth mission was not a preserve of any particular religion, because each religion was connected to the Earth through different worldviews. Hence the chapter points to how indigenous knowledge systems and Catholic principles interacted in the care of the Earth through the narratives of the women engaged in sustainable agriculture.

Most importantly, the chapter supplements other studies on the KATC that are devoid of the Earth mission discourse.[29] For example, Johannson, in the evaluation of programmes offered at KATC as part of the study of small-scale farming women

25 Siwila, Tracing the Ecological Footprints of our Foremothers, 131.

26 Phiri, I.A. 1996. The Chisumphi Cult: The Role of Women in Preserving the Environment. In: R.R. Ruether (ed). *Women Healing the Earth: Third World Women on Ecology, Feminism, and Religion*. Maryknoll: Orbis, 161-171.

27 Kanene, K.M. 2016. Indigenous Practices of Environmental Sustainability in the Tonga Community of Southern Zambia. *JAMBA: Journal of Disaster Risk Studies*, 8(1):331.

28 Mwale, N. 2014. African Traditional Religion in the Context of Climate Change: A Zambian Perspective. *Journal of Humanities*, 13:1-14.

29 Mtanga, N., Mulauzi, F. & Mwale, I. The Role of Kasisi Agricultural Training Centre in Providing Information on Organic Farming to the Small-Scale Farmers; Phakati. Participatory Rural Development and Technology Transfer.

in sustainable agriculture in Zambia, concluded that the courses had an impact on the lives of the participating small-scale farming women through their ability to spread their knowledge to neighbouring small-scale farmers.[30] These studies had, however, neglected the religious mission of the Church through agriculture. Therefore, the chapter hopes to make a modest contribution by bringing out the voices and contributions of women to the care of the Earth in the Zambian context.

A Historical Description of the Catholic Church and Sustainable Agriculture in Zambia

According to the Zambia National Agricultural policy, agriculture was identified as the key driver of the economy in order to supplement mining, which was the largest contributor of foreign exchange earnings and national revenue.[31] With regard to productivity, agriculture generated between 16 and 20 per cent of the Gross Domestic Product and provided livelihood for more than 70 per cent of the population. With the absorption of about 67 per cent of the labour force, it remained the main source of income and employment for both rural women and men.[32] The Food Agricultural Organisation also revealed that the Government of the Republic of Zambia has made improvements in mainstreaming gender equality and women's empowerment in the agriculture and rural sector.[33] For example, the Government had allocated financial resources to advance gender equality in agriculture and started various initiatives to improve women's productive capacities and strengthen resilience to shocks. Despite these initiatives, women continued to face challenges of unequal access and control over productive resources and sustainable agriculture. For this reason, the Church had stepped into projects for the empowerment of women in Agriculture.

As alluded to earlier, the Catholic Church through the Jesuit Apostolate established the KATC in order to meet the agricultural needs of the people. Having arrived in the country at Chikuni in 1905, and strongly associated with the plough and the Bible in Southern Province, the Jesuits founded the Kasisi mission station in late 1905, where they abandoned the plough in pursuit of sustainable agriculture. The Kasisi mission was built near the Ngwerere River, a perennial stream that the indigenous Soli and Lenje people called Kasisi and regarded as sacred. The farming centre was established in 1974 with the aim of empowering rural communities and improving livelihoods through research, training, extension courses, co-operative development and market linkages. The centre is located in the rural east district of Lusaka province.

---

30   Johannson, Tiyeseko.

31   Government of the Republic of Zambia (GRZ). 2013. *National Agriculture Policy*. Lusaka: Ministry of Agriculture and Livestock, 2.

32   GRZ, National Agriculture Policy, 3.

33   Food Agricultural Organisation, *National Gender Profile*, xi.

The guiding aim of the mission is improving livelihoods and facilitating holistic and sustainable rural development aimed at curbing climate change.[34] The intention was to grow healthier food and work towards a better environment.

When the Centre initially opened, a two-year course was offered for families in conventional agriculture, [35] until 1990 when there was a shift to organic sustainable agriculture and short courses. After the 1990s, the Centre taught farming techniques that did not require fertilisers and pesticides, and that required reduced water input or irrigation in order to promote organic ecologically sustainable agriculture.[36] These practices were driven not only by the rising cost of fertilisers, which a simple farmer could not afford, but also by the drying up of reservoirs. As noted by Habel, the poor of the Earth are most vulnerable in times of ecological disaster.[37] These shifts towards sustainable agriculture also coincided with Pope John Paul II's letter to the world for the World for Peace day of 1 January 1990, called 'Peace with all Creation,' that was exclusively dedicated to ecological concerns. The highlights of the letter included the Church's stewardship role, the ecological crisis, causes of ecological degradation, the application of scientific and technological advances to ecological problems, and a call to action.

Though a Catholic institution, Kasisi is ecumenical in nature as it includes people of different faiths in its ecological agenda. About two-thirds of the farmers who took courses at the Centre were women. This was underpinned by the idea that when African women were successful in farming, their children were better fed and educated and their families moved out of poverty.[38] Most importantly, the focus on women signified that the Centre embraced and targeted the poor, those with less power and influence, the most vulnerable and the marginalised as informed by the Catholic social teachings and Jesuit spirituality.[39]

Narratives of Women's Contributions towards the Care of the Earth

The narratives of two women in the public sphere were trailed in order to understand how they had contributed to the care of the common home through the mission of the Church and as part of the Earth mission through sustainable agriculture, as exemplified in their experiences. The trajectories pointed to how the care of the

34   Nkole, N. 2015. Organic farming - Future for Small-Scale Farmers. *Daily Mail*, 3 June.

35   Phakati, Participatory Rural Development and Technology Transfer, 61.

36   Changula, L.L. 2008. Kasisi Agricultural Training Centre Strategic Plan. Unpublished Manuscript.

37   Habel, Earth Mission, 119.

38   Swan, Canadian Jesuit Favours Oxen over Tractors in Helping Zambian Farmers.

39   DeBerri, E.P., Hug, J.E., Henriot, P.J. & Schultheis, M.J. 2003. *Catholic Social Teaching: Our Best Kept Secret*. New York: Orbis Books; Changula, Kasisi Agricultural Training Centre Strategic Plan.

Earth, through their adoption of sustainable agricultural practices, corresponded with improved livelihood, suggesting that as the Earth was taken care of, so was their well-being over time.

Mama Zimba and Mama Thole (not their real names) were residents in villages near Kasisi mission. They were mothers and members of the Catholic Church. Mama Zimba was a married woman with six (6) children and like many other rural women, she did not complete her secondary school education. She dropped out in junior secondary owing to financial challenges that her parents faced at the time. She was married at the early age of 15 years. Given that her husband was not in any form of employment, farming became her main source of income and livelihood. However, food security remained a challenge owing to the poor rainfall and cost of fertilisers. With the poor rains in most farming seasons, "we could not grow enough food so feeding my family was a problem... my maize never lasted a year."[40] Similarly, Mama Thole was also a farmer and engaged in vegetable farming using water from the well. However, in the dry season the well would dry up and she would be unable to grow the vegetables. This also posed a challenge for food security and an income for sustenance.

These accounts paint the reality of the ecological crisis at hand, which is associated with changes in the rainfall patterns. These experiences are confirmed by studies on the environmental crisis in Zambia, which is driven by numerous factors. For example, it was argued that the exploitative use of natural resources and irresponsible attitudes towards ecology threatened the life-supporting climate on Earth, thereby persistently intimidating the sustainable future of the natural world and humanity.[41] According to the Environmental Council of Zambia, the liberalisation of the Zambian economy contributed to the rate of ecological degradation in the country.[42] This was through the high electricity tariffs and reduction of the fiscal support to the forestry department, which heightened deforestation levels. In addition, the economic emphasis on agribusiness resulted in the use of mechanised commercial farming that is dependent on chemicals which are hazardous to ecology. As highlighted in the *Laudato Si*, the ecological crisis could not be detached from the broken human relationship with God, neighbours and the Earth.[43] Habel also observed that forests, rivers, arable lands, atmosphere and the oceans are all suffering degradation at the

40   Zimba, B. 2018. Personal Communication. 20 March, Chongwe.

41   Mulongo, L.S., Kerre, P., Omboto, P.L & Oseko, J.K. 2010. Natural Resources for Justice, Peace and Reconciliation. *African Ecclesial Review: Reconciliation through Justice and Peace*, 52(1):547-560.

42   Environmental Council of Zambia. 2001. *State of Environment in Zambia 2000*. Lusaka: ECZ.

43   Laudato Si, 2015.

hands of humans and are calling for someone to hear their cries and articulate their plights.[44]

The accounts of the women on the ecological crisis further confirm the conclusions that have been raised in eco-feminist studies: that women suffer the most in the face of a failing ecological crisis. For example, Chirongoma argued that ecological issues were women's issues because they were more vulnerable to sickness, starvation and death from toxins, droughts and famines.[45] In spite of this reality, the chapter argues that women were making strides to change these narratives. For example, the narratives of Mama Zimba and Mama Thole began to change after undergoing the training programmes at Kasisi in 2012. The courses took two (2) weeks and covered sustainable agriculture, organic vegetable production, cooperative management, agri-business, biological pest management, food processing and preservation, small animal production, animal traction and donkey utilisation and participatory guarantee system. Kalinda affirmed that the training programmes were inspired by the Catholic social teachings and deemed as an essential step in educating individuals on the principles of sustainable management and introducing skills necessary for organic sustainable agriculture.[46] As emphasised in the *Laudato Si*, that ecological education which provides information and seeks to form habits needed to occur everywhere in society, the training ignited the idea of being taught as disciples and advocates for the Earth mission.[47]

The participation of these women in the training did not suggest that they had no knowledge on how to care for the Earth. As demonstrated by Siwila, women were connected to nature through teachings on reproductive health and motherhood.[48] Phiri also showed how women were connected to the environment as providers for their homes and families, through ecological preservation and agricultural activities in indigenous African societies.[49] The training of women was also important in that, as Chirongoma has argued, women (especially mothers) are the best teachers and if we teach our children and those around us to revere nature and to consider the preservation of ecology as a divine commission, then the present and the next generations will also make it their priority.[50] The chapter therefore shows the

44   Habel, Earth Mission, 119.

45   Chirongoma, Gleaning for Gender Justice, 2.

46   Kalinda, H. 2018. Promoting Sustainable Organic Agriculture in Zambia - Deputy Executive Director Kasisi Agriculture Farming Centre, *The Solidaridad News*, 15 May.

47   Laudato Si, 2015.

48   Siwila, 2014. Tracing the Ecological Footprints of our Foremothers, 138-139.

49   Phiri, 1996. The Chisumphi Cult.

50   Chirongoma, S. 2012. Karanga-Shona Rural Women's Agency in Dressing Mother Earth: A Contribution towards an Indigenous Eco-feminist Theology. *Journal of Theology for Southern Africa*, 138.

integration of Catholic and Indigenous projests through the women's engagement in caring for the Earth.

Towards the end of the training, Mama Zimba and Mama Thole were able to cultivate home gardens and diversify their crops, which included rape, pumpkin leaves, onion, tomato, green pepper, kale, carrot and cabbage. Other crops included maize, soya beans, sweet potatoes, green manures, cowpeas and cassava. By diversifying crops, farmers attracted more beneficial insects, improved their diets and safeguarded themselves against over-reliance on a single crop.[51] It must however be noted that crop rotation and multi-cropping were not new, as these were practices that used to be associated with traditional agriculture. They had only been done away with by subsidised agriculture, which encouraged Earth-damaging practices perpetuated by mono-crop farming. As revealed by the Ministry of Agriculture and Co-operatives Annual report, the institutionalised government support to the production of hybrid maize (mono-cropping) led to a decline in the yield of traditional staple foods such as sorghum, cassava, relish-like pumpkin leaves, beans and groundnuts.[52] Therefore, the adoption of new agricultural practices from KATC signifies the value attached to Earth friendly agriculture production.

In addition, the women contribute towards the care of the Earth through the adoption of organic farming. As Mama Zimba stated:

> Only manure is used. So we first make manure and after that, we start making holes. Then after making the holes we put manure into the holes. Then in October we start putting seeds in the holes... we don't put chemicals.[53]

The trainee farmers at Kasisi were discouraged from using synthetic fertilisers but were instead encouraged to restore soil fertility through the use of compost and animal manure, green manures (*Sunn hemp* and velvet beans) and planting of nitrogen-fixing shrubs, trees and cover crops (like cowpeas).[54] This went hand in hand with land management practices that conserved and built soils, such as no-till farming, mulching, crop rotation and improved fallows.[55] The women were encouraged to use renewable resources sustainably, such as soil, trees and water, as affirmed by Mama Thole, a farmer. This resonated with the argument that natural resources and the ecosystem were the bedrock of agricultural production and that

---

51   Kalinda, Promoting Sustainable Organic Agriculture in Zambia.

52   Ministry of Agricultural and Co-operatives. 1988. Soils and Research Branch: Adaptive Research and Planning Teams Annual Report. Lusaka.

53   Zimba, B. 2018. Personal Communication. 20 March. Chongwe.

54   Kalinda, Promoting Sustainable Organic Agriculture in Zambia.

55   Phakati, Participatory Rural Development and Technology Transfer, 62.

sustainability of livelihoods was dependent upon a vibrant ecosystem.[56] This ignited the sacredness of the Earth which in turn called for the care of the Earth, as religion and nature interacted through the act of farming.

It was common practice among many Zambian communities to burn the whole bush and the crop fields during dry season. This was done as part of the culture of regenerating the vegetation although it is detrimental to the soil. For instance, among the Bemba of Northern Zambia, the practice was known as *chitememe* and involved cutting trees and burning them prior to the start of the rainy season (spring).[57] However, the flames are detrimental to the soils, as they destroy organic matter and make the soil poor. The women's action of letting go of this practice, signifies hearing the cry of the Earth and reconciling with the Earth.[58] It also shows the moral responsibility to care for the present and future generations, especially the poor, by protecting ecology. This was underpinned by the Catholic social teachings of stewardship and the common good. The principle of the common good implies that the goods of the Earth should be used for the benefit of all, from a balanced social, cultural and community standpoint.[59]

The women also adopted agroforestry as a practice to use nature responsibly. For example, they planted trees like the *musangu* and *moringa* to improve soil fertility and provide a natural windbreaker for the land. At the same time, the trees were a source of firewood and fodder for livestock. In addition, these trees have medicinal value and underpin the relevance of divine communion with the rest of the ecology. This goes hand in hand with alley farming, in which nitrogen fixing trees are planted alongside agricultural crops as a source of mulch and nutrients.[60] Tree planting was already part of indigenous society as women used to plant trees on special occasions, such as during the birth of a child and marriages. What was significant about the planting of trees in these narratives, however, was that the women had adopted drought resistant trees that not only produced protein-rich and nutritious edible leaves but also improved livestock health.

Apart from *moringa*, for instance, the leaves of *Neem* and snake bean yielded natural pesticides that could be powdered or infused as tea and applied to crops.[61] The

56   Sampson, K. 2010. Smallholder Entrepreneurs: A Key Solution to African Agricultural Development. Lilongwe: GRASP.

57   Kaunda, C.J. 2016. Towards an African Eco-gender Theology: A Decolonial Theological Perspective. *Stellenbosch* Theological Journal, 2(1):184.

58   Habel, Earth Mission, 114.

59   Klein, T.A & Laczniak, G.R. 2009. Applying Catholic Social Teachings to Ethical Issues in Marketing. *Journal of Micromarketing*, 29(3):233-244.

60   Phakati, Participatory Rural Development and Technology Transfer.

61   UNDP, Kasisi Agricultural Training Centre, 6.

women have also planted fruit trees that serve as windbreakers or living fences. KATC had helped to establish 30 community nurseries where over 5,000 seedlings are grown annually.[62] This is significant in that while it was easy for the KATC to establish community nurseries, the success of this initiative is dependent on the participants. As such, Mama Zimba and Mama Thole have taken up a leading role in the care of the Earth in their villages, including advocating for the planting of trees.

In addition, the women have embraced simple farming technologies. Oxen were used instead of tractors, as they also provided manure, and animal manure in general was used to fertilise the soils.[63] Hence Mama Zimba and Thole not only keep cattle, but also donkeys, goats and poultry whose excrement is used for the purposes of fertilizing the soils. The women have also applied scientific insights acquired from training to their farming activities. Continued extension visits and study groups are added advantages.

The Catholic Church has a responsibility to locate modern scientific understandings within a Christian vision of the ecology.[64] At Kasisi, this was translated into a research agenda on sustainable organic agriculture technologies and practices, such as the verification trials of both indigenous and exotic technology as well as technology generation trials in which new farming ideas are tested and the science behind indigenous knowledge is established and explained. The research was done in partnership with recognised local and international institutions, such as the University of Zambia, Mulungushi University and the Zambia Agricultural Research Institute. This resonated with the call that science needed to inform the Earth mission as part of the mission's call to recognise wisdom.[65]

The women have further contributed to the care of the Earth through the use of networking groups that signify solidarity. The Centre encouraged the formation of study circle groups in the villages that adopted an adult participatory education approach.[66] As such, the two women were leaders of their working groups that consisted of between 7 to 12 farmers. The meetings they held as different working groups helped them to discover the common need to care for the environment.[67] Through the initiative, the women learnt to work in groups and began to advocate for change collectively by teaching and sharing their experiences with others in the communities. As such, they are agents of change and role models for other women

62   Kalinda, Promoting Sustainable Organic Agriculture in Zambia.
63   UNDP, Kasisi Agricultural Training Centre, 7.
64   Paul. J. 1965. Pastoral Constitution on the Church in the Modern World. *Gaudium et Spes*, 7 December.
65   Habel, Earth Mission, 120.
66   Changula, Kasisi Agricultural Training Centre Strategic Plan.
67   Zimba, B. 2018. Personal Communication. 22 March. Chongwe.

in the villages. As lead farmers, both women managed a demonstration plot on their farms that was also a referral project for other farmers. This signifies that women are making strides to care for the Earth in their own contexts, a dimension that deserved to be captured in the mission of the Church to the Earth.

Ultimately, the women's care of the Earth corresponds with improved livelihoods as they point to the ability to supplement their income from the gardens and rain fed crops and hiring out donkeys for fetching water, transporting harvest and ripping fields. Apart from these, their confidence, leadership abilities, family relationships, nutrition in their diet and financial positions have changed. This is accompanied by changes in their perspective on agriculture, knowledge and skill in practicing organic agriculture, collaboration with other farmers, participation in markets, interests and capacity in gardening and animal rearing. Other benefits are that the women are able to send their children and other dependents to school, build houses, acquire water pumps and pipes to irrigate the gardens and invest in solar energy, among other things.

While the women have made these economic gains, they understand and appreciate ecology as a living entity that deserves care. This is corroborated by Habel's call to the sanctity of the Earth. While the mission of the Centre was to mitigate human suffering and ecological depletion, women were also enabled to recognise their duty to protect their common natural resources. Most importantly, agriculture was not only viewed as a matter of commerce and profit but also as protecting the community, family and individual's lives. This emphasised the solidarity underpinned by the Catholic social teaching. In *Gaudium et Spes*, on the Church in the Modern World, the Second Vatican Council stated that the joys and hopes and the sorrows and anxieties of people today, especially those who are poor and afflicted, are also the joys and hopes, sorrows and anxieties of the Disciples of Christ.[68]

Conclusion

The chapter traced the mission of the Church to the care of the common home, the Earth, through the contributions of women in Zambia's rural set-up. The chapter attempted to demonstrate that the narratives of the women changed as they have taken to caring for the environment through engagement in sustainable agriculture. The trajectories pointed to the confessions of what was wrongly done to the environment, adopting environmentally friendly practices, advocating for the care of the Earth and reaping the rewards through improved livelihoods. The chapter argued that while the Church is behind this success, the trajectories of the

---

68   Paul, J. Pastoral Constitution on the Church in the Modern World.

women need to be documented and celebrated because the women are in essence the implementers of the ecological education they have received. Moreover, it is these women who would transmit this knowledge to future generations. Seen through a gender lens as an approach to sustainable agricultural initiatives which incorporates care for our common home, the chapter agrees that gender identities are social, cultural and political constructs that depend on a range of factors, such as class, age, profession, urban or rural settings, kinship and marital status.[69] In this case, the women's narratives are largely shaped by their context, whose contributions are examples of other women's strides to care for the Earth.

69   Myrttinen, H., Naujoks, J. & El-Bushra, J. 2014. *Re-thinking Gender in Peacebuilding*. London: International Alert.

References

Ayre, C.W. 2010. Eco-salvation: The redemption of all creation. *Worldviews*, 232-242. https://doi.org/10.1163/156853510X507338

Banks, R. & Stevens, P. 1997. *The Complete Book of Everyday Christianity: An A-Z Guide to Following Christ in Every Aspect of Life*. Illinois: Intervarsity Press.

Changula, L.L. 2008. Kasisi Agricultural Training Centre Strategic Plan. Unpublished manuscript.

Chirongoma, S. 2018. Gleaning for Gender Justice in *Laudato Si*: Envisioning a radial eco-feminist conversion. Conference on the radical ecological conversion after *Laudato Si*: Discovering the Intrinsic Value of all Creatures, Human and Non-human. Rome: Pontifical Gregorian University.

Chirongoma, S. 2012. Karanga-Shona Rural Women's Agency in Dressing Mother Earth: A Contribution towards an Indigenous Eco-feminist Theology. *Journal of Theology for Southern Africa*, 142:120-144.

Chirongoma, S. 2005. Motherhood and ecological conversion of Mother Earth. *Women in God's Image*, 10 & 11:8-12.

Compendium of the Social Doctrine of the Church. 2005. Pontifical Council for Justice and Peace. Rome, Italy. Accessed on 24 May 2019.

DeBerri, E.P., Hugh, J.E., Henriot, P.J. & Schultheis, M.J. 2003. *Catholic Social Teaching: Our Best Kept Secret*. New York: Orbis Books.

Environmental Council of Zambia. 2001. *State of Environment in Zambia 2000*. Lusaka: ECZ.

Food and Agriculture Organisation. 2018. *National Gender Profile of Agriculture and Rural Livelihoods – Zambia. Country Gender assessment Series*. Lusaka: FAO.

Food and Agricultural Organisation of the United Nations – Regional Emergency Office for Southern Africa. 2010. Farming for the Future: An Introduction to Conservative Agriculture. Regional Emergency Office for Southern Africa Technical Brief 01. Johannesburg.

Government of the Republic of Zambia. 2013. *National Agriculture Policy*. Lusaka: Ministry of Agriculture and Livestock.

Habel, N. 2010. Earth Mission: The Third Mission of the Church. *Currents in Theology and Mission*, 37(2):114-25.

Johansson, K. 2003. Tiyeseko: A Study on Small-Scale Farming Women in Sustainable Agriculture in Zambia. Unpublished Advanced Paper. Stockholm, Sweden: Sodertorns Hosgkola University College.

Paul, J. 1989. The Ecological Crisis: A Common Responsibility. World Day of Peace. Post Synodical Apostolic, 8 December.

Kalinda, H. 2018. Promoting Sustainable Organic Agriculture in Zambia – Deputy Executive Director Kasisi Agriculture Farming Centre. *The Solidaridad News*, 15 May.

Kanene, K.M. 2016. Indigenous Practices of Environmental Sustainability in the Tonga Community of Southern Zambia. *JAMBA: Journal of Disaster Risk Studies*, 8(1):331. https://doi.org/10.4102/jamba.v8i1.331

Kaunda, C.J. 2016. Towards an African Eco-gender Theology: A Decolonial Theological Perspective. *Stellenbosch Theological Journal*, 2(1):177-202. https://doi.org/10.17570/stj.2016.v2n1.a09

Klein, T.A & Laczniak, G.R. 2009. Applying Catholic Social Teachings to Ethical Issues in Marketing. *Journal of Micromarketing*, 29(3):233-

244. https://doi.org/10.1177/0276146709334530

Lang, M.K. 2018. The Role of Religion in Agriculture: Reflections from the Bamenda Grassfields of Cameroon since Pre-colonial Times. *Mgbakoigba: Journal of African Studies,* 7(2):54-73.

Mckenna, J. 2016. Pope Francis says Destroying the Environment Is a Sin. *The Guardian,* 1 September.

Ministry of Agricultural and Co-operatives. 1988. Soils and Research Branch: Adaptive Research and Planning Teams Annual Report. Lusaka.

Mtanga, N., Mulauzi, F. & Mwale, I. 2014. The Role of Kasisi Agricultural Training Centre in Providing Information on Organic Farming to the Small-scale Farmers in Kasisi Area of Chongwe District, Zambia. Proceedings of the 21st Standing Conference for Eastern, Central and Southern African Library and Information Association (SCECSAL), 305-312.

Mulongo, L.S., Kerre, P., Omboto, P.L. & Oseko, J.K. 2010. Natural Resources for Justice, Peace and Reconciliation. *African Ecclesial Review: Reconciliation through Justice and Peace,* 52(1):547-560.

Munro, J. 2000. Gender and Peacebuilding. Prepared for Canadian International Development Agency.

Mwale, N. 2014. African Traditional Religion in the Context of Climate Change: A Zambian Perspective. *Journal of Humanities,* 13:1-14.

Myrttinen, H., Naujoks, J. & El-Bushra, J. 2014. *Re-thinking Gender in Peacebuilding.* London: International Alert.

Nkole, N. 3 June 2015. Organic Farming – Future for Small-Scale Farmers. *Daily Mail.*

Phakati, J. 2000. Participatory Rural Development and Technology Transfer: Empowering Small-scale Farmers with Appropriate Technology Skills. Proceedings of the Workshop of the Animal Traction Network for Eastern and Southern Africa, 344.

Phiri, I.A. 1996. The Chisumphi Cult: The Role of Women in Preserving the Environment. In: R.R. Ruether (ed). *Women Healing the Earth: Third World Women on Ecology, Feminism, and Religion.* Maryknoll: Orbis. 161-171.

Pope, F. 2015. *Laudato Si: Our Care for Our Common Home.* 24 May.

Sampson, K. 2010. *Smallholder Entrepreneurs: A Key Solution to African Agricultural Development.* Lilongwe: GRASP.

Siwila, L.C. 2014. Tracing the Ecological Footprints of our Foremothers: Towards an African Feminist Approach to Women's Connectedness with Nature. *Studia Historiae Ecclesiasticae,* 40(2):131-147.

Swan, M. 2015. Br. Paul Desmarais, SJ: Reaping the Benefits of Organic Farming in Zambia. *The Guardian,* 22 April.

United Nations Development Programme. 2015. *Kasisi Agricultural Training Centre.* Equator initiative Case Study Series. New York: UNDP.

WOMEN SHAPING THE NARRATIVES WITHIN THE "FIRE CHURCHES" ENVIRONMENT IN GABORONE, BOTSWANA

Maitseo Bolaane[1]
Gwen Lesetedi[2]

Abstract

Botswana has witnessed a mushrooming of so-called "fire churches," which are marked by the 'gospel of prosperity,' encouraging their believers to believe God for wealth, health and marriage. These churches have also opened up avenues for women to take up leadership roles and participate in ministry. This is quite a departure from the mainstream or African Initiated churches where they have clear separate gender roles. This chapter provides a descriptive analysis of the leadership role played by women in the charismatic 'fire churches.' Taking the ethnographic approach, it analyzed brochures, posters, and church websites through

---

[1]   Maitseo M.M. Bolaane graduated with a PhD from the University of Oxford. She is an Associate Professor, and Head of the History Department, Faculty of Humanities at the University of Botswana, teaching various courses in African history (including the understanding of China, Globalisation & Changing Power Relations). She has been involved with the University of Botswana - University of Tromsø Collaborative Programme for San Research and Capacity Building for some time. She is now Director of the San Research Centre at the University of Botswana. Among her key publications is a book examining the impact of wildlife conservation policy on San communities: *Chiefs, Hunters and San in the creation of the Moremi Game Reserve, Okavango Delta: Multiracial interactions and Initiatives, 1956-1979* (2013), a co-edited book on *Parallel Issues and Mutual Challenges for San and Sami People in Research* (2015), and a co-authored book titled *Botswana* (1997). She is one of the editors of a newly released book *Botswana Women Write* (2019). In addition, she has published several peer-reviewed journal articles, book chapters, technical reports, conference proceedings and encyclopedia articles, and reviewed several journal articles and book chapters.

[2]   Dr Gwen N. Lesetedi is a staunch gender activist and is currently a senior lecturer in the Sociology Department, University of Botswana. She holds a PhD (Sociology) from the University of Cape Town, South Africa; MA (Demography) from the Georgetown University, Washington DC., USA; Post-graduate Diploma, Regional Institute of Population Studies, from the University of Ghana, Accra, Ghana; and BA (Sociology and Public Administration) from the University of Zambia, Lusaka, Zambia. She started her working career as a demographer in the then Central Statistics Office (now Statistics Botswana) where she worked for ten years and left to join the University of Botswana in 1994. She has also been a part-time research associate with Women and the Law in Southern Africa (WLSA) since 1994 and conducted studies, most of which have culminated in co-authored publications on the Family, Domestic Violence and HIV and AIDS. She has conducted extensive research and published on gender and development. Her most recent publication is entitled, A Theoretical Perspective on Women and Poverty in Botswana published in the *Journal of International Women's Studies in 2018.*

Facebook and WhatsApp. The study was also based on the authors' observations during visits to some of the 'fire churches' in Gaborone (and its vicinity) and interacting with some of the church members. The study has profiled one of the women in Gaborone to illustrate the various leadership roles played by women in 'fire churches' in the country. Traditionally, churches have been criticised for perpetuating customs and perceptions that women should not hold leadership positions. However, there is an acknowledgement and acceptance of women taking up leadership roles in the 'fire churches.' They lead worship services, preach and engage in training activities. In addition, they use their 'feminine touch' or 'power dress code' to negotiate a public space in the church and this boosts their confidence. Despite embracing gender inclusiveness, there is a need for more comprehensive research regarding the gender relations prevailing in these churches.

Introduction

The chapter is a review of the new Pentecostal and charismatic movement popularly known as 'fire churches' which marks religious innovation in Botswana. Gabriel Famau has written broadly on 'the emergence of 'fire churches' and how they are positioning themselves through the use of new media in Botswana. His research has helped in building background information for this chapter.[3] Botswana has witnessed a spectacular growth of prophetic Christianity, also popularly referred to as 'fire churches,' who preach the 'prosperity gospel,' a doctrine that emphasises the importance of 'personal empowerment,' associated with God's will for people to be blessed with success, well-being and material wealth.[4] The teaching encourages believers to contribute generously to the ministry with assurance to receive blessings of health, marriage and wealth. These churches lay emphasis on how worshippers giving to God or to his anointed prophets/prophetesses will make them rich, healthy and blessed. In this regard the worshippers offer cash or buy merchandise, which include pamphlets, bracelets, car stickers, CDs, anointed oil and holy water. It is not only in terms of emphasis on prosperity that they are different from mainstream churches but also on issues of gender. To a large extent, mainstream churches have clear separate gender roles. For instance, roles like preaching, being pastor or elder are strictly for men, while women can lead the singing, clean the church or serve as ushers.[5]

3   See Faimau, G. 2018. The Emergence of Prophetic Ministries in Botswana: Self-Positioning and Appropriation of New Media. *Journal of Contemporary African Studies*, 36(3):369-385; Faimau, G. and Behrens, C. 2016. Facebooking Religion and the Technologisation of the Religious Discourse: A Case Study of a Botswana-based Prophetic Church. *Online - Heidelberg Journal of Religions on the Internet*, 11[http://online.uni-hd.de]. See also, Faimau, G. 2017. Religious Testimonial Narratives and Social Construction of Identity: Insights from Prophetic Ministries in Botswana. *Cogent Social Sciences*, 3(13):1-16 and Togarasei, L. 2018. History and Characteristics of Pentecostal Christianity in Zimbabwe. In: L. Togarasei (ed). *Aspects of Pentecostal Christianity in Zimbabwe*. Cham: Springer, 33-48.

4   See Faimau, The Emergence of Prophetic Ministries in Botswana, 373-374.

5   Mapuranga, T.P. 2018. Pastors, Preachers and Wives: A Critical Reflection on the Role of Pentecostalism in Women Empowerment in Zimbabwe. In: Togarasei (ed). *Aspects of Pentecostal*

The focus of this chapter is on the emerging women leadership roles and how these women shape narratives and negotiate public religious space in 'fire churches.' This study examines the spaces that these churches provide within their environment which enables women to hold positions of power and decision making. We are also trying to understand if women are affirming their integrity of 'Mother Earth' and 'Mother Nature' within these churches and how they are doing it. The chapter will also show how women are increasingly taking up more active roles in the church hierarchy, taking advantage of the application of technology in church activities and facilitating their occupation of public space. This study took an ethnographic approach by reviewing and analyzing social artefacts such as brochures, posters, car stickers, church websites, etc. This is similar to the digital ethnographic study method of data collection used by Faimau in his study on the emergence of prophetic ministries in Botswana. The method in digital ethnographic study included the content analysis of the ministries' websites, Facebook pages and YouTube channels.[6]

In this study, however, we did not extend our analysis to YouTube channels. We relied mainly on posters, pamphlets and the churches' websites. Most of the posters and pamphlets were sourced from noticeboards around the campus of the University of Botswana. The churches display posters and widely distribute these resources as a way of lobbying about the services offered by their churches. These pamphlets and posters are more noticeable especially when a particular church is hosting an event or a prophet. The posters are mainly displayed on the noticeboards while pamphlets are put in places like classrooms, outside the library and the halls of residence. Information on the churches was also easily accessed via social media, like Facebook and WhatsApp. In addition to analyzing social artefacts, this study was also based on the authors' observations during visits to a few 'fire churches' in Gaborone as well as our interactions with some of the members of these 'fire churches.' Interviews were also conducted with some members of the 'fire church,' and one woman, Dr Pearl Seloma, has been profiled to throw more light on women's leadership roles in the church. In addition, the study secured an interview with a senior member of the Zion Christian Church (ZCC) – which falls under the African independent churches for comparison analysis. The chapter is divided into several sections. It begins with a discussion on the role of women in churches. Under this section the role of women in churches is discussed within the context of 'Mother Earth' and 'Mother Nature.' The role of women in churches in Botswana is also discussed. The

---

Christianity in Zimbabwe. 139-150. The author analyses the ideology of patriarchy and how it reinforces the role of women simply as 'helpers' to their male counterparts, be it their husband, brothers or fathers, promoting women domesticity.

6   Faimau, The Emergence of Prophetic Ministries in Botswana, 376.

chapter also provides a description of 'fire churches' in Botswana before presenting the findings of the study and the conclusion.

The Role of Women in the Church

The general traditional discourse has been projecting women as largely passive, vulnerable, poor, and with no sense of leadership. Since the 1990s, African theologians have been looking at gender within the context of Africa's traditional society, discussing the exploitation, oppression and marginalization of women and how they are still treated like men's property.[7] According to one of the leading scholars, Mercy Amba Oduyoye, African women's theology developed in the context of global challenges and situations in Africa's religio-cultural context that called for transformation.[8] African Women's theologies were promoted through a movement called *Circle of Concerned African Women Theologians*.[9] Through this movement, African theologians engaged with gender issues, biblical and theological interpretation and feminist analysis to expose harm and injustices in society and the teachings and practices of the church.[10]

Scholars argue that in most of the African traditional societies women are treated as second-class citizens.[11] The literature draws examples from how women are being portrayed in some proverbs, which refer to women as "old cooking pots,"

7   Daniel, K. 2010. The Role of Women in Church in Africa. *International Journal of Sociology and Anthropology*, 2(6):128; Oduyoye, M. 1995. *Daughter to Anowa: African Women and Patriarchy*. New York: OrbisBooks, 1-218. See also, Pui-lan, K. 2004. Mercy Amba Oduyoye and African Women's Theology. *Journal of Feminist Studies in Religion*, 20(1):7-22; Nkomazana, F. 2008. The Experiences of Women within Tswana Cultural History & Its Implications for the History of Church in Botswana. *Studia Historiae Ecclesiasticae*, 2:83-116. See also, Nkomazana, F. 2018. The Role of Women, Theology, and Ecumenical Organisations in the Rise of Pentecostal Churches in Botswana. In: A. Afolayan, O. Yacob-Haliso and T. Falola (eds). *African Histories and Modernities Pentecostalism and Politics in Africa*. Cham: Palgrave Macmillan. 184-186; Oduyoye, M.A. and Kanyoro, R.A. 1992. *The Will to Arise: Women, Tradition, and the Church in Africa*. New York: Orbis Books.

8   Oduyoye, M.A. 2001. *Introducing African Women's Theology*. Cleveland: The Pilgrim Press, 38. For further reading see Oduyoye, *Daughter to Anowa: African Women and Patriarchy* and Oduyoye and Kanyoro, *The Will to Arise*.

9   Fiedler, R.N. 2019. A History of the Circle of Concerned African Women Theologians (1989-2007). Mzuzu: Mzuni Press, 6-8.

10 Oduyoye, *African Women and Patriarchy*, 38-41; Kanyoro, M. 2001. Engendered Communal Theology: African Women's Contribution to Theology in the Twenty-First Century. *Feminist Theology, FT*, 27:36-56; Dube, 2007. 'God Never Opened the Bible to Me': Women Church Leaders in Botswana. In: F. Nkomazana and L. Lanner (eds). *Aspects of the History of the Church in Botswana*. 210-216; Togarasei, L. 2008. Fighting HIV and AIDS with the Bible: Towards HIV and AIDS Biblical Criticism. In E. Chitando (ed). *Mainstreaming HIV in Theology and Religious Studies: Experiences and Explorations*. Geneva: WCC. 211.

11 See Oduyoye, *African Women and Patriarchy*, 4-5 & Kanyoro, African Women's Contribution to Theology, 37-38.

"large wooden stirring spoons," and "hoes," usually with a derogatory meaning.[12] In support of this view an example could be drawn from a Setswana proverb which says *Ga dike di etelelwa ke manamagadi pele* (women cannot lead), because they are considered passive. As noted by Daniel, in some cases "women themselves accept this situation."[13] However, Daniel also observes that African society recognises the woman's diverse roles as a mother, wife, educator and nurturer and makes reference to traditional priesthood, which embraces both women and men.[14] As widely acknowledged by African scholars, this demonstrates that African women have always been wielding considerable influence in society. Women's liberation movements and feminist theologians associate a woman with being 'Mother Earth,' 'Mother Nature' and 'Mother Africa' (as in line with the theme of the 5th Pan-African Circle of Concerned African Women Theologians Conference, 1-4 July 2019, University of Botswana).

The name 'Mother Earth' is associated with Greek mythology, where Gaia, the great goddess, is equated to 'Mother Earth' and 'Mother Nature.'[15] According to the narration, Gaia created herself out of 'primitive chaos.'[16] As 'Mother Nature,' Gaia personifies the entire ecosystem on Earth. The goddess was considered to have created the universe and was therefore worshiped as the universal Mother. According to Greek mythology, it is from the fertile womb of the goddess that all life begins, and therefore 'Mother Nature' or 'Mother Earth' nurtures, heals and supports all life in this planet. In the same context, it is unto 'Mother Earth' that all living things "must return after their allotted span of life is over."[17] Using the framework of spirituality, life and death is understood in this context where a mother would give birth to a child, breast feed, be caring, loving and nurture into adulthood. When human beings die, they are buried in the soil, and return to 'Mother Nature.' In real life, a mother is not only the first object of attachment that we encounter, but she provides food, takes care of our health and hygiene and answers our every need. She provides guidance until the child is grown up enough to fend for himself or herself. Understood through feminine perspective, 'Mother Nature' is viewed as always working to achieve and maintain harmony, wholeness and balance within the environment.[18]

---

12   Daniel K. 2010. The Role of Women in the Church in Africa. *International Journal of Sociology and Anthropology*, 2(6):128.

13   Daniel, The Role of Women in Church in Africa, 128.

14   Daniel, The Role of Women in Church in Africa, 129-130.

15   March J. 1998. *Cassell's Dictionary of Classical Mythology*, London: Cassell and Co, 324.

16   March. *Cassell's Dictionary of Classical Mythology*, 324. See also, David, K. and Osborne, L. 2007. *Greek medicine.net*, Blog Online Store (greekmedicine.net/introductions.htm/)

17   March. 1998. Dictionary of Classical Mythology, 324.

18   David and Osborne, *Greek medicine.net*, Blog Online Store, 1.

The role of women in the Bible is highly recognised and appreciated by theologians, and reference is made to parts of the Bible which preaches equality and does not discriminate between male and female. They make reference to some verses in the Bible to support their position. However, some feminist theologians also make reference to the contradictory nature of biblical materials.[19] The text of Galatians 3:28 consider them equal in the eyes of Jesus Christ: "There is neither Jew nor Gentile, neither slave nor free, nor is there male and female, for you are all one in Christ Jesus." In addition, Matthew 23:8 emphasises the same message that we "have only one teacher and all of you are equal as brothers and sisters." Some chapters in the Bible make reference to women participating as deacons, and companions of Jesus and Paul and others (Romans 16:1-7). As noted by Mary McKenna, women pastoral functions included teaching and caring for the sick, a role associated with being 'Mother Earth,' 'Mother nature.'[20]

To underscore the role of women in church, we wish to make reference to some women in the Bible who played prominent roles when travelling with Jesus Christ. In the Gospel of Luke 8:2-3, Mary Magdalene is listed among the women who travelled with Jesus Christ and helped support his ministry "out of their resources."[21] Mary Magdalene, Mary mother of James, and Salome were amongst those who witnessed the crucifixion of Jesus, and were also present at his burial (see Matthew 27:55-56). Together with a group of women, which included Jesus's mother, they were the first to witness the empty tomb, and the first to testify to Jesus's resurrection (see Mathew 28:1-10; Luke 2 & 24:11; Mark 16:9). Mainstream churches, such as Anglican and Lutheran, consider Mary Magdalene to be a saint, while other protestant churches honour her as a heroine of faith. We should also note the Catholic emphasis on Mary (the mother of Jesus, "the blessed virgin Mary"). In the Bible, women are not only appreciated for truly understanding Jesus's teachings, but also noted for their sense of independence and boldness in holding the torch and a bowl of myrrh and visiting Jesus's tomb. However, Ehrman argues that despite being one of the female central figures, central as in being one of the followers of Jesus, unlike Paul the Apostle, Mary Magdalene has left behind no writings of her own.[22]

---

19 Daniel, The Role of Women in Church in Africa, 129-130. See also Dube, M.W. 2007. 'God Never Opened the Bible to Me': Women Church Leaders in Botswana. In: F. Nkomazana and L. Lanner (eds). *Aspects of the History of the Church in Botswana*. Pietermaritzburg: Cluster Publications. 210-216; Dube, M.W. 1996. Readings of Semoya: Batswana Women's Interpretations of Matt 15:21-28. *SEMEIA*, (73):11-129.

20 McKenna, M.L. 1967. *Women in the Church Role and Renewal*. New York: PJ Kennedy, Sons, 153.

21 Ehrman, B.D. 2006. Truth and Fiction in The Da Vinci Code: A Historian Reveals What We Really Know about Jesus, Mary Magdalene, and Constantine. Oxford: Oxford University Press, 267.

22 Ehrman, Jesus, Mary Magdalene, and Constantine, 267.

Although the general view is that the role played by women in African mainstream and some independent churches is inferior, incapable due to their nature of being biologically female, the roles of women in the new Pentecostal charismatic movement are largely similar to those in the Bible. They embrace the values of feminism and motherhood through these churches, as will be demonstrated later in the chapter. Some women have had the opportunity to perform pastoral functions in the Botswana contemporary church as they are operating within today's world, emphasizing equal rights and some dignity for both female and male. Some of these roles include leadership. In the 'fire churches,' women have a strong voice which is not only confined to singing and clapping hands, but involves taking up leadership roles as prophetesses, church elders or even as founders of churches. The acknowledgement of gender roles and the expressive ways of praise and worship are characteristics of 'fire churches' which sets them apart from mainstream churches.

According to Charlotte Spink (2003:22), women are attracted to 'fire churches' or 'churches of prosperity' because these churches have broken away from the traditional religious norms. Women are not restricted to holding the traditional roles only aligned to that of 'Mother nature' or 'Mother Earth'; they can aspire to hold any position within the church structures. The principle of 'prosperity' also encourages women to realise their ambitions and become prosperous and independent. The church provides a conducive environment or 'space' where all this can be achieved and career opportunities are provided through the church hierarchies.[23] The style of worship practiced in the church is also appealing to a lot of worshippers, not only women. It is similar to what you would find in a night club or at a party but in a much safer environment. In such a space women can feel free and safe without having to risk their lives in the name of seeking entertainment at a club.

In addition, the church also provides social support and networks, which can stand in the place of weakening family ties. These networks offer the same stability that you would find in a family, like emotional and social support in times of need. By extension, through these networks young females have opportunities to meet marriage partners. Since these churches break away from the traditional modes of religion, they encourage all women to always look beautiful and smart when coming to church. They dress up in the latest styles with their hair nicely done and wearing jewellery. Space is also provided for not only women, but even young people to aspire to hold any position in the church. Leadership training (including in-house training) is provided for all church members despite their age and gender. This is an outright rejection of a lopsided male dominance in the church, making the 'fire

---

23   Spink, C. 2003. Panacea or Painkiller? The Impact of Pentecostal Christianity on Women in Africa. *Critical Half*, 1(1):20-25.

churches' quite appealing to the young people and women. This is contrary to what happens in most mainline churches and African Independent Churches, where leadership positions are strictly for men and the elderly.

Male dominance and control over females is practiced uiversally in a social system referred to as patriarchy.[24] It cuts across all social institutions, starting in the family and spreading across all other institutions, including religion. All religions all over the world reflect male dominance in their hierarchical structures.[25] The dominant role of the Creator or God in most religions is male, while females are associated with motherhood roles, such as 'Mother nature.'[26] In some organizations women are not allowed to hold senior positions or even preach, as in the case of the Zion Christian Church as presented in the narration above. The Catholic Church, on the other hand, which falls under the mainline churches, also holds similar positions to that of the ZCC church when it comes to the roles that women play in the organization. The church does not allow women to hold senior positions or become priests. A priest plays the role of Christ, who is a man, and therefore this role cannot be played by a woman.[27] In the Catholic Church, all the senior positions, starting with the Pope, all the cardinals, archbishops, bishops and priests are men. Women are usually relegated to household-related chores like cleaning the church, or looking after the sick and comforting the bereaved. However, a review of the literature on Botswana has shown that in the Pentecostal movement, women have always been involved in the running of the church and holding key leadership positions.[28]

Prior to the emergence of African Initiated Churches (AICs) in the 1950s, mainstream churches had dominated Christianity with minimal regard for women. According to Langford they were usually assigned gender-specific roles but not ordained as pastors.[29] Nkomazana observes that women "were relegated to the background and not recognised for their efforts."[30] However, the University of Botswana theologians argue that AICs and Pentecostal churches and their theology recognised the role

24   Lim, Y.C.L. 1997. Capitalism, Imperialism and Patriarchy: The Dilemma of Third-World Women Workers in Multinational Factories. Dhaka: The University Press Limited, 220.

25   Klingorová, K. and Havlíček, T. 2015. Religion and Gender Inequality: The Status of Women in the Societies of World Religions. *Moravian Geographical Reports*, 23(2):1-10.

26   Klingorová and Havlíček. Religion and Gender Inequality: The Status of Women in the Societies of World Religions, 3.

27   Klingorová and Havlíček, Religion and Gender Inequality, 3.

28   Nkomazana, F. 2000. The Profile of Reverend Mrs Rebecca Motsitsi of the Pentecostal Holiness Church in Botswana. *Religion, & Gender in BOLESWA Occasional Papers in Theology & Religion*, 1(7):44-59; The Role of Women, Theology, and Ecumenical Organisations, 181-202. See also Dube. 'God Never Opened the Bible to Me': Women Church Leaders in Botswana, 210-216.

29   Langford, J. 2017. Feminism and Leadership in the Pentecostal Movement. *Feminist Theology*, 26(1):69-79.

30   Nkomazana, The Role of Women, Theology, and Ecumenical Organisations, 184.

p0layed by women in the church.[31] Amanze's book, *Botswana Handbook of Churches*, has recorded a few churches founded and established by women, laying a research foundation for Botswana theologians.[32] Nkomazana published a profile of a female reverend to show an increase in women establishing new ministries.[33] In her paper titled "Women Church Leaders in Botswana," Dube discusses the strategies used by women to assume active leadership in the church and society, noting alternative ways of women's empowerment.[34] In a separate publication on "Botswana Women's Interpretation of Matthew 15:21-28," she demonstrates how Botswana women were inspired by the Bible stories to break cultural barriers that had been hindering them in directly playing various meaningful roles in the life of the church.[35] In addition to these works on Botswana is Tshinamo's study on "Women Church Leaders in Botswana," showing an increase in the number of women penetrating the church's public space and seeking ordination and leadership positions.[36] A good illustration is a profile of "Reverend Rebecca Motsisi of the Pentecostal Holiness Church in Botswana" by Nkomazana.[37] This profile is evidence that Rebecca, in pastoring her own congregation, demonstrated that women were not only playing key roles in the economic development of the country, but were also capable church leaders.

Studies conducted by Dube and Nkomazana have shown that in the Pentecostal movement women explore their 'Mother Nature.'[38] Women were viewed as being friendly, approachable, good public relation officers, good communicators, charismatic and able to negotiate their space within the church environment. Like in the case of Mary Magdalene in the Bible, who is not only noted for her beauty but also for supporting Jesus Christ's ministry, as it will be demonstrated later in the analysis of posters, women in 'fire churches' are also very particular about their appearance, especially those at the pulpit. Aspects of 'Mother Nature' and 'Mother Earth' are also associated with ensuring that the church environment is kept clean and orderly. In most churches women often multi-task and take care of the cleaning of the church, arranging of the chairs and the decorations. Through women church clubs, associations and organizations they build social networks and extend

---

31   See Dube, Women Church Leaders in Botswana, 210-216.

32   Amanze, J. 1994. *Botswana Handbook of Churches*. Gaborone: Pula Press.

33   Nkomazana, The Profile of Reverend Mrs Rebecca Motsitsi, 44-59.

34   Dube, Women Church Leaders in Botswana, 210-216.

35   Dube, M.W. 1994. Reading of Semoya: Batswana Women's Interpretations of Matt 15: 21-28. *SEMEIA*, (73):111-129.

36   Tshinamo, G. 1999. Women Church Leaders in Botswana: A Documentation. Unpublished MA Dissertation. Gaborone: University of Botswana, 110.

37   Nkomazana, The Profile of Reverend Mrs Rebecca Motsitsi, 44-59.

38   Dube, Women's Interpretations of Matt 15:21-28, 11-29 & Women Church Leaders in Botswana, 210-216. See also Nkomazana, The Profile of Reverend Mrs Rebecca Motsitsi, 44-59 & Nkomazana, The Role of Women, Theology, and Ecumenical Organisations, 194.

spirituality, fellowship, caring and comforting services through visits to the sick and the elderly. However, the Botswana theologians, such as Nkomazana, note that women worshippers of the charismatic and Pentecostal movement also meet outside the church structure for worship, Bible reading, healing, prayer and testimony.[39] In other words, they do not only focus on cooking and catering at weddings and funerals, but take advantage of opportunities through their churches, Christian organizations and institutions to gain key positions in church. The majority serve as Sunday school teachers and on local, regional and national church committees. They go for training for ministerial positions and some even compete for church positions in inter-denominational organizations, such as Evangelical Fellowship Botswana (EFB) and Botswana Council of Churches. Some go to the extent of leading women organizations. For illustration, Nkomazana gives a good example of a prophetess who is the founder and leader of the 'Battle Cry Ministries' and currently general secretary of EFB.[40] Another good example in Gaborone is that of Pastor Felicity Chijena, born in Tutume (a village north-east of Botswana), serving as the Botswana Group Pastor and overseeing more than 48 churches under Christ Embassy.

Mainline churches may no longer be as attractive as 'fire churches' because of their nature of being confined to their places of worship as well as conforming to hierarchical structures which are predominantly and essentially male. To a large extent mainline churches, such as the Dutch Reformed Church in Botswana, systematically excluded its womenfolk from being ordained as ministers, keeping them away from leadership roles.[41] A good illustration here is when some 'concerned group' within the Dutch Reformed Church in Mochudi (a village south of Botswana) were refusing Moniemang Kgosiemang to be ordained as a priest and she ended up leaving the main church to establish her own. From March to November 2004, a certain journalist, Lekopanye Mooketsi of *Mmegi* newspaper, devoted time to expose gender discrimination within the Dutch Reformed Church in Botswana. The journalists Mooketsi and Sharon Mothala ran headlines such as "Botswana: Dutch Church Threatened with Legal Action," "Dispute Over Female Priest Goes to Court," "Out You Go" and "Kgosiemang expulsion splits Church." The Mochudi branch witnessed a dispute over the ordaining of the first female priest by the Dutch Reformed Church in Botswana. The "concerned group," composed of some church choir members, instructed a law firm in Gaborone to challenge the ordination of Reverend Kgosiemang.[42] They were opposing the ordination on the basis that

---

39   Nkomazana, The Role of Women, Theology, and Ecumenical Organisations Botswana, 190.

40   Nkomazana, The Role of Women, Theology, and Ecumenical Organisations, 190.

41   Mooketsi, L. 2004. Botswana Dutch Church Threatened with Legal Action & Botswana: Dispute Over Female Priest Goes to Court. *Mmegi*, 18 November.

42   Ibid.; Kgosiemang: Expulsion Splits Church. *Mmegi*, 4 March, 20 May & 18 November; See also Mothala, S. 2017. Out You Go: Dutch Reformed Churches Fire Members. *The Voice*, 24 November.

the church constitution discriminated against women ministers. Kgosiemang was dismissed from church leadership in a dramatic fashion during a church service, invoking section 10 of the church order or constitution, terminating her services. The discrimination against Kgosiemang was not based on her leadership qualities but on the fact that she was a woman.

'Fire Churches' or 'Prophetic Churches' in Botswana

The Batswana[43] are a highly religious people, with Christianity being the most dominant religion, and women are always the majority at a church gathering. Christianity was introduced amongst the Batswana in the 19th century by the London Missionary Society (LMS).[44] According to the 2011 Population and Housing Census, 79 per cent of the population is classified as Christians.[45] Based on their doctrines and practices, there are three main categories of Christianity in Botswana: the mainline churches, African Initiated churches and Evangelical or Pentecostal or Charismatic churches.[46] Churches which are classified as mainline include Anglican, Catholic, Lutheran and Seventh Day Adventists, just to mention a few. These are missionary founded churches associated with international denominations and they preach the gospel of salvation and shared resources. The African Initiated Churches can be described as a form of indigenous religion which practices a combination of Christian worship and traditional ancestral worship. Under this category you find churches like the Spiritual Healing Church of Botswana, St John Apostolic Faith Mission, Head Mountain, Head Mountain of God Apostolic Church in Zion Botswana, Eloyi Christian Church, and the Zion Christian Church.[47]

The third and final category is the Pentecostal and Charismatic, also popularly referred to as 'fire churches.' These churches preach the gospel of prosperity and focus on being born again and Holy Spirit filled.[48] They encourage the members to

---

43 Batswana in this context refers to the people of Botswana or citizens of Botswana (it is the plural form of Motswana).

44 Nkomazana, F. 1999. London Missionary Society, Church & State in Colonial Bechuanaland: The Case of Bangwato, 1867-1923. *Scriputura: International Journal of Bible, Religion and Theology in Southern Africa*, 71(4):303-312. See also Tlou, T. and Campbell, A. 1984 & 1997. *History of Botswana*. Gaborone: Macmillan, 181-193.

45 Kgosimore, M., Sebolai, B., Macheng, B.J. and Mabote, M.M. 2014. Religious Perspectives in Botswana: Population and Housing Census 2011 Dissemination Seminar. Gaborone: Statistics Botswana, 326.

46 Nkomazana, The Role of Women, Theology, and Ecumenical Organisations, 188.

47 Kealotswe, O.N. 1994. *An African Independent Church Leader Bishop Smart Mthembu of the Head Mountain of God Apostolic Church in Zion Botswana*. Studies on the Church in Southern Africa V. Gaborone: University of Botswana Department of History & Department of Theology and Religious Studies, 4-5.

48 Heuser, A. 2016. Charting African Prosperity Gospel economies. *Herv.teol. stud*, 72(4):1-9. See also, Nkomazana, The Role of Women, Theology, and Ecumenical Organisations, 193.

strive to attain wealth. In other words, they take worshipping as a business entity.[49] Botswana has witnessed an increase in the number of 'fire churches' over the past two decades. In May 2015 the Department of Civil and Registration had registered 1,936 churches, the majority being New or Modern Pentecostal Churches under which the prophetic churches or 'fire churches' fall.[50] Although referred to as churches, the preferred word of reference is 'ministry.' The use of the word 'ministry' allows for fluidity of membership, as an individual can be part of a ministry despite belonging to another church.[51] Narratives have been told of worshippers from mainline churches attending sermons, healing or prayer sessions of prophetic churches whenever they feel the need for spiritual upliftment. However, for the purpose of this study they will be referred to as the prophetic church or 'fire churches.'

In Botswana, like in other parts of sub-Saharan Africa, the 'fire churches' have become increasingly attractive because of their charismatic nature and how they capture the public space. Women make a statement through their dress code when coming for 'fire church' attendance. They are associated with eloquence in preaching the 'Word,' the congregation praying in tongues, or the church's music band playing some 'swinging gospel highlife.'[52] In her essay, Meyer addresses the new public appearance of Pentecostalism in Ghana, where she describes Christianity as a brand that has become increasingly present in the public sphere since the liberalization and commercialization of state-controlled and state-owned media.[53]

In this paper Meyer looks at technologies of transmission intrinsic to booklets, radio, TV, video and the computer, and how loudspeakers are crucial mediators of the divine message aiming to reach the congregation. The new Pentecostalism is seeking to capture the public space not only through images but also through sound systems. In the case of Botswana, the public appearance of Christianity is also being evoked by visual technologies, including billboards advertising along roadsides, large posters on walls and noticeboards of key places such as the University of Botswana, and stickers on cars and bedroom doors. The divine message is also popularised through the easy accessibility of booklets such as the *Rhapsody of Realities, Daily Devotional* of

49   Togarasei, L. 2012. Mediating the Gospel: Pentecostal Christianity and Media Technology in Botswana and Zimbabwe. *Journal of Contemporary Religion,* 27(2):257-274. Retrieved 20 September 2019.

50   Faimau and Beherens, Facebooking Religion and the Technologisation of the Religious Discourse, 68.

51   Faimau and Beherens. Facebooking Religion and the Technologisation of the Religious Discourse, 68.

52   See Meyer, B. 2003. Impossible Representations. Pentecostalism, Vision and Video Technology in Ghana. *Working Papers,* Department of Anthropology and African Studies. Mainz: Johannes Gutenberg University, 1-22.

53   Meyer, Pentecostalism, Vision and Video Technology in Ghana, 6. See also Meyer, B. 2010. There is a Spirit in that Image: Mass-Produced Jesus Pictures and Protestant-Pentecostal Animation in Ghana. *Comparative Studies in Society and History,* 52(1):100-130.

Christ Embassy,[54] video, DVD and CD technology. In this context, the Pentecostal movement assumes a key role in commodifying Christianity and feeding Botswana's urban and peri-urban new image-economy through gospel concerts, sale of music, sermons and booklets.

Technology is widely used in the 'fire churches' during worship as well as in the spread of the word of God and promotion of their church. Modern technology includes print media and electronic media. Print media is quite effective in the spreading of the gospel. Churches produce booklets, pamphlets, magazines and posters which are displayed everywhere. They also make use of electronic media by spreading the word of God through radio, television, computers, digital projectors and electronic billboards, just to mention a few. The computer has also allowed for the use of social media, like the internet and e-mails. Music on CDs, DVDs and audio cassettes have been used to spread the gospel. Not only do they contain music, but some also have recordings of sermons and scriptures. In addition to spreading the word of God, these are also sold to raise funds for the church.

However, the most common form of media technology utilised by the churches is the mobile phone. Its main advantage is that most people have access to a mobile phone and therefore it can be used to reach members in all corners of society. The mobile phone is used to send prayers, bible verses, inspirational messages, blessings, prophecies and other religious messages. It can also be used to send church notices informing the members about church activities.[55] In this way the congregants can network and keep in touch. The use of technology has contributed to the growth of the 'fire churches.'[56] The use of technology can also be linked to women taking up more leadership roles in these churches in comparison to mainline churches. In a study conducted in Spain on gender and religion on a group of immigrant women, it was found that the use of technology has made information more readily available to them and as a result they felt empowered.[57] Some of the women attested to the fact that they could access information on their own without having to go through the traditional means like waiting to attend a church service or participate in a Bible study.

---

54 Christ Embassy church under the international leadership of Pastor Chris Oyakhilome has booklets titled *Rhapsody Realities: Daily Devotional*, Charlotte: Loveworld. The church uses the booklets to reach the whole world with the gospel. One of the popular Pentecostal churches in Botswana is Christ Embassy.

55 Togarasei, L. 2012. Mediating the Gospel: Pentecostal Christianity and Media Technology in Botswana and Zimbabwe, *Journal of Contemporary Religion*, 27(2):259.

56 Faimau, The Emergence of Prophetic Ministries in Botswana, 376.

57 Díez Bosch, M., Lluís Micó, J. and Sabaté Gauxachs, A. 2018. A Phone of My Own. Gender, Religion and Technology. *Journal of Applied Ethics*, 9:9-10.

Although the study cited above was on immigrant women, the same principles apply to other women in similar circumstances. In all this, the issue of competence, type of technological device and access to technology has to be taken into account. The majority of the women interviewed owned a mobile phone and most of them admitted to not being digitally competent and using the phone mainly for talking. However, because the women felt empowered, they could come out into the public sphere and participate in the religious organizations beyond their traditional roles.[58] They were able to communicate with fellow women and were also exposed to the outside world.

In this regard we concur with Meyer's observation that 'fire churches' are a power which cannot be neglected in scholarship because they project a notion of Christian modernity which acknowledges the realities of belief systems in matters of the evil machinations of demons and superstitions, "which a good Christian is supposed to leave behind."[59] Therefore the 'fire churches' are attractive to members because they have a way of bringing hope for a better and more prosperous life. Like in the case of Ghana, while defining themselves through new audio-visual media, Botswana 'fire churches' inform the popular imagination which gives rise to new forms of consciousness and participation.[60] They run prayer programs from morning to late at night and are not restricted to church attendance on Sundays only. 'Fire church ministries' allow the old and the young, men and women to interact in one public space. They all sing and dance, responding to music complemented with sophisticated instruments like guitars and keyboards.

To a large extent, public articulation takes some form of popular entertainment which attracts large gatherings. Unsurprisingly, one of the most notable features of these churches is that the congregants are quite youthful. In other words, these churches attract the young people – most of them with ages ranging from twenties to fifties.[61] The church leadership is characterised by a youthful leadership of prophets, prophetesses, deacons, deaconesses, and apostles asserting their presence by occupying the public space. A pastor or prophet is central in their teachings and

---

58   Díez Bosch, Lluís Micó and Sabaté Gauxachs. A Phone of My Own. Gender, Religion and Technology, 10.

59   Meyer, Impossible Representations, 8 & 9.

60   Meyer, Impossible Representations, 5.

61   This is based on personal observation during visits to the 'Gospel of God's Grace Ministries' in Kopong led by Prophet Cedric, and Christ Embassy (the Gaborone Bus Station Branch) led by Pastor Felly (27 Oct. & 3 Nov. 2019). These churches have a vibrant and youthful (male and female) band which leads the singing, and the atmosphere is charismatic. The church use drums, guitars, keyboards, etc. During church services there are video cameras which record everything taking place within the church. The multimedia team use the video from different cameras inside the church and then show them live on various TV sets for access by all members in the church, including those sitting at the back or outside in the overflows and tents.

doctrine. A prophet/prophetess provides spiritual guidance and healing, and in some cases can be the key to worshippers remaining in the church to receive counselling.[62] A youthful church leader will attract young worshippers. The hierarchical structure of the prophetic church is organised so that the prophet/prophetess is at the top, with the congregants at the bottom.[63] Between the prophet/prophetess and the congregants are the senior pastor and the pastor. In Gaborone there are cases where churches such as Christ Embassy have youthful female pastors and female deacons. On the whole, unlike other religions such as Hinduism, Christianity is female-dominated in attendance. Therefore, this study is an attempt to understand how women in Botswana 'fire churches' are building their own niche, creating a meaningful space within the church.[64] In this charismatic ministry, females as religious practitioners are the center of attention and their dress code is equally attractive, as illustrated later in the chapter.[65]

Some of the 'fire church' leadership in countries such as Nigeria and South Africa run their own media ministries (e.g. TB Joshua and Major 1 Bushiri) and are accessed throughout the world. These African ministries which have since gone international have influenced and gradually facilitated the growth of the 'fire churches' movement in countries such as Botswana, where some members (including founders of churches) constantly cross the borders to receive deliverance from these popular prophets.[66] Given the charismatic nature and the new image-economy of the 'fire churches,' in recent years some of the Botswana popular culture music celebrities like Vee Mampeezy (Odirile Sento) and Shumba Ratshega (Moses Malapela)

---

62   A good example is that of Christ Embassy, where at the bus station branch in Gaborone a female pastor carries such responsibility and so does a female deacon at a branch in Tlokweng (personal observation).

63   Faimau, The Emergence of Prophetic Ministries in Botswana, 376.

64   Kgosimore, Sebolai, Macheng and Mabote. 2014. Religious Perspectives in Botswana, 326.-327 & Langford, Feminism and Leadership in the Pentecostal Movement, 75-79; See also, Mapuranga, Pentecostalism in Women Empowerment in Zimbabwe, 143-144.

65   As noted in footnotes 58 and 59, there is evidence of female leaders in various churches in the country. This point has been expanded with illustration under the section 'Women Shaping Narrations in Botswana Fire Churches'. See also, Rantopole, I. 2019. *Mosadi thari ya setshaba- moruti. Daily News*, 11 July. In this article, the Archbishop of Presbyterian Apostolic Church in Zion described Keikothae Tlhatseng as Mosadi thari ya setshaba (woman/mother is the cradle of the nation). Tlhatseng was being inaugurated as a new leader of the Saviour Apostolic Church in Kanye. Studies show that in the early 1950s the first woman founder of an independent church in South Africa used to visit colonial Botswana to conduct prayers. African Theologians in Botswana have argued that healer and prophetess Christinah Nku prepared the ground for the emergence of Pentecostalism in Botswana. But it was only in 1992 that the first Pentecostal church was founded and led by a woman in Botswana. See Nkomazana, The Role of Women, Theology, and Ecumenical Organisations in the Rise of Pentecostal Churches in Botswana, 192-193.

66   Authors of this chapter have relatives, cousins, friends and colleagues at the University of Botswana who are members of mainstream churches such as the UCCSA (United Congregational Church of Southern Africa) and Roman Catholic who often cross the border to seek deliverance at the ECG Church of Prophet Bushiri. Some would even travel as far as Nigeria for TB Joshua. When they return from either South Africa or Nigeria they maintain their membership with their churches, 2019.

became 'Born Again.' Some even founded their own churches.[67] Because of the public impact of the new Pentecostal churches, some church members are doubling as staunch members to mainline churches on Sundays but during the course of the week they attend the charismatic churches for night deliverance. Some youthful church ministers follow the example of Moruti Tiego, who when he noticed the resistance of the United Congregational Church of Southern Africa (UCCA) to embrace charismatic renewal in praying, ended up leaving the church to become a Pentecostal-charismatic leader of his own church in Gaborone. Some members are confessing that nowadays in Botswana, to retain their youthful members some of the mainstream churches, e.g. the Catholic Church, started running prayer groups and song groups in the charismatic mode.[68]

Women Shaping Narrations in Botswana 'Fire Churches'

As already stated, the study is based on the analysis of posters and pamphlets which were sourced from around the University of Botswana main campus in Gaborone. Altogether sixteen (16) posters and pamphlets were analysed. The posters were put up on noticeboards around the main lecture halls while the pamphlets were placed at the entrances of these buildings on campus. What stood out with most of the posters and pamphlets was that they were very eye-catching – printed in bright colours on glossy paper. They were printed on different sised paper with some of them quite small and others bigger than an A4. They contained a lot of information about the church and the activities they were promoting. The churches had exotic sounding names. For example, the churches had names like 'Dynamic Kingdom Development,' 'Forward in Faith Ministries (International)' and 'Bethel Church for All Nations.' The posters also provided information about the leadership, e.g. who was hosting the service and the position they held in the church. In one of the posters it was stated that Prophet P.M. and K.P. Ramocha, a married couple, were going to host the event. The couple were young – between the ages of 30 and 50 years. Most of the posters displayed pictures of young individuals or youthful-looking couples.

The men and women displayed on the posters were always smartly dressed, following the modern dress code and the latest fashion trends. They would be wearing very expensive outfits, with the women adorning themselves with beautiful hairstyles and expensive jewellery, including pearls. Most of these outfits were what you would see in expensive boutiques. This is in line with the doctrine of prosperity

---

67   See Batlotleng, B. 2017. Shumba Ratshega turns to God. *Daily News,* Gaborone, 26 July.

68   WhatsApp communication with church deaconess, 5 Nov. 2019.

and encouraging congregants to always be smartly dressed.[69] Positions held by the individual in church, like pastor, prophet, prophetess, deacon or deaconess were included in the poster along with their academic qualifications, like professor or doctor. There was also quite a lot of use of Bible verses, like 1 Timothy 2:8-10, 1 Peter 3:4, Isaiah 52:2 and Romans 13:11-14. In addition, the posters carried messages which are very attractive, e.g. "Surely the Lord is in this place, the house of God" and "Life Changing All Night." They also have catch phrases, as seen on a poster from the church called 'Life Impact Church Crusade' which said, "Come and Experience the Power of God" and also stated, "Come and Listen to the Testimony of an ex-Wizard." These churches also have international links. For instance, one of the churches hosted T.D. Jakes, a famous televangelist from the United States of America. The event was held at the University of Botswana Indoor Sports Stadium, and worshippers were required to buy tickets which cost between P250 for the general stands and P1200 for the Very Important Visitors. It was advertised in the same way that a musical show would be advertised – even offering an 'early bird special.'

Information was included on how to access church services, where these churches are located and how they could be reached. None of the posters we studied provided a landline number but rather a series of cell phone numbers for easy accessibility. Details on the venues of these events were included, such as tents, shops and warehouse which had been converted into churches, while some operated from schools. Most of the churches are situated near a mall or within walking distance of the bus/taxi rank, making it easier to access them. For instance, on most of the church posters it was stated that the venues were within walking distance of the Gaborone taxi rank. Times for worship services were specified on the posters and they also allocated time for specific activities, e.g. 9 am-10 am youth sessions responding to various issues raised by the youth. From the posters and pamphlets one could deduce that these churches are active in live broadcasting – through TV or radio. They utilise a lot of social media like You Tube, Facebook and WhatsApp, and even maintain websites. This extensive use of technology makes it possible for the churches to reach wider audiences. More importantly, the use of technology empowers women, making them more confident to participate in the public sphere.[70]

The posters and pamphlets also revealed that the 'fire churches' did not only offer deliverance and spiritual guidance but they also tackled topical issues like financial management, career development and leadership development. The 'Leadership

---

69   For modest dressing the authors analyzed the church posters, but also based on personal observation of church members.

70   See Díez Bosch, M., Lluís Micó, J. and Sabaté Gauxachs, A. 2018. A Phone of My Own. Gender, Religion and Technology. *Journal of Applied Ethics*, 9:7-9.

Development Interdenominational Church' is an example of a church where they offered both spiritual guidance and ran Life Skills Workshops. These workshops covered money and budgeting skills, how to choose and pursue a career, time management and goal setting prioritisation, problem solving skills and employability skills. In addition, the workshops offered personal grooming and character building, cleanliness and hygiene, organizational skills, social skills and manners, and coping with emotions. In running these workshops, they also presented the church as having a multi-racial community of compassionate worshippers. A church like 'Disciples of Christ' emphasises worshipping God, ministering to society and advancing God's kingdom through evangelism and love. Such a message was appealing and associated with 'Mother Nature.'

In the selected posters we studied, some churches displayed the popular biblical message, John 3:16, "For God so loved you that he gave his only begotten son (Jesus) that when you believe, you will not perish." At the 'Disciples of Christ Church' worship is free and they even run a free counselling and prayer line. However, the workshops cost about P600, covering refreshments and resource materials. The church and the workshops are run by a husband-and-wife team referred to as the Prophet and the Prophetess. The wife is also referred to as the 'coach princess,' acknowledging her feminine side. By looking at the names that appear on the posters, most of the churches being advertised were run by both Batswana and Non-Batswana men and women. Women in posters were displayed as partners in the ministry.

In the posters analysed, there were women who held more senior positions than men. They held the position of prophetess, which is the highest position in these churches.[71] One of the posters advertising the Youth Annual conference held at the 'Bethel Church for All Nations' had a picture of Senior Pastor Kebangwe, who is female and held a much higher position than her male counterpart, Pastor Julius. A poster also showed a woman as the founder of a ministry. Female evangelist Fatima Ezekiel was listed as the founder of the 'Divine Fortress Worldwide' ministry. She was said to have an event referred to as the "Emerald Women and an Empowered Woman and An Unravelling Force." In most of these churches women held various positions, ranging from worship director to pastor and/or elder. Accessing the church websites showed that women preached on Sunday mornings.[72] In one of the posters analysed, an event for women organised by an all-woman ministry team was advertised. The 'Women of Purpose International' organised "The 2019 Purpose and Grace Conference" hosted by Pastor Tekolo Modungwa, a former senior civil servant, with guest speaker Pastor Lindey McCauley and facilitator Dr Kopano

71   See Faimau, 2018, The Emergence of Prophetic Ministries in Botswana, 376.

72   Authors accessed church websites.

Mpuang-Allmond. According to the pamphlet the title of the conference was "A desert blossoms to a rose" – a deliberate affirmative action focusing on women. The ticket to the conference was P200, which included a raffle ticket. The raffle prizes showed that the conference acknowledged the feminine side of the participants. The 1st prize was a massage, 2nd prize facial make-up and 3rd prize plain hair plaiting. However, the conference also covered topics like 'leadership principles' and 'great purpose,' while falling within the conference theme of 'Purpose and Grace.'

In addition to the analysis of poster and pamphlets, we conducted an interview with a deaconess belonging to the 'fire church' Christ Embassy which is also known as the 'Believers Love World Ministry.' This is an international church with branches in South Africa, Canada, the United States of America and Nigeria. The church is also the publisher of *Rhapsody of Realities*, a daily devotional which has been translated into over 130 languages across the world, including into 8 languages in Botswana alone (e.g. Setswana, Ikalanga, Chikuhane, Shekgalagari, Thimbukushu, Sebirwa, and Chetswapong). The Church uses various social media platforms, e.g. WhatsApp, Youtube and Facebook, to reach a wider audience.

Dr Pearl Seloma, a senior lecturer in the Department of African Languages and Literature, Faculty of Humanities at the University of Botswana, talked to the authors about how she has been applying her expertise and skills of translation to serve the church in translating the *Rhapsody of Realities* into some languages spoken in Botswana. In addition to her impressive academic record, she is a deaconess as well as registrar of the foundation school run by the church.[73] These are senior positions at the Botswana Christ Embassy Church. Sometimes the church runs Setswana online church services where Dr Seloma, who teaches a course at UB on 'Introduction to Rhetoric and Public Speaking,' participates in preaching.[74] In her interview she emphasised the fact that in her church everyone is encouraged to develop the mindset of a potential leader and the church offers training in this regard. She also pointed out that most of the Christ Embassy church leadership roles are held by women, like Pastor Felly, and this is further illustrated in her interview.

Interview with Deaconess and Registrar of Christ Embassy Foundation School in Botswana, University, Gaborone, 22 September 2019

> In the Christ Embassy Church women hold leadership roles. For instance, our Botswana group pastor (an overseer of 45 Christ Embassy Churches in Botswana) is a woman. There are three female subgroup pastors and only 2 male subgroup pastors. Each subgroup pastor is an overseer of 7 or more churches. I am not only

---

73   Interview with Dr Pearl Seipone Seloma, University of Botswana, 1 March 2017 & 03 Nov 2019.

74   Interview with Dr Pearl Seloma, University of Botswana, 22 September 2019.

a Deaconess, but also have other leadership responsibilities. I am the Registrar of Christ Embassy Foundation School in Botswana of over 45 churches (that is, internal Bible School with one class per week for 6 weeks and 1 mid-term exam and final exam). I ensure that the Foundation School teachers are trained and Bible exams are moderated for quality assurance, amongst other duties. Every three months there must be a formal graduation in the subgroup churches. The graduating students wear graduation gowns and are given trophies of excellent performance. In our Gaborone church, we have 5 deaconesses and 2 deacons. Our church encourages everyone who joins to develop a mindset of potential leaders. We undergo leadership training, young and old, because the Gospel is free but not cheap, hence as leaders we need to demonstrate it through good works and sound leadership, not only through preaching the Word of God.

The international link in the 'fire church' movement also provides an opportunity for women in key positions to travel abroad for training. A good example of this is at Christ Embassy where Dr Seloma and her colleagues in leadership often travel to South Africa, London and Nigeria for the purposes of training on the translation of the *Rhapsody of Realities, Daily Devotional*.[75] According to Dr Seloma of UB, also a female Deacon providing leadership at the Tlokweng church service, her church is an international church ministry which has a branch in five (5) continents.[76] Seloma affirms that although the Christ Embassy Church President is a man, Pastor Chris Oyakhilome, there are regional pastors and the one who oversees the Southern African Region is a woman, Pastor Ose Oyakhilome (a wife of Pastor Chris). Christ Embassy has a male pastor for Southern Africa Zone 3, then below him are Group Pastors, and the Botswana one is Pastor Felicity. Below this female pastor there are subgroup pastors. In Botswana, out of five (5) pastors, three (3) are women. Each subgroup Pastor oversees about 6 to 12 satellite churches under the leadership of ordained pastors, nominated church coordinators and members of the deaconry, some of whom are women (including an academic from the University of Botswana). Below them are Cell Leaders in every church.[77]

The authors of this chapter also attended church services where female pastors like Modungwa of 'Holy Land International Ministries' (who was ordained with her husband in November 2015) had acted as marriage officers or officiated at funerals. These women have been licensed or ordained like men to preside over weddings or funerals. Keikothae Tlhatseng of the 'Saviour Apostolic Church' in Kanye (south of Botswana) and Felicity Chijena of 'Christ Embassy' in Gaborone are also good examples. In most of these churches, women held various positions ranging from worship director to pastor and/or elder. Accessing the church websites and studying

75   Interview with Pearl Seloma, University of Botswana, 22 September 2019.
76   Interview with Dr Seloma, 22 September 2019.
77   See interview with Dr Seloma, 22 September 2019.

the details in church posters showed that women preached on Sunday mornings.[78] Through the different times that the authors attended these services, female pastors displayed their affluence in wearing expensive dresses, dress suits or skirt/trouser and jacket suits. They displayed hairstyles with long weaves or wigs and jewellery, like pearls. We have observed during church services and also by studying posters, that female church leaders complement their expensive suits with brooches, handbags and flawless makeup. Similarly, male pastors appear clean-shaven and wear full suits of various colours, adding accessories such as matching neckties, pocket handkerchiefs, cufflinks and expensive looking leather shoes. This is in contrast to the mainline churches or African Initiated churches, where the church officials leading in worship, who are mainly males, are usually dressed in robes.

The dress code of the leaders (both men and women) of the 'fire churches' is more appealing to the young generation. This is similar to what we see in boutiques today, like attractive and expensive tight-fitting clothes. The leaders of 'fire churches' seem to want to portray the 'modern' or 'western' look because they hardly wear any clothes made from African print material, including the popular southern African print material (known as *leteisi* in Botswana). They also seem to be depicting the corporate world to look professional. It is widely believed that to be taken seriously women should wear what they call 'power dressing' or 'power suits.' In a way they are also affirming their femininity. Despite the senior positions that they might hold and the official responsibilities that they are required to perform, women are still required to play their 'mothering' roles, like cooking for the family at home. One of the female pastors told one of the authors that she still acts as mother to her family and the congregants; she is often called upon to look after the sick and provide comfort to the bereaved. She also takes part in the cleaning of the church and its surroundings, making sure that everything is in order – that the chairs are well organised and the flowers are nicely arranged. If there is a need to supply refreshments or snacks for the congregants, this also falls on her shoulders.

In contrast to the various leadership roles that women can hold in the 'fire churches,' in some of the African Initiated Churches it is totally the opposite. The interview below further illustrates how some African Initiated Churches view women's leadership in churches in Botswana.

> ZCC is an African independent church rooted in African culture and tradition, dominated by men who play a leading role in the main church activities. Men are responsible for marching, which is associated with prayer in ZCC, and they take the lead while women follow. Women are mere followers in support of men. From Monday to Sunday at every prayer, except the Wednesday afternoon one,

---

78   See e.g. Christ Embassy, Gaborone, Botswana, Join Our Sunday Online Service with Pastor Felly Chijena. https://www.facebook.com/cegaborone1

men are in the lead. When men are not present, people would pronounce that "*Baruti ga bayo*" [priests have not yet arrived], because in ZCC "*baruti*" [priests] are men. On Sunday, which is the main church activity, men lead all activities. Before arrival of the male church leadership, women cannot start, even though their number is significant and they are always ready for church services. However, on Wednesdays (2-5) women are given an opportunity to exercise 'leadership,' e.g. reading the Bible and sharing spiritual messages, including matters of welfare. But women can only enter the church provided men have come to sprinkle the church space with holy water. The men sprinkle the water before the church service starts. When women lead, it is only in the absence of men. During the Wednesday service men stay far away because they are not supposed to listen to what women are discussing. In ZCC men and women's church uniforms are defined.

The respondent holds the position of secretary of the Zion Christian Church, Bobonong branch (Central District). Prior to holding this senior position he was a headmaster of a local primary school.[79] The quote above is in total contrast to what is emerging in the 'fire churches,' where women can hold leadership positions and even rise to the rank of prophetess or be founders of their own ministries.

Conclusion

Churches have always been criticised for perpetuating customs and perceptions that women cannot hold leadership positions. However, based on our analysis of posters and pamphlets from 'fire churches' as well as some interviews, this is changing very fast. These churches have opened avenues for women to take up leadership roles and participate in any aspect of the church. At the same time, female pastors and prophetesses use their 'feminine touch' or 'power dress code' to negotiate a public space in the church and this boosts their confidence. They also engage in training activities and lead online church services to improve their profile. The posters, which were widely circulated, played a prominent role in the distribution of information concerning church activities and the pastors/apostles responsible for hosting the events that were being advertised. Most of the posters included both male and female pastors. There were a few exceptions where one poster depicted an all-male team and others showed only females. Some were advertising an event hosted by a female evangelist and others a women's conference hosted by an all-female team. The posters showed women holding senior positions in churches, some of them even as prophetesses, church elders or founders of ministries.

The analysis of posters and websites (online church service) demonstrate that the church environment does facilitate women taking up leadership roles, like what

79   Interview, 27 Sept 2019.

was described in the interview with the deaconess from the Christ Embassy Church in Botswana. They encourage the general membership, not only women, to strive for leadership positions. Overall, there is an acknowledgement and acceptance of women taking up leadership roles, which sets these churches apart from mainstream churches and Africa Initiated Churches. The analysis of these posters has established that women are gradually occupying the religious space and that the skills acquired in church do equip women to participate in the public space. Women's leadership abilities are embraced in the 'fire churches' through their positions as prophetesses, deaconesses and founders of churches. The 'fire churches' provide space for women to go beyond the traditional religious norms of being mother to the congregation and only participating in activities like cleaning the church, cooking or flower arrangements. These churches encourage women to aspire to hold leadership positions within the organization while continuing to perform their traditional roles. Despite this rosy picture of the 'fire churches' and their approach to being all-inclusive in terms of gender, criticisms have arisen as to whether this is sustainable in the long term or if it is just a passing phase. In conclusion, there is a need for more research in order to get a more comprehensive picture regarding the gender relations prevailing in the various church organizations.

References

Amanze, J. 1994. *Botswana Handbook of Churches*. Gaborone: Pula Press.

Amanze, J. 2002. *African Traditional Religions & Culture in Botswana*. Gaborone: Pula Press.

Batlotleng, B. 2017. Shumba Ratshega turns to God. *Daily News*, Gaborone, 26 July.

Daniel, K. 2010. The Role of Women in Church in Africa. *International Journal of Sociology and Anthropology*, 2(6):126-139.

David, K. and Osborn, L. 2007. *Greek medicine.net*. Blog Online Store.

Díez Bosch, M., Lluís Micó, J. and Sabaté Gauxachs, A. 2018. A Phone of My Own. Gender, Religion and Technology. *Journal of Applied Ethics*, 9:7-10.

Dube, M.W. 2007. 'God Never Opened the Bible to Me': Women Church Leaders in Botswana. In: F. Nkomazana and L. Lanner (eds). *Aspects of the History of the Church in Botswana*. Pietermaritzburg: Cluster Publications. 210-216.

Dube, M.W. 1994. Readings of Semoya: Batswana Women's Interpretations of Matt 15: 21-28. *SEMEIA*, (73):11-129.

Ehrman, B.D. 2006. *Truth and Fiction in The Da Vinci Code: A Historian Reveals What We Really Know about Jesus, Mary Magdalene, and Constantine*. Oxford: Oxford University Press.

Faimau, G. 2018. The Emergence of Prophetic Ministries in Botswana: Self-Positioning and Appropriation of New Media. *Journal of Contemporary African Studies*, 36(3):369-385. https://doi.org/10.1080/02589001.2018.1490009

Faimau, G. 2017. Religious Testimonial Narratives and Social Construction of Identity: Insights from Prophetic Ministries in Botswana. *Cogent Social Sciences*, 3:1-16. https://doi.org/10.1080/23311886.2017.1356620

Faimau, G. and Behrens, C. 2016. Facebooking Religion and the Technologization of the Religious Discourse: A Case Study of a Botswana-based Prophetic Church. *Online - Heidelberg Journal of Religions on the Internet*, 11 http://online.uni-hd.de [Accessed August, 2019].

Fiedler, R.N. 2019. *A History of the Circle of Concerned African Women Theologians (1989-2007)*. Mzuzu: Mzuni Press.

Forbes, B.D. and Jeffrey, H.M. (eds). 2000. *Religion and Popular Culture in America*. Berkeley and Los Angeles: University of California Press.

Heuser, A. 2016. Charting African Prosperity Gospel economies. *Herv. teol. stud.*, 72(4):1-9. https://doi.org/10.4102/hts.v72i4.3823

Hoffman, B.G. 1997. Reviewed Work(s): Daughters of Anowa: African Women and Patriarchy by Mercy A. Oduyoye. *African Studies Review*, 40(1):201-203. https://doi.org/10.2307/525062

Kanyoro, M. 2001. Engendered Communal Theology: African Women's Contribution to Theology in the Twenty-First Century. *Feminist Theology*, 27:36-56. https://doi.org/10.1177/096673500100002704

Kasomo, D. 2010. The Role of Women in the Church in Africa. *International Journal of Sociology and Anthropology*, 2(6):126-139.

Kealotswe, O.N. 1994. *An African Independent Church Leader Bishop Smart Mthembu of the Head Mountain of God Apostolic Church in Zion Botswana*. Studies on the Church in Southern Africa V. Gaborone: University of Botswana Department of History & Department of Theology and Religious Studies.

Kgosimore, M., Sebolai, B., Macheng, B.J. and Mabote, M.M. 2014. Religious Perspectives. In: *The 2011 Population and Housing Census Analytical Report.* Gaborone: Statistics Botswana.

Klingorová, K. and Havlíček, T. 2015. Religion and Gender Inequality: The Status of Women in the Societies of World Religions. *Moravian Geographical Reports*, 23(2):1-10. https://doi.org/10.1515/mgr-2015 -0006

Lim, Y.C.L. 1997. *Capitalism, Imperialism and Patriarchy: The Dilemma of Third-World Women Workers in Multinational Factories.* Dhaka: University Press Limited.

Langford, J. 2017. Feminism and Leadership in the Pentecostal Movement. *Feminist Theology*, 26(1):69-79. https://doi.org/10.1177 /0966735017714402

Mapuranga, T.P. 2018. Pastors, Preachers and Wives: A Critical Reflection on the Role of Pentecostalism in Women Empowerment in Zimbabwe. In: L. Togarasei (ed). *Aspects of Pentecostal Christianity in Zimbabwe.* Cham: Springer. 139-150. https://doi.org/10 .1007/978-3-319-78565-3_10

March, J. 1998. *Cassell's Dictionary of Classical Mythology.* London: Cassell and Co.

McKenna, M.L. 1967. *Women in the Church Role and Renewal.* New York: PJ Kennedy, Sons.

Meyer, B. 2010. "There is a Spirit in that Image" Mass-Produced Jesus Pictures and Protestant-Pentecostal Animation in Ghana. *Comparative Studies in Society and History*, 52(1):100-130. https://doi.org/10.1017 /S001041750999034X

Meyer, B. 2003. Impossible Representations. Pentecostalism, Vision and Video Technology in Ghana. *Working Papers*, Department of Anthropology and African Studies. Mainz: Johannes Gutenberg University, 1-22.

Meyer, B. 1995. 'Delivered from the Powers of Darkness,' Confessions about Satanic Riches in Christian Ghana. *Africa*, 65(2):236-55. https:// doi.org/10.2307/1161192

Mooketsi, L. 2004. Botswana Dutch Church Threatened with legal Action. *Mmegi*, 4 March.

Mooketsi, L. 2004. Botswana: Dispute Over Female Priest Goes to Court. *Mmegi*, 18 November.

Mooketsi, L. 2004. Kgosiemang: Expulsion Splits Church. *Mmegi*, 20 May.

Mothala, S. 2017. "Out You Go" Dutch Reformed Churches Fire Members. *The Voice*, 24 November.

Morris, R.C. 2002. A Room with a Voice: Mediation and Mediumship in Thailand's Information Age. In: F.D. Ginsburg, L. Abu-Lughod and B. Larkin (eds). *Media Worlds Anthropology on New Terrain.* Berkeley and Los Angeles: University of California Press. 319-336.

Nkomazana, F.1999. London Missionary Society, Church & State in a Colonial Bechuanaland: The Case of Bangwato, 1867-1923. *Scriputura: International Journal of Bible, Religion and Theology in Southern Africa*, 71(4):303-312. https://doi.org/10.7833/71-0-1234

Nkomazana, F. 2000. The Profile of Reverend Mrs Rebecca Motsitsi of the Pentecostal Holiness Church in Botswana. *Religion & Gender in BOLESWA Occasional Papers in Theology & Religion*, 1(7):44-59.

Nkomazana, F. 2008. The Experiences of Women within Tswana Cultural History & Its Implications for the History of Church in Botswana. *Studia Historiae Ecclesiasticae*, XXXIV(2):83-116.

Nkomazana, F. 2018. The Role of Women, Theology, and Ecumenical

Organizations in the Rise of
Pentecostal Churches in Botswana.
In: A. Afolayan, O. Yacob-Haliso and
T. Falola (eds). *African Histories and
Modernities Pentecostalism and Politics
in Africa.* Cham: Palgrave Macmillan.
184-186. https://doi.org/10.1007/978
-3-319-74911-2_10

Oduyoye, M. and Kanyoro, R.A. 1992.
*The Will to Arise: Women, Tradition,
and the Church in Africa.* Maryknoll,
New York: Orbit Books.

Oduyoye, M. 1995. *Daughter to Anowa:
African Women and Patriarchy.* New
York: Orbit Books.

Oduyoye, M. 2001. *Introducing African
Women's Theology.* Cleveland: The
Pilgrim Press.

Pui-Ian, K. 2004. Mercy Amba Oduyoye
and African Women's Theology.
Journal of Feminist Studies in Religion,
20(1):7-22.

Christ Embassy. 2010. *Rhapsody of
Realities.* Johannesburg: Love World
Publishers.

Ricci, C. 1994. *Mary Magdalene and Many
Others: Women who followed Jesus.* (Paul
Burns, transl.). Minneapolis: Fortress
Press.

Shanduka, T. and Togarasei, L. Health and
Well-Being in Zimbabwe's Pentecostal
Churches. In: L. Togarasei (ed). *Aspects
of Pentecostal Christianity in Zimbabwe.*
Cham: Springer. 151-163. https://doi
.org/10.1007/978-3-319-78565-3_11

Spink, C. 2003. Panacea or Painkiller?:
The Impact of Pentecostal Christianity
on Women in Africa. *Critical Half,*
1(1):20-25.

Tlou, T. and Campbell, A. 1984 &
1997. *History of Botswana.* Gaborone:
Macmillan.

Togarasei, L. 2012. Mediating the
Gospel: Pentecostal Christianity and
Media Technology in Botswana and
Zimbabwe. *Journal of Contemporary
Religion,* 27(2):257-274. https://doi.o
rg/10.1080/13537903.2012.675740

Togarasei, L. 2008. Fighting HIV and
AIDS with the Bible: Towards HIV
and AIDS biblical criticism. In: E.
Chitando (ed). *Mainstreaming HIV
in Theology and Religious Studies:
Experiences and Explorations,* 211–222.
Geneva: WCC.

Togarasei, L. 2018. History and
Characteristics of Pentecostal
Christianity in Zimbabwe. In: L.
Togarasei (ed). *Aspects of Pentecostal
Christianity in Zimbabwe,* Cham:
Springer. 33-48. https://doi.org/10
.1007/978-3-319-78565-3_3

CONTRIBUTING AUTHORS

DR MMAPULA DIANA KEBANEILWE, Senior Lecturer, University of Botswana, https://orcid.org/0000-0001-5190-3419

MR KGOMOTSO SCOTCH, Master of Theology Student, University of Botswana, https://orcid.org/0000-0002-9785-6299

REV. DR. PEGGY MULAMBYA-KABONDE, Minister of Religion with the Methodist Church in Britain/United Reformed Church in the UK; First female General Secretary, United Church of Zambia, Southern Africa Circle Coordinator of African women Theologians. Affiliated to World Communion of Reformed Churches (WCRC) and Oxford Institute of Methodists Theological Studies, https://orcid.org/0000-0002-4582-9408

DR. FIFAMÈ FIDÈLE HOUSSOU GANDONOU, Théologienne Pasteure de Paroisse et enseignante à l'Université Protestante d'Afrique de l'Ouest (UPAO/Porto-Novo), https://orcid.org/0000-0002-9490-4996

PROF. ESTHER MOMBO, Faculty of Theology, St. Paul's University, https://orcid.org/0000-0002-7186-547X

DR. MASTER OBOLETSWE MATLHAOPE, General Secretary, Association of Evangelicals in Africa (AEA), https://orcid.org/0000-0003-3681-8309

REV. DR. ANGELINE SAVALA, Senior Lecturer, Masinde Muliro University of Science and Technology, https://orcid.org/0000-0002-9914-1975

REV. DR. TABE JENNET OTOB BENONI-WANG, Registrar/Lecturer of Dogmatics, Presbyterian Theological Seminary, Kumba Cameroon, https://orcid.org/0000-0002-5072-6032

NELLY MWALE, Lecturer, University of Zambia, Department of Religious Studies; Research Fellow, Institute for Theology and Religion, University of South Africa, https://orcid.org/0000-0002-4556-9239

PROF MAITSEO BOLAANE, Associate Professor & Head of Department of History, University of Botswana, https://orcid.org/0000-0002-8151-9490

DR. GWEN N. LESETEDI, PHD, Senior Lecturer, University of Botswana, Department of Sociology, https://orcid.org/0000-0003-4346-6882

* 9 7 8 1 9 9 1 2 0 1 3 0 0 *